STUDY GUIDE FOR WEITEN'S

PSYCHOLOGY
Themes & Variations
Briefer Version

FOURTH EDITION

STUDY GUIDE FOR WEITEN'S

PSYCHOLOGY
Themes & Variations
Briefer Version

FOURTH EDITION

RICHARD B. STALLING
Bradley University

RONALD E. WASDEN
Bradley University

Brooks/Cole • Wadsworth
I⟨T⟩P® An International Thomson Publishing Company

Belmont, CA • Albany, NY • Boston • Cincinnati • Johannesburg • London • Madrid • Melbourne
Mexico City • New York • Pacific Grove, CA • Scottsdale, AZ • Singapore • Tokyo • Toronto

For permission to use material from this text, contact us:
web   www.thomsonrights.com
fax   1-800-730-2215
phone   1-800-730-2214

Printed in the United States of America.
3 4 5 6 7 8 9 10

Wadsworth Publishing Company
10 Davis Drive
Belmont, CA 94002

International Thomson Publishing Europe
Berkshire House
168-173 High Holborn
London, WC1V 7AA, United Kingdom

Nelson ITP, Australia
102 Dodds Street
South Melbourne
Victoria 3205 Australia

Nelson Canada
1120 Birchmount Road
Scarborough, Ontario
Canada M1K 5G4

International Thomson Editores
Seneca, 53
Colonia Polanco
11560 México D.F. México

International Thomson Publishing Asia
60 Albert Street #15-01
Albert Complex
Singapore 189969

International Thomson Publishing Japan
Hirakawa-cho Kyowa Building, 3F
2-2-1 Hirakawa-cho, Chiyoda-ku
Tokyo 102, Japan

International Thomson Publishing Southern Africa
Building 18, Constantia Square
138 Sixteenth Road, P.O. Box 2459
Halfway House, 1685 South Africa

ISBN 0-534-36674-0

Contents

To the Student

The two of us have written about eight study guides across the last couple of decades, and we've used a number of them written by others as well. Our goal in writing this study guide was to make it the best that we have ever written or used. We're pleased with the organization, the clear way in which each component parallels each part of the text, the fact that the practice material is in close proximity to the learning objectives, and the variety of the examples. We hope you find it as helpful a resource as we have tried to make it.

The first and major section of each chapter in the study guide is the Review of Key Ideas, consisting of approximately 20 learning objectives and several questions or exercises relating to each objective. The learning objectives tell you what you are expected to know, while the exercises quiz you, sometimes tutor you, and occasionally try to make a joke. Answers are provided at the end of each set of exercises.

The second section is the Review of Key Terms, which asks you to match 20 to 60 terms from the chapter with their definitions. The third section is the Review of Key People, a matching exercise confined to the major researchers and theorists presented in each chapter. Finally, the Self-Quiz for each chapter gives you some idea of whether or not your studying has been on target.

What's the best way to work with this book? We suggest that you try this: (1) read each learning objective; (2) read the text subsection that relates to that learning objective;

(3) answer the questions. After you complete the objectives, do the matching exercises and take the self-quiz. Of course, you may find a different procedure that works for you. Whatever method you use, the learning objectives will serve as an excellent review. At the end of your study of a particular chapter you can quiz yourself by reading over the learning objectives, reciting answers aloud, and checking your answers. This procedure roughly parallels the SQ3R study technique introduced in the Application section of Chapter 1 of the text.

In Chapter 16 of your text Wayne Weiten, the author, illustrates a topic in social psychology by saying that "Years ago, one of my teachers told me that I had an 'attitude problem.' " Well, years ago—about 25, to be specific—we were Wayne's teachers in college, and although we don't recall reprimanding him, if we did, we apologize. Because now the tables are turned; now we are being instructed by and taking correction from Wayne.

We wish to acknowledge the help of a few people. First, we wish to thank Wayne Weiten, our former student. It has been a pleasure to work with him; he is an excellent teacher and superb writer, which make our task much easier. If this guide achieves what we hope it does, Wayne deserves much of the credit. Our thanks also to Faith Stoddard of Brooks/Cole, who always works patiently with the two of us, and to Gail Reynolds, who transformed our copy into its final form.

Rick Stalling and Ron Wasden

STUDY GUIDE FOR WEITEN'S

PSYCHOLOGY
Themes & Variations
Briefer Version

FOURTH EDITION

1 THE EVOLUTION OF PSYCHOLOGY

REVIEW OF KEY IDEAS

FROM SPECULATION TO SCIENCE: HOW PSYCHOLOGY DEVELOPED

1. **Summarize Wundt's accomplishments and contributions to the evolution of psychology.**

   1-1.   If you ask most college graduates to name the founder of psychology they might well mention the name of a famous psychologist (for example, maybe Sigmund Freud), but they almost certainly would *not* say Wilhelm Wundt. Yet among psychologists Wundt is generally acknowledged to be the "_____" of our field.

   1-2.   Wundt established the first experimental psychology _____ in Leipzig, Germany, in 1879. He also established the first _____ devoted to publishing psychological research.

   1-3.   Who is the founder of psychology? _____ When did psychology, as an independent field of study, begin? _____

   What was the subject matter of Wundt's psychology? _____

   Answers: **1-1.** founder **1-2.** laboratory, journal **1-3.** Wilhelm Wundt, 1879, consciousness.

2. **Compare structuralism and functionalism and discuss their impact on the subsequent development of psychology.**

   2-1.   Which "school" is characterized by each of the following descriptions? Place an "S" for structuralism or "F" for functionalism in the appropriate blanks.

   _____   Concerned with the <u>purpose</u> (or function) of consciousness.

   _____   Trained human beings to <u>introspect</u> about consciousness.

   _____   Assumed that consciousness could be broken down into <u>basic elements</u> (in the same way that physical matter is comprised of atoms).

   _____   Interested in the <u>flow</u> of consciousness.

   _____   Focused on the <u>adaptive</u> (evolutionary) value of consciousness.

_____ Emphasized <u>sensation</u> and <u>perception</u> in vision, hearing, and touch.

_____ Founded by <u>William James</u>.

2-2. While neither structuralism nor functionalism survived as viable theories of psychology, functionalism had a more lasting impact. What was that impact?

Answers: 2-1. F, S, S, F, F, S, F **2-2.** The emphasis of functionalism on the practical (or the adaptive or purposeful) led to the development of two areas of modern psychology: behaviorism and applied psychology.

3. Summarize Watson's view on the appropriate subject matter of psychology, nature versus nurture, and animal research.

3-1. A literal translation of the root words of psychology (*psyche* and *logos*) suggests that psychology is the study of the _____. For both Wundt and James, this was the case: they studied human _____. For Watson, however, the subject matter of psychology was _____.

3-2. Watson believed that psychology could not be a science unless it, like the other sciences, concentrated on _____ rather than unobservable events.

3-3. Which of the following are observable behaviors? Place an "O" in the blank if the event is observable and an "N" if it is not.

_____ writing a letter

_____ feeling angry

_____ saying "Please pass the salt"

_____ passing the salt

_____ perceiving a round object

_____ experiencing hunger

_____ walking rapidly

3-4. Watson largely discounted the importance of genetic inheritance. For Watson, behavior was governed by the _____.

3-5. Watson also made a shift away from human introspection by using _____ as the subjects for research. Why the change in orientation? First, animal behavior is observable; human consciousness is not. Second, the environment of laboratory animals, in contrast to that of humans, is subject to much more _____.

Answers: 3-1. soul (or mind), consciousness, behavior **3-2.** observable **3-3.** O, N (you can't see or hear your own or another person's feelings of anger; you may see the results of anger), O, O, N (you can't see or hear perception), N (you can't see or hear hunger), O **3-4.** environment **3-5.** animals, control.

4. Summarize Freud's principal ideas and why they inspired controversy.

4-1. Recall that for Wundt, the subject matter of psychology was human consciousness. For Freud, a major subject of study was what he termed the _____. With this concept, Freud asserted that human beings are (<u>aware/unaware</u>) of most of the factors that influence their thoughts and behavior.

4-2. There is a word beginning with *s* that means the same thing as feces. This word, however, may be more likely to cause laughter, embarrassment, or anger than the word feces. Why do two words that mean the same thing produce such differing reactions? Freud would assert that our more emotional response to one of the words would be caused by the _____.

4-3. Although generally not accessible to us, the unconscious is revealed in several ways, according to Freud. Freud thought, for example, that the unconscious is revealed in mistakes, such as "_____ of the tongue," or the symbolism in nighttime _____.

4-4. Freud's ideas were (and still are) quite controversial. The general public tended to find Freud's ideas unacceptable because of his emphasis on _____. And scientific psychologists, with their increasing emphasis on observable behavior, rejected Freud's notion that we are controlled by _____ forces. Nonetheless, Freud's theory gradually gained prominence and survives today as an influential theoretical perspective.

Answers: 4-1. unconscious, unaware **4-2.** unconscious **4-3.** slips, dreams **4-4.** sex (sexuality, sexual instincts), unconscious.

5. Summarize Skinner's work, views, and influence.

5-1. Summarize Skinner's viewpoint with regard to the following topics.

(a) Mental events:

(b) The fundamental principle of behavior:

(c) Free will:

(d) The factors that control human (and lower animal) behavior:

Answers: 5-1. (a) They cannot be studied scientifically and are not useful in building a science of behavior. (b) Organisms will tend to repeat responses followed by positive outcomes (and *not* to repeat responses followed by neutral or negative outcomes). (c) Free will is an illusion (because, he says, behavior is under the lawful control of the environment). (d) external stimuli (or environmental events).

6. Summarize Rogers's and Maslow's ideas and the contributions of humanistic psychology.

6-1. Both Rogers and Maslow, like other _____ psychologists, emphasized the (similarities/differences) between human beings and the other animals.

6-2. While Freud and Skinner stressed the way in which behavior is *controlled* (by unconscious forces or by the environment), Rogers and Maslow emphasized human beings' _____ to determine their own actions.

6-3. Rogers and Maslow also asserted that human beings have a drive to express their inner potential, a drive toward personal _____.

6-4. Perhaps the greatest contribution of the humanistic movement has been in producing (scientific findings/new approaches) in psychotherapy.

Answers: **6-1.** humanistic, differences **6-2.** freedom **6-3.** growth (expression) **6-4.** new approaches.

7. Explain how historical events since World War I have contributed to the emergence of psychology as a profession.

7-1. World War I ushered in the field of *applied* psychology, primarily the extensive use of _____ testing. World War II created demand for yet another applied area, the field of _____ psychology.

7-2. World War II brought an increased need for screening recruits and treating emotional casualties. With the increased demand, the Veterans' Administration began funding many new training programs in _____ psychology.

7-3. Thus, the two wars accelerated the development of psychology as a/an _____ field in contrast to its previous development as primarily a research or academic endeavor.

Answers: **7-1.** intelligence (or ability or mental), clinical **7-2.** clinical **7-3.** applied (or professional).

8. Describe two recent trends in research in psychology that reflect a return to psychology's intellectual roots.

8-1. Two recent trends in research in psychology involve the reemergence of areas largely discarded or ignored by the behaviorists. What are these two areas?

8-2. Think about sucking on a lemon. When you do, the amount of saliva in your mouth will actually increase a measurable amount. While it would be enough to describe your observable response as a function of my observable instruction, it is also obvious that thinking, or cognition, is involved: My instruction changed your _____ image, which was accompanied by a change in salivation.

8-3. The study of mental imagery, problem solving, and decision making involves _____ processes. The second more recent trend also concerns "internal" processes. Research on electrical stimulation of the brain, brain specialization, and biofeedback involves _____ processes.

Answers: **8-1.** cognition (consciousness or thinking) and physiological (or biological) processes **8-2.** mental (cognitive) **8-3.** cognitive, physiological (biological).

9. Explain why Western psychology traditionally had scant interest in other cultures and why this situation has begun to change.

4

9-1.   In part because they assumed that they were discovering general principles, psychologists saw little need to test their theories in other cultures. The situation has begun to change in recent years primarily due to (a) increased communication and trade worldwide and the resulting _____ interdependence; and to (b) increased diversity of ethnic groups within the countries of the Western World, including the _____ mosaic characteristic of the United States.

9-2.   This new orientation of psychological research is directed toward testing the generality of earlier findings; exploring both the differences and _____ among cultural groups; looking for ways to reduce intergroup _____ ; and, in general, understanding the role that culture plays in human behavior.

Answers: **9-1.** global (worldwide); multicultural (cultural) **9-2.** similarities, misunderstandings (conflict, hostility).

10.   Summarize the basic tenets of evolutionary psychology.

10-1.   The most recent major perspective to arise in psychology is _____ psychology, a field that examines behavioral processes in terms of survival value for a species.

10-2.   According to evolutionary psychologists, all aspects of human behavior—including not only aggression and mate selection but perception, language, personality, and cognition—are strongly influenced by the _____ value that these factors have had for the human species.

10-3.   While Darwin's influence is clear in other psychological theories (e.g., James, Freud, and Skinner), the new emphasis on natural selection is (less/more) comprehensive and widely researched than the earlier versions.

10-4.   The viewpoint has its critics. Some charge that the theory is not subject to scientific _____ and that evolutionary conceptions are simply post hoc accounts rather than explanations. Nonetheless, evolutionary psychology has gained a high degree of acceptance as a major new perspective in psychology.

Answers: **10-1.** evolutionary **10-2.** survival (adaptive) **10-3.** more **10-4.** test (evaluation).

PSYCHOLOGY TODAY: VIGOROUS AND DIVERSIFIED

11.   List and describe seven major research areas in psychology.

11-1.   Read over the descriptions of the research areas in Figure 1.6. Then match the names of the areas with the correct research topics by placing the appropriate letters in the blanks. (Note that the separation between these areas is *not* always perfect. For example, a personality theorist might also be a psychometrician with an interest in genetics or child development. Nonetheless, the following topics have been chosen so that one answer is correct for each.)

A. Experimental   _____ attitude change, group behavior

B. Physiological   _____ personality and intelligence assessment, test design, new statistical procedures

C. Cognitive   _____ personality assessment, personality description

D. Developmental   _____ "core" topics (e.g., perception, conditioning, motivation)

E. Psychometrics   _____ influence of the brain, bodily chemicals, genetics

F. Personality   _____ child, adolescent, and adult development

G. Social   _____ memory, decision making, thinking

11-2. In case you want to remember the list of seven research areas, here's a mnemonic device: *Peter Piper Picked Some Exquisite California Dills.* List the seven research areas by matching them with the first letter of each word.

Answers: 11-1. G, E, F, A, B, D, C **11-2.** physiological, psychometrics, personality, social, experimental, cognitive, developmental.

12. List and describe the four professional specialties in psychology.

12-1. Review Figure 1.7. Then match the following specialties with the descriptions by placing the appropriate letter in the blanks.

A. Clinical

____ Treatment of less severe problems and problems involving family, marital, and career difficulties.

B. Counseling

____ Treatment of psychological disorders, behavioral and emotional problems

C. Educational and school

____ Involves work on curriculum design and achievement testing in school settings.

D. Industrial and organizational

____ Psychology applied to business settings; deals with personnel, job satisfaction, etc.

Answers: 12-1. B, A, C, D.

PUTTING IT IN PERSPECTIVE: SEVEN KEY THEMES

13. Discuss the text's three organizing themes relating to psychology as a field of study.

13-1. When my (R. S.'s) older daughter Samantha was about three years old, she pulled a sugar bowl off a shelf and broke it while I was not present. Later, when I surveyed the damage, I said, "I see you've broken something." She said, "How do yer know, did yer see me do it?" I was amused, because while it was obvious who had broken it, her comment reflected psychology's foundation in direct observation. **Theme 1** is that psychology is _____. Empiricism is the point of view that knowledge should be acquired through _____.

13-2. We would ordinarily think that if one theory is correct, any other used to explain the same data must be wrong. While scientists do pit theories against each other, it is also the case that apparently contradictory theories may both be correct—as with the explanation of light in terms of both wave and particle theories. Thus, **Theme 2** indicates that psychology is _____ _____.

13-3. Psychology tolerates (and in fact encourages) different theoretical explanations because:

13-4. Psychology does not evolve in a vacuum. Social trends influence what is studied in psychology, and findings in psychology in turn affect what is going on in society. As stated in **Theme 3**, psychology evolves in a _____ context.

14. **Discuss the text's four organizing themes relating to psychology's subject matter.**

14-1.   When looking for an explanation of a particular behavior, someone might ask: "Well, why did he do it? Was it greed or ignorance?" The question implies that if one cause is present another cannot be, and it illustrates the very human tendency to reason in terms of (<u>one cause</u>/multiple causes).

14-2.   What influences the course of a ball rolled down an inclined plane? Gravity. And also friction. And the presence of other objects, and a number of other factors. That is the point of **Theme 4**: even more than is the case for physical events, behavior is determined by _____ _____.

14-3.   Among the multiple causes of human behavior is the category of causes referred to as *culture*. Cultural factors include the customs, beliefs, and values that we transmit across generations—what we eat, how we walk, what we wear, what we say, what we think, and so on. **Theme 5** indicates that our behavior is shaped by our _____ heritage.

14-4.   For example, I (R. S.) have observed that many American students traveling abroad initially think that their European lecturers talk down to them; the lecturers, in turn, may regard our students as spoiled and insolent. Perhaps closer to the truth is that there is a clash of customs invisible to both cultures. While we are shaped by our _____ _____, we are often _____ (aware/<u>unaware</u>) of the precise rules and customs that affect us.

14-5.   **Theme 6** relates to the influence of heredity and environment. What is the current consensus about the effect of heredity and environment on behavior?

14-6.   The scientific method relies on observation, but observation by itself isn't sufficient. Why isn't it?

14-7.   **Theme 7** indicates that our experience is subjective. What does this mean?

15. **Discuss three important considerations in designing a program to promote adequate studying.**

    15-1.   Three features of successful studying are listed below. Elaborate them by providing some of the details asked for.

        (a) A schedule: When should you plan your study schedule? Should you write it down? Do the routine or simpler tasks first, or begin with the major assignments?

        (b) A place: What are the major characteristics of a good study place?

        (c) A reward: When should you reward yourself? What kinds of rewards are suggested?

Answers: 15-1. (a) It's probably useful to set up a general schedule for a particular quarter or semester and then, at the beginning of each week, plan the specific assignments you intend to work on during each study session. Put your plans in writing. It's probably best to tackle the major assignments first, breaking them into smaller components as needed. (b) Find a place to study with minimal distractions: little noise, few interruptions. (c) Reward yourself shortly after you finish a particular amount of studying; snacking, watching TV, or calling a friend are suggested. **Suggestion:** You are studying now. Is this a good time for you? If it is, why not *write out your weekly schedule now.* Include schedule preparation as part of your study time.

16. **Describe the SQ3R method and explain what makes it effective.**

    16-1.   Below are descriptions of an individual applying the five steps of the SQ3R method to Chapter 1 of your text. The steps are not in the correct order. Label each of the steps and place a number in the parentheses to indicate the correct order.

    (   ) _____ Vanessa is taking introductory psychology using this book. She looks at the title of the first subsection of the chapter. After wondering briefly what it means for psychology to have "parents," she formulates this question: How was the field of psychology influenced by philosophy and physiology?

    (   ) _____ She turns to the back of Chapter 1 and notes that there is a chapter review. She turns back to the first page of the chapter, sees that the outline on that page matches the review at the end, and browses through some of the other parts of the chapter. She has a rough idea that the chapter is going to define the field and discuss its history.

    (   ) _____ Keeping in mind the question she has posed, she reads the section about the meeting of psychology's "parents" and formulates a tentative answer to her question. She also asks some additional questions: "Who was Descartes?" and "What method did philosophers use?"

    (   ) _____ She answers her first question as follows: "Philosophy (one of the parents) posed questions about the mind that made the study of human thinking and actions acceptable; physiology (the other parent) contributed the scientific method." She decides to note down her answer for later review.

(   ) _____ When she has finished steps 2 through 4 for all sections, Vanessa looks over the entire chapter, section by section. She repeats the questions for each section and attempts to answer each one.

16-2. What makes the SQ3R technique so effective?

Answers: 16-1. (2) Question (1) Survey (3) Read (4) Recite (5) Review **16-2.** It breaks the reading assignment into manageable segments; it requires understanding before you move on.

17. Summarize advice provided on how to get more out of lectures.

17-1. Using a few words for each point, summarize the four points on getting more out of lectures.

Answers: 17-1. Listen actively, read ahead, organize in terms of importance, ask questions.

18. Summarize advice provided on improving test-taking strategies.

18-1. Is it better to change answers on multiple-choice tests or to go with one's first hunch?

18-2. Following are situations you might encounter while taking a test. Reread the section on general test-taking tips and then indicate what you would do in each situation.

(a) You run into a particularly difficult item:

(b) The answer seems to be simple, but you think you may be missing something:

(c) The test is a timed test:

(d) You have some time left at the end of the test:

18-3. Following are samples of the situations mentioned under the discussion of tips for multiple-choice and essay exam questions. Based on the suggestions, what would you do?

(a) In a multiple-choice test, item c seems to be correct, but you have not yet read items d and e.

(b) You know that items a and b are correct, are unsure of items c and d, and item e is an "all of the above" option.

(c) You have no idea which multiple-choice alternative is correct. You note that option *a* has the word "always" in it, items *b* and *c* use the word "never," and item *d* says "frequently."

(d) You have read the stem of a multiple-choice item but you have not yet looked at the options.

Answers: 18-1. In general, changing answers seems to be better. Available research indicates that people are more than twice as likely to go from a wrong answer to a right one as from a right answer to a wrong one. **18-2.** (a) Skip it and come back to it if time permits. (b) Maybe the answer is simple! Don't make the question more complex than it was intended to be. (c) Budget your time, checking the proportion of the test completed against the time available. (d) Review, reconsider, check over your answers. **18-3.** (a) Read all options. (b) Answer *e*. (c) Answer *d*. (Still good advice and generally the best procedure to follow. But note that some professors, aware of the strategy, may throw in an item in which "always" is part of a correct answer! It's sort of like radar detectors: someone builds a better detector and someone else builds radar that can't be detected.) (d) Try to anticipate the correct answer *before* reading the options.

REVIEW OF KEY TERMS

Applied psychology
Behavior
Behaviorism
Clinical psychology
Cognition
Culture

Empiricism
Evolutionary psychology
Functionalism
Humanism
Introspection
Psychoanalytic theory

Psychology
SQ3R
Structuralism
Testwiseness
Theory
Unconscious

_____ **1.** Examines behavioral processes in terms of their adaptive or survival value for a species.

_____ **2.** The branch of psychology concerned with practical problems.

_____ **3.** School of thought based on notion that the task of psychology is to analyze consciousness into its basic elements.

_____ **4.** Observation of one's own conscious experience.

_____ **5.** School of thought asserting that psychology's major purpose was to investigate the function or purpose of consciousness.

_____ **6.** The theoretical orientation asserting that scientific psychology should study only observable behavior.

_____ **7.** An observable activity or response by an organism.

_____ **8.** Freudian theory that explains personality and abnormal behavior in terms of unconscious processes.

_____ **9.** According to psychoanalytic theory, that portion of the mind containing thoughts, memories, and wishes not in awareness but nonetheless exerting a strong effect on human behavior.

_____ **10.** The psychological theory asserting that human beings are unique and fundamentally different from other animals.

_____ **11.** Widely shared customs, beliefs, values, norms, and institutions that are transmitted socially across generations.

_____ **12.** The branch of psychology concerned with the diagnosis and treatment of psychological disorders.

_____ 13. Mental processes or thinking.

_____ 14. The science that studies behavior and the physiological and cognitive processes that underlie it, and it is the profession that applies this knowledge to solving various practical problems.

_____ 15. The point of view that knowledge should be based on observation.

_____ 16. A system of ideas used to link together or explain a set of observations.

_____ 17. A five-step procedure designed to improve study skills.

_____ 18. Ability to use the characteristics and formats of a test to maximize one's score.

Answers: 1. evolutionary psychology **2.** applied psychology **3.** structuralism **4.** introspection **5.** functionalism **6.** behaviorism **7.** behavior **8.** psychoanalytic theory **9.** unconscious **10.** humanism **11.** culture **12.** clinical psychology **13.** cognition **14.** psychology **15.** empiricism **16.** theory **17.** SQ3R **18.** testwiseness.

REVIEW OF KEY PEOPLE

Sigmund Freud   Carl Rogers   John B. Watson
William James   B. F. Skinner   Wilhelm Wundt

_____ 1. Founded experimental psychology and the first experimental psychology laboratory.

_____ 2. Chief architect of functionalism; described a "stream of consciousness."

_____ 3. Founded behaviorism.

_____ 4. Devised the theory and technique known as psychoanalysis.

_____ 5. Identified operant conditioning.

_____ 6. A major proponent of "humanistic" psychology.

Answers: 1. Wundt **2.** James **3.** Watson **4.** Freud **5.** Skinner **6.** Rogers.

SELF-QUIZ

1. Structuralism is the historical school of psychology that asserted that the purpose of psychology was to:
   a. study behavior
   b. discover the smaller elements that comprise consciousness
   c. explore the unconscious
   d. examine the purposes of conscious processes

2. Of the two parents of psychology, physiology and philosophy, which provided the method? What is the method?
   a. philosophy; logic, reasoning
   b. philosophy; intuition, introspection
   c. physiology; observation, science
   d. physiology; anatomy, surgery

3. Who is Wilhelm Wundt?
   a. He founded the first experimental laboratory.
   b. He founded the American Psychological Association.
   c. He discovered the classically conditioned salivary reflex.
   d. He founded behaviorism.

4. For John B. Watson, the appropriate subject matter of psychology was:
   a. animal behavior
   b. the unconscious
   c. consciousness
   d. human physiology

5. Which of the following represents a major breakthrough in the development of applied psychology?
   a. the use of the method of introspection
   b. Binet's development of the intelligence test
   c. establishment of the first animal laboratory
   d. Wundt's founding of experimental psychology

6. Within the field of psychology, Freud's ideas encountered resistance primarily because he emphasized:
   a. human consciousness
   b. human behavior
   c. introspection
   d. the unconscious

7. Which of the following would be considered the major principle of operant conditioning?
   a. Human behavior derives in part from free will; animal behavior is determined by the environment.
   b. Humans and other animals tend to repeat responses followed by positive outcomes.
   c. The majority of human behavior is based on thoughts, feelings, and wishes of which we are unaware.
   d. Human beings are fundamentally different from other animals.

8. Which of the following theorists would tend to emphasize explanations in terms of freedom and potential for personal growth?
   a. Carl Rogers
   b. Sigmund Freud
   c. B. F. Skinner
   d. Wilhelm Wundt

9. Recent research trends in psychology involve two areas largely ignored by early behaviorists. These two areas are:
   a. observable and measurable responses
   b. cognition (thinking) and physiological processes
   c. classical and operant conditioning
   d. the effect of environmental events and the behavior of lower animals

10. Which core psychological research area is primarily devoted to the study of such topics as memory, problem solving, and thinking?
   a. physiological
   b. social
   c. cognitive
   d. personality

11. Which of the following schools of psychology objected both to attempts to break consciousness into constituent elements and to attempts to analyze behavior into stimulus-response bonds?
   a. structuralism
   b. functionalism
   c. behaviorism
   d. Gestalt

12. The assertion that "psychology is empirical" means that psychology is based on:
   a. introspection
   b. logic
   c. observation
   d. mathematics

13. In looking for the causes of a particular behavior, psychologists assume:
    a. one cause or factor
    b. multifactorial causation
    c. free will
    d. infinite causation

14. Contemporary psychologists generally assume that human behavior is determined by:
    a. heredity
    b. environment
    c. heredity and environment acting jointly
    d. heredity, environment, and free will

15. What does SQ3R stand for?
    a. search, question, research, recommend, reconstitute
    b. silence, quietude, reading, writing, arithmetic
    c. summarize, quickly, read, research, reread
    d. survey, question, read, recite, review

Answers: 1. b **2.** c **3.** a **4.** a **5.** b **6.** d **7.** b **8.** a **9.** b **10.** c **11.** d **12.** c **13.** b **14.** c **15.** d.

THE RESEARCH ENTERPRISE IN PSYCHOLOGY

REVIEW OF KEY IDEAS

LOOKING FOR LAWS: THE SCIENTIFIC APPROACH TO BEHAVIOR

1. **Explain science's main assumption, and describe the goals of the scientific enterprise in psychology.**

   1-1. A major assumption of science is that events occur in a(an)_____ manner.

   1-2. The three interrelated goals of psychology and the other sciences are: (a) measurement and description, (b) understanding and prediction, and (c) application and control. Match each of the following descriptions with the goal it represents by placing the appropriate letters in the blanks. (There is considerable overlap among these goals; pick the closest match.)

   _____ Muscle relaxation techniques are found to be useful in reducing anxiety and improving concentration and memory.

   _____ A psychologist develops a test or procedure that measures anxiety.

   _____ Researchers find that when individuals are exposed to an object they happen to fear (e.g., a cliff, rats, roaches, snakes, spiders, etc.), their concentration and memory deteriorate.

   Answers: 1-1. lawful (predictable, consistent, regular, orderly) **1-2.** c, a, b.

2. **Explain the relations between theory, hypotheses, and research.**

   2-1. A theory is a system of ideas used to explain a set of observations. One could devise an exhaustive description of human behavior, but the description wouldn't be a theory unless it also included concepts that would _____ why the behavior occurs.

   2-2. Researchers can't test a theory all at once, but they can test one or two hypotheses derived from a theory. For example, evolutionary theory asserts that humans form groups because this behavioral tendency has had survival value. To reflect on this idea, one could test the _____ that certain specific aspects of group-oriented behavior occur in all cultures.

2-3. The relationship between theory, hypothesis, and research is this: theories suggest _____ (questions or predictions), which are then tested in _____. If the hypotheses are supported, confidence in the _____ is strengthened. If the findings fail to support the hypothesis, confidence in the theory decreases and the theory may be revised or discarded. In this way theory building is a gradual process with the result that over time theories (<u>remain fixed/are subject to revision</u>).

Answers: **2-1.** explain **2-2.** hypothesis **2-3.** hypotheses, experiments (research), theory, are subject to revision.

3. Outline the steps in a scientific investigation.

3-1. Following are the five steps generally used in performing a scientific investigation. Fill in the missing key words.

(a) Formulate a testable _____.

(b) Select the research _____ and design the study.

(c) _____ the data.

(d) _____ the data and draw _____.

(e) _____ the findings.

3-2. Following are descriptions of various phases in the project by Holmes and his co-workers (Wyler et al., 1968). Indicate which step of this study is being described by placing a letter from the previous question (a, b, c, d, or e) in the appropriate blank.

_____ The authors prepared a report of their findings that was accepted for publication in a technical journal.

_____ The patients' responses were expressed as numbers and analyzed with statistics. The data indicated that high scores on the life change questionnaire were associated with high scores on physical illness.

_____ Holmes and his co-workers thought that life change might be associated with increased illness. Before they began they made precise operational definitions of both life change and illness.

_____ The researchers decided to use a survey procedure involving administering questionnaires to a large number of people.

_____ The researchers gathered questionnaire data from 232 patients.

Answers: **3-1.** (a) hypothesis (b) method (c) collect (d) analyze, conclusions (e) report (publish, write up) **3-2.** e, d, a, b, c.

4. Discuss the advantages of the scientific approach.

4-1. We all tend to agree with the idea that "haste makes waste." We are also likely to agree with a commonsense saying that has the opposite implication: "a stitch in time saves nine." What are the two major advantages of the scientific approach over the commonsense approach?

Answers: 4-1. First, scientific descriptions generally have a *clarity and precision* lacking in commonsense proverbs. While we have a general idea about the meaning of haste, for example, we don't know precisely when or in what way or how much haste we should avoid. Second, science has an *intolerance for error* or for contradictory conclusions; commonsense sayings are likely to be contradictory. (Note that the proverbs in our example have contradictory messages: one says to slow down, the other says to hurry up.)

LOOKING FOR CAUSES: EXPERIMENTAL RESEARCH

5. **Describe the experimental method of research, explaining independent and dependent variables, experimental and control groups, and extraneous variables.**

   5-1. Schachter proposed that affiliation is caused (in part) by level of anxiety. What was his independent variable? _____ The dependent variable? _____

   5-2. The variable that is manipulated or varied by the experimenter is termed the _____ variable. The variable that is affected by, or is dependent on, the manipulation is termed the _____ variable.

   5-3. What is the name of the variable that *results from* the manipulation? _____ What is the name of the variable that *produces* the effect? _____

   5-4. The group of subjects that receives the experimental treatment is known as the _____ group; the group that does not is known as the _____ group.

   5-5. Control and experimental groups are quite similar in most respects. They differ in that the experimental group receives the experimental _____ and the control group does not. Thus, any differences found in the measure of the _____ variable are assumed to be due to differences in manipulation of the _____ variable.

   5-6. In Schachter's study, the experimental group was subjected to instructions that produced a high level of _____. Results were that the experimental group was higher than the control group on the dependent measure, the tendency toward _____ with others.

   5-7. An extraneous variable is any variable other than the _____ variable that seems likely to cause a difference between groups as measured by the _____ variable.

   5-8. To review the parts of an experiment: Suppose a researcher is interested in the effect of a drug on the running speed of rats. The _____ group is injected with the drug and the _____ group is not. Whether or not the rats received the drug would be the _____ variable, and running speed would be the _____ variable.

   5-9. Suppose also that the average age of the experimental rats is two years while the average age of the control rats is three months. What is the extraneous variable in this experiment? _____ Why does this variable present a problem?

5-10. Researchers generally control for extraneous variables through random _____ of subjects to groups. Write a definition of this procedure:

Answers: 5-1. anxiety, affiliation **5-2.** independent, dependent **5-3.** dependent, independent **5-4.** experimental, control **5-5.** treatment, dependent, independent **5-6.** anxiety, affiliation **5-7.** independent, dependent **5-8.** experimental, control, independent, dependent **5-9.** age, any difference between groups could be due to age rather than the independent variable **5-10.** assignment, All subjects have an equal chance of being assigned to any group or condition.

6. Explain the major advantages and disadvantages of the experimental method.

6-1. What is the major advantage of the experimental method?

6-2. What are the two major disadvantages of the experimental method?

6-3. Suppose a researcher is interested in the effect of excessive coffee drinking on health (e.g., 15 cups per day over an extended period of time). What would be a major *disadvantage* of using the experimental method to examine this particular question?

Answers: 6-1. The major advantage is that it permits researchers to make cause-effect conclusions **6-2.** The major disadvantages are that (a) precise experimental control may make the situation so artificial that it does not apply to the real world, and (b) ethical or practical considerations may prevent one from manipulating independent variables of interest **6-3.** To the extent that excessive coffee drinking is a suspected factor in health problems, it would be unethical and perhaps impossible to require an experimental group to drink that many cups daily.

LOOKING FOR LINKS: DESCRIPTIVE/CORRELATIONAL RESEARCH

7. Distinguish between positive and negative correlations and explain how the size of a correlation coefficient relates to the strength of an association.

7-1. Some examples will help illustrate the difference between positive and negative correlations. Which of the following relationships are positive (direct) and which are negative (inverse)? (Indicate with a + or − sign.)

_____ The better that students' grades are in high school, the better their grades tend to be in college.

_____ The more alcohol one has drunk, the slower his or her reaction time.

_____ The higher the anxiety, the poorer the test performance.

_____ The greater the fear, the greater the need for affiliation.

7-2. Which of the following indicates the *strongest correlational relationship*?

(a) 1.12   (b) –.92   (c) .58   (d) .87

Answers: 7-1. +, –, –, +**7-2.** b (not *a*, because correlations cannot exceed +1.00 or –1.00).

8. Explain how correlations relate to prediction and causation.

8-1. Suppose you have data indicating that the more money people make (e.g., the higher their annual incomes), the less depressed they report being on a mood survey. Thus, if you know the incomes of people in that group you should be able to _____, with some degree of accuracy, their self-reported depressed mood.

8-2. The accuracy of your prediction will depend on the size of the correlation coefficient. Which of the following correlation coefficients would allow you to predict with the greatest accuracy?

(a) +.41   (b) +.54   (c) –.65   (d) +.20

8-3. What kind of conclusion is justified on the basis of the previous relationship, a conclusion involving prediction or one involving a statement about causation? _____

8-4. Consider the (hypothetical) relationship discussed in the earlier question: You discover that the more money people make, the greater their happiness. Which of the following conclusions is justified? Explain.

(a) Money makes people happy.

(b) Happiness causes people to earn more money.

(c) Both happiness and money result from some unknown third factor.

(d) None of the above.

8-5. Again consider the relationship between money and happiness. Assume that money does not cause happiness and happiness does not cause money. What possible *third factor* can you think of that could cause both? (I'm asking you to make a wild speculation here just to get the idea of how third variables may operate.)

8-6. We aren't justified in making causal conclusions from a correlation, but we can predict. Let's examine what prediction means in the case of our hypothetical example. If the relationship really exists, what prediction would you make about people who are rich? What prediction would you make concerning people who are unhappy?

Answers: 8-1. predict 8-2. c 8-3. prediction (Generally one can't make causal conclusions from a correlation.) 8-4. d. While any of the statements is a *possible* causal explanation of the relationship, we don't know which one(s) may be correct because the data are correlational. Therefore, *no causal conclusions* are justified! 8-5. For example, poor health might cause one to be both unhappy *and* poverty stricken (while good health would cause one to be both happy and wealthy). Intelligence or aggressiveness or stubbornness or a number of other physiological or behavioral factors could be causally related *both* to income and to happiness without those two factors being causes of one another 8-6. You would predict that a group that was rich would also be happy and that a group that was unhappy would be poor. No causation is implied in these statements.

9. **Discuss three descriptive/correlational research methods.**

   9-1.   List the three descriptive methods described.

   9-2.   An in-depth and generally highly subjective or impressionistic report of a single individual (derived from interviews, psychological testing, and so on) is termed a _____ _____. Observation of human beings or animals in their natural environments, conducted without directly intervening, is known as _____ _____. The method that uses questionnaires or interviews to find out about specific aspects of human attitudes or opinions is known as the _____ technique.

   Answers: 9-1. naturalistic observation, case studies, and surveys 9-2. case study, naturalistic observation, survey.

10. **Explain the major advantages and disadvantages of descriptive/correlational research.**

   10-1.   Describe one major advantage and one major disadvantage of the descriptive approach.

   Answers: 10-1. An advantage is that descriptive methods allow researchers to study phenomena that they could not study with experimental methods; thus, descriptive methods broaden the scope of phenomena studied. A disadvantage is that one generally cannot make cause-effect conclusions from descriptive data.

LOOKING FOR FLAWS: EVALUATING RESEARCH

11. **Describe the four common flaws in research (sampling bias, placebo effects, distortions in self-report, and experimenter bias).**

   11-1.   Dr. Brutalbaum distributes a questionnaire in an attempt to find out how the students in a particular course react to his teaching. Unfortunately, the day he selects for the evaluation is the day before a scheduled vacation, and about half the students are absent. He knows, however, that he does not have to test the entire class, and the sample that remains is large enough. Is the sample representative? Define the concept representative sample. Which of the four common flaws is illustrated?

11-2. Brutalbaum is now concerned about class attendance and decides to find out what proportion of students miss class regularly. He distributes a questionnaire that asks students to indicate how many classes they have missed during the course of the semester. Which of the four common flaws is he likely to encounter?

11-3. A student in Brutalbaum's class orders some audio tapes that promise sleep learning for psychology students. (Brutalbaum is dubious, because from his observations students sleep a lot in his classes but still don't seem to learn much.) The student obtains an appropriate sample of psychology students, distributes the tapes to a random half, *tells the experimental subjects about the anticipated sleep-learning benefits*, and instructs them to use the tapes each night for one month. He has no contact with the remaining random half, his "control" group. After the next test the student analyzes the results. The mean test score of the experimental group is statistically significantly higher than that of the control group. He concludes that the higher grades are due to the taped messages.

(a) For review: What is the independent variable?

(b) What are the names of two flaws (of the four discussed in the text) illustrated in this study? (Note that these two flaws overlap somewhat in meaning.)

(c) What two procedures could have been used to correct the student's experiment?

Answers: 11-1. Probably not representative. A representative sample is one that is similar in composition to the population from which it is drawn. In this case, it seems likely that students who attend are different from those who do not (e.g., perhaps more enthusiastic, harder working, etc.). Thus, the flaw illustrated is *sampling bias* **11-2.** He is likely to encounter distortions in self-report, which may include the *social desirability bias*, misunderstanding of the questionnaire, memory errors, and response set (e.g., tendencies to agree or disagree regardless of content) **11-3.** (a) the tapes (versus no tapes) (b) Through contact with the experimental group the experimenter may have produced a *placebo effect* and unintentionally influenced subjects through *experimenter bias*. (c) A fake or *placebo condition* (in which subjects receive a fake experimental treatment) and a *double-blind procedure* (in which *neither the experimenter nor subjects* would know who is in the experimental group and who is in the control group).

LOOKING AT ETHICS: DO THE ENDS JUSTIFY THE MEANS?

12. Discuss the pros and cons of deception in research with human subjects.

12-1. In the space below present one or two of the arguments in favor of using deception and one or two arguments against.

Answers: 12-1. On the con side, deception is, after all, lying; it may undermine people's trust in others; it may cause distress. On the pro side, many research issues could not be investigated without deception; the "white lies" involved are generally harmless; research indicates that deception studies are not actually harmful to subjects; the advances in knowledge obtained may improve human well-being.

13. **Discuss the controversy about the use of animals as research subjects.**

13-1. What is the major reason that some people object to using animal subjects in research? In view of this objection, what moral considerations are raised by those who favor using animals in research?

Answers: 13-1. Many people believe that it is morally wrong to use animals in research, especially in painful or harmful treatments that would be unacceptable for human subjects. In defense of the practice, others cite the significant advances in treatment of a variety of mental and physical disorders that have resulted from animal research. The question to some degree involves the issue of whether or not saving human lives or finding remedies for human illnesses justifies the sacrifice or pain inflicted on research animals.

PUTTING IT IN PERSPECTIVE

14. **Explain how this chapter highlighted two of the text's unifying themes.**

14-1. **Theme 1** is that psychology is _____, which means that its conclusions are based on systematic _____ and that it tends to be (skeptical/credulous).

14-2. In what way did the discussion of methodology suggest that psychology tends to be skeptical of its results?

14-3. Which of the methodological problems discussed point up psychology's awareness of the subjective nature of our experience?

Answers: 14-1. empirical, observation (experience), skeptical **14-2.** Researchers constantly look for methodological flaws, and they subject their results to critical scrutiny by other scientists. **14-3.** Scientists try to guard against subjective reactions, both their own and those of their subjects, by maintaining a skeptical attitude and by building in appropriate experimental controls, including ones for placebo effects and experimenter bias.

APPLICATION: FINDING AND READING JOURNAL ARTICLES

15. **Describe the *Psychological Abstracts* and explain how its author and subject indexes can be used to locate information.**

15-1. *Psychological Abstracts* contains abstracts or a concise _____ of articles published in psychological journals. To find information about a particular article, consult either the author index or the _____ index found at the back of each monthly issue of the *Abstracts*. Cumulative _____ are published annually.

15-2. If you know the author's name you can easily find the article. Next to the author's name, each article he or she has published within the period is identified by a particular number, its _____ number.

15-3. Once you know the index number you can find the abstract. As you can see in Figure 2.13 in your text, the abstract provides not only a summary but the exact reference for the article, including publication date, page numbers, and name of the _____ in which the article was published.

15-4. The subject index works the same way as the author index, but it's a little more like looking through the yellow pages of a phone book (e.g., do you look under cars, automobiles, or rental?). As with the author index, you can locate the abstract once you find the index _____ of a particular article. A quick glance at the abstract will then tell you whether the article is likely to be of interest.

15-5. The availability of personal computers has made the search easier. The information contained in *Psychological Abstracts* from 1887 on is now stored in the _____ databases PsycINFO and PsychLIT. The advantage of computerized over manual searches is that the former are much faster, more precise, and more thorough. With a computerized search you are much (<u>less/more</u>) likely to miss relevant articles, and by pairing two topics you can find precisely those articles that are relevant to your particular question.

Answers: 15-1. summaries, subject, indexes **15-2.** index **15-3.** journal **15-4.** number **15-5.** computerized, less.

16. Describe the standard organization of journal articles reporting on psychological research.

16-1. In the blanks below list the six parts of the standard journal article in the order in which they occur. (As a hint, the initial letters of each section are listed on the left.)

A _____

I _____

M _____

R _____

D _____

R _____

16-2. In the blanks below match the names of the sections of the standard journal article with the descriptions.

_____ States the hypothesis and reviews the literature relevant to the hypothesis.

_____ A list of all the sources referred to in the paper.

_____ A summary.

_____ Presents the data; may include statistical analyses, graphs, and tables.

_____ Describes what the researchers did in the study; includes subjects, procedures, and data collection techniques.

_____ Interprets or evaluates the data and presents conclusions.

Answers: 16-1. abstract, introduction, method, results, discussion, references **16-2.** introduction, references, abstract, results, method, discussion.

REVIEW OF KEY TERMS

Case study
Confounding of variables
Control group
Correlation
Correlation coefficient
Data collection techniques
Dependent variable
Double-blind procedure
Experiment
Experimental group
Experimenter bias

Extraneous variables
Hypothesis
Independent variable
Journal
Naturalistic observation
Operational definition
Participants
Placebo effects
Population
Random assignment
Replication

Research methods
Sample
Sampling bias
Social desirability bias
Statistics
Subjects
Survey
Theory
Variables

_____ 1. Any of the factors in an experiment that are controlled or observed by an experimenter or that in some other way affect the outcome.

_____ 2. A tentative statement about the expected relationship between two or more variables.

_____ 3. Precisely defines each variable in a study in terms of the operations needed to produce or measure that variable.

_____ 4. The persons or animals whose behavior is being studied.

_____ 5. Differing ways of conducting research, which include experiments, case studies, surveys, and naturalistic observation.

_____ 6. A research method in which independent variables are manipulated and which permits causal interpretations.

_____ 7. A condition or event that an experimenter varies in order to observe its impact.

_____ 8. The variable that results from the manipulation in an experiment.

_____ 9. The group in an experiment that receives a treatment as part of the independent variable manipulation.

_____ 10. The group in an experiment that does not receive the treatment.

_____ 11. Any variables other than the independent variables that seem likely to influence the dependent measure in an experiment.

_____ 12. Distribution of subjects in an experiment in which each subject has an equal chance of being assigned to any group or condition.

_____ 13. A link or association between variables such that one can be predicted from the other.

_____ 14. The statistic that indicates the degree of relationship between variables.

_____ 15. A research method in which the researcher observes behavior in the natural environment without directly intervening.

_____ 16. An in-depth, generally subjective, investigation of an individual subject.

_____ 17. A questionnaire or interview used to gather information about specific aspects of subjects' behavior.

_____ 18. Procedures for making empirical observations, including questionnaires, interviews, psychological tests, and physiological recordings.

_____	19. Mathematical techniques that help in organizing, summarizing, and interpreting numerical data.
_____	20. A repetition of a study to determine whether the previously obtained results can be duplicated.
_____	21. A group of subjects taken from a larger population.
_____	22. A larger group from which a sample is drawn and to which the researcher wishes to generalize.
_____	23. Exists when a sample is not representative of the population from which it was drawn.
_____	24. Occurs when a researcher's expectations influence the results of the study.
_____	25. Effects that occur when subjects experience a change due to their expectations (or to a "fake" treatment).
_____	26. Occurs when an extraneous variable makes it difficult to sort out the effects of the independent variable.
_____	27. The tendency to answer questions about oneself in a socially approved manner.
_____	28. A research strategy in which neither the subjects nor experimenters know which condition or treatment the subjects are in.
_____	29. A periodical that publishes technical and scholarly material within a discipline.
_____	30. A system of interrelated ideas used to explain a set of observations.
_____	31. The persons or animals whose behavior is being studied; also referred to as subjects.

Answers: 1. variables **2.** hypothesis **3.** operational definition **4.** subjects (or participants) **5.** research methods **6.** experiment **7.** independent variable **8.** dependent variable **9.** experimental group **10.** control group **11.** extraneous variables **12.** random assignment **13.** correlation **14.** correlation coefficient **15.** naturalistic observation **16.** case study **17.** survey **18.** data collection techniques **19.** statistics **20.** replication **21.** sample **22.** population **23.** sampling bias **24.** experimenter bias **25.** placebo effects **26.** confounding of variables **27.** social desirability bias **28.** double-blind procedure **29.** journal **30.** theory **31.** participants (or subjects).

REVIEW OF KEY PEOPLE

Neal Miller   Robert Rosenthal   Stanley Schachter

_____	1. Studied the effect of anxiety on affiliation.
_____	2. Studied experimenter bias, a researcher's unintended influence on the behavior of subjects.
_____	3. Asserted that the benefits of animal research (e.g., the resulting treatments for mental and physical disorders) far outweigh the harm done.

Answers: 1. Schachter **2.** Rosenthal **3.** Miller.

SELF-QUIZ

1. Which of the following is a major assumption of science?
   a. Events occur in a relatively orderly or predictable manner.
   b. Cause and effect is indicated by correlational relationships.
   c. In contrast to the behavior of lower animals, human behavior is in part a function of free will.
   d. Events are largely randomly determined.

2. An experimenter tests the hypothesis that physical exercise helps people's mood (makes them happier). Subjects in the experimental group participate on Monday and Tuesday and those in the control group on Wednesday and Thursday. What is the *independent* variable?
   a. the hypothesis
   b. day of the week
   c. the exercise
   d. the mood (degree of happiness)

3. Regarding the experiment described in the previous question: What is the *dependent* variable?
   a. the hypothesis
   b. day of the week
   c. the exercise
   d. the mood (degree of happiness)

4. Regarding the experiment described above: What is an *extraneous* (confounding) variable?
   a. the hypothesis
   b. day of the week
   c. the exercise
   d. the mood (degree of happiness)

5. The major advantage of the experimental method over the correlational approach is that the experimental method:
   a. permits one to make causal conclusions
   b. allows for prediction
   c. is generally less artificial than correlational procedures
   d. permits the study of people in groups

6. In looking through some medical records you find that there is a strong relationship between depression and chronic pain: the stronger the physical pain that people report, the higher their scores on an inventory that measures depression. Which of the following is the best statement of conclusions?
   a. Depression tends to produce chronic pain.
   b. Chronic pain tends to produce depression.
   c. Both chronic pain and depression result from some unknown third factor.
   d. Depression could have caused the pain, pain could have caused the depression, or both pain and depression could have been caused by an unknown third factor.

7. In an experiment, neither the experimenter nor the subjects know what treatment condition they are in (e.g., whether they are in the experimental or control group). What has occurred?
   a. a confounding or extraneous variable
   b. the double-blind has been used
   c. experimenter bias
   d. a correlation coefficient

8. In his experiment on anxiety and affiliation, Schachter defined anxiety in terms of the specific instructions given by "Dr. Zilstein." In Schachter's experiment, then, anxiety was
   a. existentially defined
   b. conditionally defined
   c. operationally defined
   d. undefined

9. Suppose that researchers find an inverse relationship between alcohol consumption and speed of response: the more alcohol consumed, the slower the response. Which of the following fictitious statistics could possibly represent that correlation?
   a. – 4.57
   b. –.87
   c. .91
   d. .05

10. In the Schachter experiment on anxiety and affiliation, need to affiliate (to have the company of others) was the
    a. independent variable
    b. dependent variable
    c. extraneous variable
    d. intervening variable

11. An instructor wishes to find out whether a new teaching method is superior to his usual procedures, so he conducts an experiment. Everyone in his classes is quite excited about the prospect of learning under the new procedure, but of course he cannot administer the new teaching method to everyone. A random half of the students receive the new method and the remaining half receive the old. What is the most obvious flaw in this experiment?
    a. Subjects should have been systematically assigned to groups.
    b. The sample is not representative of the population.
    c. Placebo effects or experimenter bias are likely to affect results.
    d. Distortions in self-report will affect results.

12. What procedure helps correct for experimenter bias?
    a. extraneous or confounding variables
    b. sleep learning or hypnosis
    c. a higher standard for statistical significance
    d. use of the double-blind procedure

13. With regard to the topic of deception in research with human subjects, which of the following is true?
    a. Researchers are careful to avoid deceiving subjects.
    b. Some topics could not be investigated unless deception was used.
    c. It has been empirically demonstrated that deception causes severe distress.
    d. All psychological research must involve some deception.

14. Which of the following is among the six standard parts of a psychological journal article?
    a. conclusions
    b. bibliography
    c. data summary
    d. results

15. The Author Index in the *Psychological Abstracts* provides:
    a. names of current APA members
    b. registration and biographical information about frequent authors
    c. index numbers that locate article summaries
    d. names of authors who specialize in abstractions

Answers: 1. a **2.** c **3.** d **4.** b **5.** a **6.** d **7.** b **8.** c **9.** b **10.** b **11.** c **12.** d **13.** b **14.** d **15.** c.

THE BIOLOGICAL BASES OF BEHAVIOR

REVIEW OF KEY IDEAS

COMMUNICATION IN THE NERVOUS SYSTEM

1. **Describe the main functions of the two types of nervous tissue.**

   1-1.   One of the major types of nervous tissue provides very important services to the other type: such as removing waste, supplying nutrients, insulating, and providing structural support. Individual members of this kind of nervous tissue are called _____.

   1-2.   The other type of nervous tissue receives, integrates, and transmits information. Individual members of this type of tissue are called _____.

   1-3.   While most neurons just receive and transmit information from one neuron to another, two kinds of neurons are specialized for additional tasks. Name the two types and describe their specialization below.

   Answers: 1-1. glia cells **1-2.** neurons **1-3.** Sensory neurons receive information from the outside environment, while motor neurons activate the muscles.

2. **Describe the various parts of the neuron.**

   2-1.   The neuron has three basic parts: the dendrites, the cell body or soma, and the axon. The major mission of the average neuron is to receive information from one neuron and pass it on to the next neuron. The receiving part is the job of the branch-like parts called _____. They then pass the message along to the nucleus of the cell, called the cell body, or _____. From there the message is sent down the _____ to be passed along to other neurons.

   2-2.   Many axons are wrapped in a fatty jacket called the _____, which permits for faster transmission of information and prevents messages from getting on to the wrong track. Like the covering on an electrical cord, myelin acts as an _____ material.

2-3. When the neural message reaches the end of the axon it excites projections called terminal _____, which then release a chemical substance into the junction that separates them from other neurons. This junction between neurons is called the _____.

2-4. Identify the major parts of a neuron in the figure below. Note that the arrow indicates the direction of the flow of information.

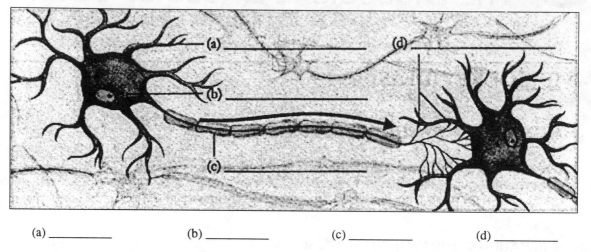

(a) _____   (b) _____   (c) _____   (d) _____

Answers: 2-1. dendrites, soma, axon. **2-2.** myelin sheath, insulating. **2-3.** buttons, synapse. **2-4.** (a) dendrites, (b) cell body or soma, (c) axon, (d) terminal buttons.

3. Describe the neural impulse.

3-1. When it is at rest, the neuron is like a tiny battery in that it contains a weak (<u>negative/positive</u>) charge. When the neuron is stimulated, the cell membrane becomes more permeable. This allows positively charged _____ ions to flow into the cell, thus lessening the cell's negative charge.

3-2. The change in the charge of the cell caused by the inflow of positively charged sodium ions is called an _____, which travels down the _____ of the neuron. After the firing of an action potential, there is a brief period in which no further action potentials can be generated. This brief period is called the absolute _____ period.

3-3. The text likens the neuron to a gun in that it either fires or it does not fire. This property of the neuron is called the _____ law. Neurons transmit information about the strength of a stimulus by variations in the number of action potentials generated. For example, in comparison to a weak stimulus, a strong stimulus will generate a (<u>higher/lower</u>) rate of action potentials.

Answers: 3-1. negative, sodium **3-2.** action potential, axon, refractory **3-3.** all-or-none, higher.

4. Describe how neurons communicate at chemical synapses.

4-1. A neuron passes its message on to another neuron by releasing a chemical messenger into the gap or _____ that separates it from other neurons. The sending neuron, called the _____ neuron, releases a chemical messenger into the synaptic cleft, which then excites the _____ neuron.

4-2. The chemical messenger that provides this transmitting service is called a _____. The chemical binds with specifically tuned receptor sites on the postsynaptic neurons. In other words, the receptor sites accept some neurotransmitters and reject _____. Thus a specific receptor site and a specific neurotransmitter act in the manner of a lock and _____.

4-3. When the neurotransmitter combines with a molecule at the receptor site it causes a voltage change at the receptor site called a _____ potential (PSP). One type of PSP is excitatory and (increases/ decreases) the probability of producing an action potential in the receiving neuron. The other type is inhibitory and _____ the probability of producing an action potential.

4-4. Whether or not a neuron fires depends on the number of excitatory PSPs it is receiving and the number of _____ PSPs it is receiving. PSPs (do/do not) follow the all-or-none law.

4-5. Put the five steps of communication at the synapse in their correct order (by using the numbers 1 through 5):

_____ (a) The reuptake of transmitters by the presynaptic neuron.

_____ (b) The enzyme inactivation or drifting away of transmitters in the synapse.

_____ (c) The synthesis and storage of transmitters.

_____ (d) The binding of transmitters at receptor sites on the postsynaptic membrane.

_____ (e) The release of transmitters into the synaptic cleft.

Answers: 4-1. synaptic cleft, presynaptic, postsynaptic **4-2.** neurotransmitter, others, key **4-3.** postsynaptic, increases, decreases **4-4.** inhibitory, do not **4-5.** (a) 5 (b) 4 (c) 1 (d) 3 (e) 2.

5. Discuss how acetylcholine, the biogenic amines, GABA, and endorphins are related to behavior.

5-1. Our moods, thoughts, and actions all depend on the action of neurotransmitters. For example, the movement of all muscles depends on _____ (ACh). An inadequate supply of acetylcholine has also been implicated in the memory losses seen in _____ disease.

5-2. Three neurotransmitters, dopamine, norepinephrine, and serotonin, are collectively known as _____. Both Parkinsonism and schizophrenia have been linked with alterations in _____ activity, while the mood changes found in depression have been linked to receptor sites for _____.

5-3. Still another group of neurotransmitters, including GABA and glycine, are unlike other neurotransmitters in that they only have (excitatory/inhibitory) effects at receptor sites. Most other neurotransmitters can have either inhibitory or excitatory effects. Lowered levels of GABA in the brain may allow for heightened neural activity, which translates into feelings of _____. Tranquilizers appear to work by increasing inhibitory activity at GABA synapses, a task that would normally be accomplished by _____ itself.

5-4. Endorphins are neuropeptides produced by the body that have effects similar to those produced by the drug _____ and its derivatives. That is, they are able to reduce pain and also induce _____. Endorphins work in two different ways. Some bind to specific receptor sites and thus serve as _____. Most endorphins, however, work by modulating the activity of specific neurotransmitters. In this role they are said to serve as _____ _____.

Answers: 5-1. acetylcholine, Alzheimer's **5-2.** biogenic amines, dopamine, norepinephrine **5-3.** inhibitory, anxiety, GABA **5-4.** opium, pleasure, neurotransmitters, neuromodulators.

ORGANIZATION OF THE NERVOUS SYSTEM

6. **Provide an overview of the organization of the nervous system.**

With approximately 100 to 180 billion individual neurons to control, it is important that the central nervous system have some kind of organizational structure. This organizational structure is depicted in Figure 3.7 of the text, and it will prove helpful if you have this figure in front of you while answering the following questions.

6-1. Answer the following questions regarding the organization of the nervous system.

(a) What are the two major divisions of the nervous system?

(b) What two subdivisions make up the peripheral nervous system?

(c) What two subdivisions make up the autonomic nervous system?

(d) What are the two major divisions of the central nervous system?

6-2. With respect to the opposing roles of the sympathetic and parasympathetic nervous systems, which system:

(a) prepares the body for fight or flight?

(b) conserves the body's resources?

6-3. What are the roles of the meninges covering and the cerebrospinal fluid?

Answers: 6-1. (a) The central nervous system and the peripheral nervous system. (b) The somatic nervous system and the autonomic nervous system. (c) The sympathetic nervous system and the parasympathetic nervous system. (d) The brain and the spinal cord. **6-2.** (a) The sympathetic system. (b) The parasympathetic system. **6-3.** They serve as protective features for the brain and spinal cord.

THE BRAIN AND BEHAVIOR

7. **Describe the new brain-imaging methods (CT, PET, MRI scans) that are used to study brain structure and function.**

7-1. There are three new kinds of brain-imaging procedures that have come into recent use. One of these procedures consists of a computer-enhanced X-ray machine that compiles multiple X-rays of the brain into a single vivid picture. The resulting images are called _____ scans. An even newer device that produces clearer three-dimensional images of the brain goes by the name of magnetic resonance imaging scanner, and the images it produces are known as _____ scans.

7-2. Unlike CT and MRI scans, which can only show the structure of the brain, the positron emission tomography scanner can portray the brain's actual _____ across time. The images produced by this procedure are called _____ scans.

Answers: **7-1.** CT, MRI **7-2.** activity, PET.

8. Summarize the key structures and functions of the hindbrain and midbrain.

8-1. The brain can be subdivided into three major structures. Moving up from the top of the spinal cord, one first encounters the hindmost part of the brain, or _____. Next comes the middle part or _____. At the top we encounter the _____.

8-2. Three separate structures make up the hindbrain: the cerebellum, the pons, and the medulla. The structure that attaches to the top of the spinal cord and controls many essential functions such as breathing and circulation is called the _____. The section that forms a bridge of fibers between the brainstem and the cerebellum is called the _____. The structure that is essential for executing and coordinating physical movement is called the _____.

8-3. Helping to control sensory processes and voluntary movements is one of the major roles of the _____. It also shares a structure with the hindbrain that is essential for the regulation of sleep and wakefulness as well as modulation of muscular reflexes, breathing, and pain perception. This structure is called the _____ formation.

Answers: **8-1.** hindbrain, midbrain, forebrain **8-2.** medulla, pons, cerebellum **8-3.** midbrain, reticular.

9. Summarize the key functions of the thalamus, hypothalamus, and limbic system.

9-1. The structure that serves as a way station for all sensory information (except for smell) headed for the brain is called the _____. The thalamus also appears to play an active role in _____ sensory information.

9-2. In addition to its role in controlling the autonomic nervous system and linking the brain to the endocrine system, the hypothalamus also plays a major role in regulating basic biological drives such as fighting, _____, feeding, and _____.

9-3. An interconnected network of structures involved in the control of emotion, motivation, and memory are collectively known as the _____ system. Damage to one of these structures, the hippocampus, is found in Alzheimer's disease patients; thus it must play a key role in the formation of _____. However, the limbic system is best known for its role as the seat of _____. Electrical stimulation of particular areas of the limbic system in rats, monkeys, and human beings appears to produce intense pleasure, but the pleasure seems to be least intense in _____. The key neurotransmitter in these pleasure centers appears to be _____.

Answers: **9-1.** thalamus, integrating **9-2.** fleeing, mating **9-3.** limbic, memories, emotion, humans, dopamine.

10. **Describe the structure of the cerebrum and the key function of the four lobes in the cerebral cortex.**

    10-1.   The cerebrum is the brain structure that is responsible for our most complex _____ activities. Its folded outer surface is called the _____ cortex. The cerebrum is divided into two halves, known as the _____ and _____ cerebral hemispheres. The two hemispheres communicate with each other by means of a wide band of fibers called the _____ _____.

    10-2.   Each cerebral hemisphere is divided into four parts called lobes. Match these four lobes (occipital, parietal, temporal, and frontal) with their key function:

        (a) Contains the primary motor cortex, which controls the movement of muscles _____

        (b) Contains the primary visual cortex, which initiates the processing of visual information _____

        (c) Contains the primary auditory cortex, which initiates the processing of auditory information _____

        (d) Contains the somatosensory cortex, which registers the sense of touch _____

Answers: 10-1. mental, cerebral, right, left, corpus callosum **10-2.** (a) frontal (b) occipital (c) temporal (d) parietal.

RIGHT BRAIN/LEFT BRAIN: CEREBRAL SPECIALIZATION

11. **Summarize evidence that led scientists to view the left hemisphere as the dominant hemisphere and describe how research on cerebral specialization changed this view.**

    11-1.   Until recent years, it was believed that the left hemisphere dominated a submissive right hemisphere. Evidence for this belief came from several sources, which all seemed to indicate that the left hemisphere played the dominant role with respect to the use of _____. For example, damage to an area in the frontal lobe known as _____ area was associated with speech deficits. Also, damage to another area located in the temporal lobe was found to be associated with difficulty in speech comprehension. This area is called _____ area. Both of these areas are located in the _____ cerebral hemisphere.

    11-2.   Answer the following questions regarding split-brain research.

        (a) What was the result of severing the corpus callosum in these patients?

        (b) Which hemisphere was found to be primarily responsible for verbal and language tasks in general?

        (c) Which hemisphere was found to be primarily responsible for visual and spatial tasks?

    11-3.   What can be concluded with respect to hemispheric domination from both split-brain and intact-brain studies?

Answers: 11-1. language, Broca's, Wernicke's, left **11-2.** (a) The two cerebral hemispheres could no longer communicate with each other. (b) The left cerebral hemisphere. (c) The right cerebral hemisphere. **11-3.** Neither hemisphere dominates, rather each has its own specialized tasks.

THE ENDOCRINE SYSTEM: ANOTHER WAY TO COMMUNICATE

12. Describe the workings of the endocrine system.

12-1. Answer the following questions regarding the workings of the endocrine system.

(a) What is the role played by the hormones in the endocrine system?

(b) While many glands comprise the endocrine system, which one functions as a master gland to control the others?

(c) What structure is the real power behind the throne here?

12-2. Fill in the boxes in the diagram below showing the role of the pituitary gland in the "fight or flight" response to stress.

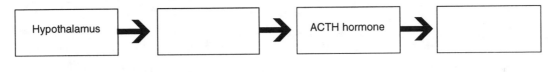

12-3. What is the role of sexual hormones:

(a) Prior to birth?

(b) At puberty?

Answers: 12-1. (a) They serve as chemical messengers. (b) The pituitary gland. (c) The hypothalamus. **12-2.** pituitary, adrenal cortex **12-3.** (a) They direct the formation of the external sexual organs. (b) They are responsible for the emergence of the secondary sexual characteristics.

HEREDITY AND BEHAVIOR: IS IT ALL IN THE GENES?

13. Describe the structures and processes involved in genetic transmission.

13-1. When a human sperm and egg unite at conception they form a one-celled organism called a _____. This cell contains 46 chromosomes, half of which are contributed by each _____, thus making 23 pairs. Each member of a pair operates in conjunction with its _____ member. The zygote then evolves to form all of the cells in the body, each of which, except for the sex cells, have _____ pairs of chromosomes.

13-2. Each chromosome is actually a threadlike strand of a _____ molecule, and along this threadlike structure are found the individual units of information, called _____, that determine our biological makeup. Like chromosomes, genes operate in _____. For example, eye color is determined by a pair of genes. If both parents contribute a gene for the same color, the child will inherit this eye color, and the two genes are said to be _____. If the parents contribute two different genes for eye color, the genes are said to be _____, and the child will inherit the eye color carried by the dominant gene. When heterozygous genes are paired, the dominant gene masks the _____ gene.

Answers: 13-1. zygote, parent, opposite, 23 13-2. DNA, genes, pairs, homozygous, heterozygous, recessive.

14. Explain the special methods used to investigate the influence of heredity on behavior.

14-1.   If a trait is due to heredity, then more closely related members of a family should show (lesser/greater) resemblance on this trait than less closely related family members. Studies using this method are called _____studies. Data gathered from family studies (can/cannot) furnish conclusive proof as to the heritability of a specific trait. Even when it is demonstrated that a particular trait is highly related to the degree of family relationship, the cause for this relationship could be either heredity or _____.

14-2.   A second method in this line of investigation is to compare specific traits across identical twins and fraternal twins. This method, called _____studies, assumes that inherited traits are much more likely to be found among _____ twins than among fraternal twins. These studies do in fact show that for many characteristics, such as intelligence and extraversion, the resemblance is closest for _____ twins. However, since identical twins are far from identical on these characteristics, _____ factors must also play a role here.

14-3.   A third method in this line of investigation is to study children who have been separated from their biological parents at a very early age and raised by adoptive parents. The idea behind these _____ studies is that if the adoptive children more closely resemble their biological parents with respect to a specific trait, then it can be assumed that _____ plays a major role. On the other hand, if the adoptive children more closely resemble their adoptive parents with respect to a specific trait it would indicate that _____ plays a major role. Studies using this method to study the inheritabilty of intelligence have found that adoptive children more closely resemble their _____ parents on this particular trait, but not by much. This would indicate that a trait such as intelligence is influenced by both heredity and _____.

Answers: 14-1. greater, family, cannot, environment 14-2. twin, identical, identical, environmental 14-3. adoption, heredity, environment, biological, environment.

15. Explain how heredity may influence behavior and how its influence may be moderated by environment.

15-1.   The answer to the question "Is it all in the genes?" now appears to be quite clear. The answer is No. However, neither is it all in the environment. What does this mean with respect to most behavioral traits?

15-2.   How can the interaction between heredity and environment be used to explain the development of schizophrenic disorders?

Answers: 15-1. They result from an interaction between heredity and environment. 15-2. One can inherit a vulnerability to schizophrenia, but the actual expression of this disorder will depend on environmental factors.

PUTING IT IN PERSPECTIVE

16. Explain how this chapter highlighted three of the text's unifying themes.

16-1. Indicate which of the three unifying themes–heredity and environment jointly influence behavior, behavior is determined by multiple causes, and psychology is empirical–is particularly illustrated in each of the following situations.

(a) The development of schizophrenic disorders.

(b) The new discoveries of cerebral specialization and the impact of heredity on behavior.

(c) The development of personal characteristics such as sarcasm and artistic interest.

Answers: 16-1. (a) Behavior is determined by multiple causes. (b) Psychology is empirical. (c) Heredity and environment jointly influence behavior.

APPLICATION: THINKING CRITICALLY ABOUT THE CONCEPT OF "TWO MINDS IN ONE"

17. Outline four popular ideas linking cerebral specialization to cognitive processes and evaluate each of these in light of currently available evidence.

17-1. Your text lists four popular ideas that have found support among some neuroscientists and psychologists. These ideas are:

(a) The two hemispheres are _____ to process different cognitive tasks.

(b) The two hemispheres have _____ modes of thinking.

(c) People vary in their _____ on one hemisphere as opposed to the other.

(d) Schools should place more emphasis on teaching the _____ side of the brain.

17-2. We will now proceed through each of these four assumptions to show how each has to be qualified in light of currently available evidence.

(a) The idea that the left and right brains are specialized to handle different kinds of information (is/is not) supported by research. However, there is evidence that this specialization hardly occurs in some persons, while in other persons the specialization is reversed, particularly among _____-handed persons. Moreover, most tasks require the ongoing cooperation of _____ hemispheres.

(b) The assertion that each hemisphere has its own mode of thinking is (plausible/confirmed). A big problem here, however, is that mode of thinking, or cognitive style, has proven difficult to both _____ and _____.

(c) The assertion that some people are left-brained while other are right-brained (is/is not) conclusive at this time. Abilities and personality characteristics (do/do not) appear to be influenced by brainedness.

(d) The notion that most schooling overlooks the education of the right brain (does/does not) really make sense. Since both hemispheres are almost always sharing in accomplishing an ongoing task, it would be _____ to teach only one hemisphere at at time.

Answers: 17-1. (a) specialized (b) different (c) reliance (dependence) (d) right **17-2.** (a) is, left, both (b) plausible, define, measure (c) is not, do not (d) does not, impossible.

REVIEW OF KEY TERMS

Absolute refractory period
Action potential
Adoption studies
Afferent nerve fibers
Agonist
Antagonist
Autonomic nervous system (ANS)
Axon
Blood-brain barrier
Central nervous system (CNS)
Cerebral cortex
Cerebral hemispheres
Chromosomes
Corpus callosum
Dendrites
Efferent nerve fibers
Endocrine System

Endorphins
Family studies
Forebrain
Genes
Hindbrain
Hormones
Hypothalamus
Limbic system
Midbrain
Myelin sheath
Nerves
Neuromodulators
Neurons
Neurotransmitters
Parasympathetic division
Peripheral nervous system

Pituitary gland
Polygenic traits
Postsynaptic potential (PSP)
Resting potential
Soma
Somatic nervous system
Spatial summation
Split-brain surgery
Symnpathetic division
Synapse
Synaptic cleft
Temporal summation
Terminal buttons
Thalamus
Twin studies

_____ 1. Individual cells in the nervous system that receive, integrate, and transmit information.

_____ 2. Neuron part that contains the cell nucleus and much of the chemical machinery common to most cells.

_____ 3. Branchlike parts of a neuron that are specialized to receive information.

_____ 4. A long, thin fiber that transmits signals away from the soma to other neurons, or to muscles or glands.

_____ 5. An insulating jacket, derived from glia cells, that encases some axons.

_____ 6. Small knobs at the end of the axon that secrete chemicals called neurotransmitters.

_____ 7. A junction where information is transmitted between neurons.

_____ 8. The stable, negative charge of an inactive neuron.

_____ 9. A brief change in a neuron's electrical charge.

_____ 10. The minimum length of time after an action potential during which another action potential cannot begin.

_____ 11. A microscopic gap between the terminal buttons of the sending neuron and the cell membrane of another neuron.

_____ 12. Chemicals that transmit information from one neuron to another.

_____ 13. A voltage change at the receptor site of a neuron.

_____ 14. A technique for assessing hereditary influence by examining blood relatives to see how much they resemble each other on a specific trait.

_____ 15. A chemical that mimics the action of a neurotransmitter.

_____ 16. A chemical that opposes the action of a neurotransmitter.

_____ 17. An entire family of internally produced chemicals that resemble opiates in structure and effects.

_____ 18. Chemicals that increase or decrease (modulate) the activity of specific neurotransmitters.

_____ 19. System that includes all those nerves that lie outside the brain and spinal cord.

_____ 20. Bundles of neuron fibers (axons) that travel together in the peripheral nervous system.

_____ 21. System made up of the nerves that connect to voluntary skeletal muscles and sensory receptors.

_____ 22. Axons that carry information inward to the central nervous system from the periphery of the body.

_____ 23. Axons that carry information outward from the central nervous system to the periphery of the body.

_____ 24. System made up of the nerves that connect to the heart, blood vessels, smooth muscles and glands.

_____ 25. The branch of the autonomic nervous system that mobilizes the body's resources for emergencies.

_____ 26. The branch of the autonomic nervous system that generally conserves bodily resources.

_____ 27. System that consists of the brain and spinal cord.

_____ 28. A semipermeable membranelike mechanism that stops some chemicals from passing between the bloodstream and brain cells.

_____ 29. Assessing hereditary influence by comparing the resemblance of identical twins and fraternal twins on a trait.

_____ 30. Part of the brain that includes the cerebellum and two structures found in the lower part of the brainstem – the medulla and the pons.

_____ 31. The segment of the brainstem that lies between the hindbrain and the forebrain.

_____ 32. Part of the brain encompassing the thalamus, hypothalamus, limbic system, and cerebrum.

_____ 33. A structure in the forebrain through which all sensory information (except smell) must pass to get to the cerebral cortex.

_____ 34. A structure found near the base of the forebrain that is involved in the regulation of basic biological needs.

_____ 35. A densely connected network of structures located beneath the cerebral cortex, involved in the control of emotion, motivation, and memory.

_____ 36. The convulated outer layer of the cerebrum.

_____ 37. The right and left halves of the cerebrum.

_____ 38. The structure that connects the two cerebral hemispheres.

_____ 39. Assessing hereditary influence by examining the resemblance between adopted children and both their adoptive and biological parents.

_____ 40. Surgery in which the the corpus callosum is severed to reduce the severity of epileptic seizures.

_____ 41. System of glands that secrete chemicals into the bloodstream that help control bodily functioning.

_____ 42. The chemical substances released by the endocrine glands.

_____ 43. The "master gland" of the endocrine system.

_____ 44. Threadlike strands of DNA molecules that carry genetic information.

_____ 45. DNA segments that serve as the key functional units in hereditary transmission.

_____ 46. Characteristics that are influenced by more than one pair of genes.

_____ 47. Can take place when several or more PSPs occur simultaneously at different receptor sites.

_____ 48. Can take place when several or more PSPs follow one another in rapid succession at a receptor site.

Answers: 1. neurons **2.** soma **3.** dendrites **4.** axon **5.** myelin sheath **6.** terminal buttons **7.** synapse **8.** resting potential **9.** action potential **10.** absolute refractory period **11.** synaptic cleft **12.** neurotransmitters **13.** postsynaptic potential (PSP) **14.** family studies **15.** agonist **16.** antagonist **17.** endorphins **18.** neuromodulators **19.** peripheral nervous system **20.** nerves **21.** somatic nervous system **22.** afferent nerve fibers **23.** efferent fibers **24.** autonomic nervous system (ANS) **25.** sympathetic division **26.** parasympathetic division **27.** central nervous system (CNS) **28.** blood-brain barrier **29.** twin studies **30.** hindbrain **31.** midbrain **32.** forebrain **33.** thalamus **34.** hypothalamus **35.** limbic system **36.** cerebral cortex **37.** cerebral hemispheres **38.** corpus callosum **39.** adoption studies **40.** split-brain surgery **41.** endocrine system **42.** hormones **43.** pituitary gland **44.** chromosomes **45.** genes **46.** polygenic traits **47.** spatial summation **48.** temporal summation.

REVIEW OF KEY PEOPLE

Alan Hodgkin & Andrew Huxley   Candice Pert & Solomon Snyder   Roger Sperry & Michael Garzzaniga
James Olds & Peter Milner   Robert Plomin

_____ 1. Unlocked the mystery of the neural impulse.

_____ 2. Known for their work with the split brain.

_____ 3. Showed that morphine works by binding to specific receptors.

_____ 4. Discovered "pleasure centers" in the limbic system.

_____ 5. One of the leading behavior genetics researchers in the last decade.

Answers : 1. Hodgkin & Huxley **2.** Sperry & Garzzaniga **3.** Pert & Snyder **4.** Olds & Milner **5.** Plomin.

SELF-QUIZ

1. Most neurons are involved in transmitting information:
   a. from one neuron to another
   b. from the outside world to the brain
   c. from the brain to the muscles
   d. from the brain to the glands

2. Neurons that are specialized to communicate directly with the muscles of the body are called:
   a. sensory neurons
   b. motor neurons
   c. actuator neurons
   d. muscle neurons

3. Which part of the neuron has the responsibility for receiving information from other neurons?
   a. the cell body
   b. the soma
   c. the axon
   d. the dendrites

4. The myelin sheath serves to:
   a. permit faster transmission of the neural impulse
   b. keep neural impulses on the right track
   c. add structural strength
   d. permit faster transmission and keep neural impulses on the right track

5. The change in the polarity of a neuron that results from the inflow of positively charged ions and the outflow of negatively charged ions is called the:
   a. presynaptic potential
   b. postsynaptic potential
   c. synaptic potential
   d. action potential

6. The task of passing a message from one neuron to another is actually carried out by:
   a. the myelin sheath
   b. the glia cells
   c. the action potential
   d. neurotransmitters

7. Which of the following neurotransmitters can only have an inhibitory effect at receptor sites?
   a. GABA
   b. dopamine
   c. norepinephrine
   d. serotonin

8. Which of the following brain-imaging techniques portray the brain's actual activity across time?
   a. CT scans
   b. PET scans
   c. MRI Scans
   d. ESB scans

9. The seat of emotion is to be found in the:
   a. reticular formation
   b. hindbrain
   c. limbic system
   d. forebrain

10. Persons having difficulty with language and speech following an accident that resulted in injury to the brain are most likely to have sustained damage in the:
    a. right cerebral hemisphere
    b. left cerebral hemisphere
    c. right cerebral hemisphere if they are a male and left cerebral hemisphere if they are a female
    d. I have no idea what you are talking about

11. In carrying out the "fight or flight" response, the role of supervisor is assigned to the:
    a. adrenal gland
    b. pituitary gland
    c. hypothalamus
    d. parasympathetic nervous system

12. Which of the following kinds of studies can truly demonstrate that specific traits are indeed inherited?
    a. family studies
    b. twin studies
    c. adoption studies
    d. none of the above since you cannot infer causation from correlational studies

13. Current evidence indicates that schizophrenia results from:
    a. genetic factors
    b. environmental factors
    c. multiple causes that involve both genetic and environmental factors
    d. completely unknown factors

14. Psychology as a science can be said to be:
    a. empirical
    b. rational
    c. analytic
    d. both b and c

15. Which of the following statements is/are correct?
    a. the right side of the brain is the creative side
    b. the right and left brains are specialized to handle different kinds of information
    c. language tasks are always handled by the left brain
    d. all of the above

Answers: 1. a **2.** b **3.** d **4.** c **5.** d **6.** d **7.** a **8.** b **9.** c **10.** b **11.** c **12.** d **13.** c **14.** a **15.** b.

## CHAPTER THREE

4 SENSATION AND PERCEPTION

REVIEW OF KEY IDEAS

OUR SENSE OF SIGHT: THE VISUAL SYSTEM

1. List the three properties of light and the aspects of visual perception that they influence.

    1-1. Before we can see anything,_____ must be present. There are three characteristics of lightwaves that directly affect how we perceive visual objects; match each of these characteristics with its psychological effect.

        (a) _____ wavelength   1. color

        (b) _____ amplitude   2. saturation (or richness)

        (c) _____ purity   3. brightness

    Answers: 1-1. lightwaves or light, (a) 1 (b) 3 (c) 2.

2. Describe the role of the lens and pupil in the functioning of the eye.

    2-1. Getting light rays entering the eye to properly focus on the retina is the job of the _____. It accomplishes this task by either thickening or flattening its curvature, a process called _____. Controlling the amount of light entering the eye is the job of the _____. It accomplishes this task by opening or closing the opening in the center of the eye called the_____.

    Answers: 2-1. lens, accommodation, iris, pupil.

3. Describe the role of the retina in light sensitivity and in visual information processing.

    3-1. The structure that transduces the information contained in light rays into neural impulses that are then sent to the brain is called the _____. All of the axons carrying these neural impulses exit the eye at a single opening in the retina called the optic _____. Since the optic disk is actually a hole in the retina, this part of the retina cannot sense incoming visual information and for this reason it is called the _____.

3-2. The specialized receptor cells that are primarily responsible for visual acuity and color vision are called the
_____. The cones are mainly located in the center of the retina in a tiny spot called the
_____. The specialized receptor cells that lie outside of the fovea and toward the periphery of
the retina are called the _____. The rods are primarily responsible for peripheral vision and for
_____vision.

3-3. Both dark and light adaptation are primarily accomplished through _____ reactions in the rods
and cones. This chemical reaction occurs more quickly in the _____, so they are quicker to
show both dark adaptation and light adaptation.

3-4. Light rays striking the rods and cones initiate neural impulses that are then transmitted to
_____cells and then to _____ cells. From here the visual information is transmitted
to the brain via the axons running from the retina to the brain, collectively known as the
_____ nerve.

3-5. The processing of visual information begins within the receiving area of a retinal cell called the
_____ field. Stimulation of the receptive field of a cell causes signals to be sent inward toward
the brain and sideways, or _____, to nearby cells, thus allowing them to interact with one
another. The most common of these interactive effects, the inhibition of one cell by another, is called lateral
_____. Lateral antagonism allows the visual system to compute the (absolute/relative) amount
of light; it occurs in the retina and along the pathway to and including the visual cortex.

Answers: 3-1. retina, disk, blind spot **3-2.** cones, fovea, rods, night **3-3.** chemical, cones **3-4.** bipolar, ganglion, optic
3-5. receptive, laterally, antagonism, relative.

4. Describe the routing of signals from the eye to the brain and the brain's role in visual information processing.

4-1. Visual information from the right side of the visual field (see Figure 4-8 in the text) exits from the retinas of
both eyes via the optic nerves and meet at the _____ chiasma, where it is combined and sent to
the _____ side of the brain. Visual information from the left side of the visual field follow a
similar pattern, meeting at the optic chiasma, and then on to the _____ side of the brain.

4-2. After leaving the optic chiasma on their way to the visual cortex, the optic nerve fibers diverge along two
pathways. Fill in the missing parts of these pathways in the figures below.

Major pathway

(a) Optic chiasma _____   _____ Visual cortex

Secondary pathway

(b) Optic chiasma _____   _____ Visual cortex

4-3. What purpose is served by having these two separate pathways dumping their information into different areas
of the visual cortex?

4-4.   Because the cells in the visual cortex respond very selectively to specific features of complex stimuli, they have been described as _____ detectors. There are three major types of cells in the visual cortex: simple cells, complex cells, and hypercomplex cells. Identify them from their descriptions given below.

    (a)   These cells are particular about the width and orientation of a line but respond to any position in their receptive field.

    (b)   These cells are very particular about the width, orientation, and position of a line.

    (c)   These cells are like complex cells, but they are particular about the length of the lines that will cause them to fire.

4-5.   Each of these groups of cells respond to particular features of incoming stimuli. This means that the cells in the visual cortex (do/do not) provide a photographic-like picture of the outside world. Rather they provide a coding system that can then be transformed into such a picture.

Answers: 4-1. optic, left, right **4-2.** (a) thalamus, lateral geniculate nucleus (b) superior colliculus, thalamus **4-3.** It allows for parallel processing (simultaneously extracting different information from the same input). **4-4.** feature (a) complex cells (b) simple cells (c) hypercomplex cells **4-5.** do not.

5.   Discuss the trichromatic and opponent process theories of color vision, and the modern reconciliation of these theories.

5-1.   The trichromatic theory of color vision, as its name suggests, proposes three different kinds of receptors (channels) for the three primary colors red, _____, and _____. The opponent process theory of color vision also proposes three channels for color vision, but these channels are red versus _____, yellow versus _____, and black versus _____.

5-2.   These two theories of color vision can be used to explain different phenomena. Use T (trichromatic) or O (opponent process) to indicate which theory best explains the following phenomena.

    _____ (a)   The color of an afterimage is the complement of the original color.

    _____ (b)   The different kinds of color blindness suggest three different kinds of receptors.

    _____ (c)   Any three appropriately spaced colors can produce all other colors.

    _____ (d)   People describing colors often require at least four different names.

5-3.   The evidence is now clear that both theories are (incorrect/correct). Each is needed to explain all of the phenomena associated with color vision. Three different kinds of cones have been found in the retina that are sensitive to one of the three primary colors; this supports the _____ theory. It has also been found that visual cells in the retina, the LGN, and the visual cortex respond in opposite (antagonistic) ways to complementary colors, thus supporting the _____ theory.

Answers: 5-1. green, blue, green, blue, white **5-2.** (a) O (b) T (c) T (d) O **5-3.** correct, trichromatic, opponent process.

6. Explain the basic premise of Gestalt psychology and describe Gestalt principles of visual perception.

6-1.   The Gestalt view of form perception assumes that form perception is not constructed out of individual elements; rather the form, or whole, is said to be _____ than the sum of its individual elements. The illusion of movement, called the _____ phenomenon, is used to support the Gestalt view of form perception because the illusion of movement (is/is not) completely contained in the individual chunks of stimuli that give rise to it. In other words, the illusion, or whole, appears to be _____ than the sum of its parts.

6-2.   Five Gestalt principles of visual perception are illustrated below. Match each illustration with its correct name.

Proximity

Similarity

Continuity

Closure

Simplicity

(a) _____

(b) _____

(c) _____

(d) _____

(e) _____

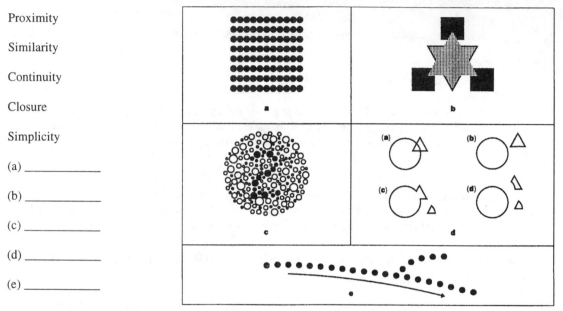

6-3.   What Gestalt principle is illustrated by:

(a)   The words printed on this page appear to stand out from the white paper they are printed on?

(b)   Things moving in the same direction together get grouped together?

Answers: **6-1.** greater (more), phi, is not, greater (more) **6-2.** (a) proximity (b) closure (c) similarity (d) simplicity (e) continuity **6-3.** (a) figure and ground (b) common fate.

7. Explain how form perception can be a matter of formulating perceptual hypotheses.

7-1.   The objects that surround us in the world outside of our bodies are called _____ stimuli; the images the objects project on our retinas are called _____ stimuli. When perceived from different angles or distances, the same distal stimulus projects (similar/different) proximal images on the retina. This forces us to make perceptual _____ about the distal stimulus.

Answers: **7-1.** distal, proximal, different, hypotheses or guesses.

8. **Describe the monocular and binocular cues employed in depth perception and cultural variations in depth perception.**

8-1.   There are two general kinds of cues that allow us to perceive depth and they are easy to remember because one kind involve the use of both eyes and are called _____ cues; the other kind require the use of only one of the eyes and are called _____ cues. Depth perception (does/does not) require the use of both binocular and monocular cues.

8-2.   Here are examples of two different kinds of binocular cues, retinal disparity and convergence. Identify each from these examples:

(a) As a person walks toward you your eyes turn inward.

(b) The images are slightly different on each retina and the differences change with distance.

8-3.   There are two general kinds of monocular cues. One kind involves the active use of the eye, such as the accommodation used for focusing the eye. The other general kind is used to indicate depth in flat pictures and thus is called a _____ cue.

8-4.   Identify the following pictoral cues below:

(a) Parallel lines grow closer as they recede into the distance.

(b) More distant objects are higher in the field than nearer objects.

(c) When objects appear to be of the same size, closer ones appear larger than more distant ones.

(d) Near objects block or overlap more distant ones.

(e) Texture appears to grow finer as viewing distance increases.

(f) Patterns of light and dark suggest shadows that can create an impression of three-dimensional space.

8-5.   What phenomenon was observed in people from pictureless societies? What does this tell us about depth cues in pictures?

Answers: 8-1. binocular, monocular, does not **8-2.** (a) convergence (b) retinal disparity **8-3.** pictorial **8-4.** (a) linear perspective (b) height in plane (c) relative size (d) interposition (e) texture gradients (f) light and shadow **8-5.** They had difficulty perceiving depth in two-dimensional pictures. Perception of depth in pictures is partly an acquired skill that depends on experience.

9. **Describe perceptual constancies and illusions in vision, and discuss cultural variations in susceptibility to certain illusions.**

9-1.   The tendency to experience stable perceptions in spite of constantly changing sensory input is called perceptual _____. The text lists several of these visual perceptual constancies; identify the ones being illustrated below.

   (a) Even though the retinal image shrinks as a friend walks away, she continues to appear her usual height.

   (b) The retinal image warps as you track a basketball through the air, but the ball always appears perfectly round.

   (c) Indoors or on the ski slope a light blue sweater always looks light blue.

9-2.   Being fooled by the discrepancy between the appearance of a visual stimulus and its physical reality is what is meant by an optical _____. Both perceptual constancies and optical illusions illustrate the point that we are continually formulating _____ about what we perceive and also that these perceptions can be quite (<u>subjective/objective</u>).

9-3.   How do cultures affect susceptibility to certain illusions?

Answers: 9-1. constancy, (a) size constancy (b) shape constancy (c) color constancy **9-2.** illusion, hypotheses, subjective **9-3.** They make us more or less susceptible (to certain illusions).

OUR SENSE OF HEARING: THE AUDITORY SYSTEM

10. **List the three properties of sound and the aspects of auditory perception that they influence.**

10-1.   Name the perceived qualities that are associated with the following properties of sound waves.

Physical Property	Description	Perceived Quality
(a) purity	kind of mixture	_____
(b) amplitude	wave height	_____
(c) wavelength	wave frequency	_____

Answers: 10-1. (a) timbre (b) loudness (c) pitch.

11. **Summarize the information on human hearing capacities and describe how sensory processing occurs in the ear.**

11-1.   Below are questions concerning human hearing capacities. Match the questions with their correct answers.

Answers	Questions
1. 90 to 120 decibels (dB).	_____ (a) What is the frequency range of human hearing?
2. 1,000 to 5,000 Hz.	_____ (b) How loud do sounds have to be to cause damage to human hearing?
3. 20 to 20,000 Hz.	_____ (c) To what frequency range is human hearing the most sensitive?

11-2. Below is a scrambled sequence of events that occurs when a sound wave strikes the ear. Put these events in their correct order using the numbers 1 through 4.

_____ Fluid waves travel down the choclea causing the hair cells on the basilar membrane to vibrate.

_____ The pinna directs air to the eardrum.

_____ The hair cells convert fluid motion into neural impulses and send them to the brain.

_____ The motion of the vibrating eardrum is converted to fluid motion by the ossicles.

Answers: 11-1. (a) 3 (b) 1 (c) 2 **11-2.** 3, 1, 4, 2.

12. Compare and contrast the place and frequency theories of pitch perception and discuss the resolution of the debate.

12-1. One theory of pitch perception assumes that the hair cells respond differentially to pitch depending on their location along the basilar membrane. This is the main idea of the _____ theory of pitch perception. A second theory assumes a one-to-one correspondence between the actual frequency of the sound wave and the frequency at which the entire basilar membrane vibrates. This is the main idea of the _____ theory of pitch perception.

12-2. Below are several facts uncovered by research. Tell which theory of pitch is supported by each of these facts.

(a) The hair cells vibrate in unison and not independently.

(b) Even when they fire in volleys, auditory nerves can only handle up to 500Hz.

(c) A wave pattern caused by the vibrating basilar membrane peaks at a particular place along the membrane.

12-3. The above facts mean that the perception of pitch depends on both _____ and _____ coding.

Answers: 12-1. place, frequency **12-2.** (a) frequency theory (b) place theory (c) place theory **12-3.** place and frequency.

OUR CHEMICAL SENSES: TASTE AND SMELL

13. Describe the stimulus and receptors for taste and discuss factors that may influence perceived flavor.

13-1. The stimuli for taste perception are _____ absorbed in the saliva that stimulate taste cells located in the tongue's _____. It is generally thought that there are four fundamental tastes; these are _____, _____, _____, _____ .

13-2. Answer the following questions regarding the role of visual input and odors on perceived flavor.

(a) Why is the same meal likely to taste better when served in a fine restaurant than in a shabby diner?

(b) Why do most persons prefer not to have their steak liquefied in a food processor?

(c) What additional effect is added to the flavor of wine by first swirling it in the glass?

Answers: 13-1. chemicals, taste buds, sweet, sour, salty, bitter **13-2.** (a) Appearance influences perceived flavor (b) It changes the texture and appearance of the steak (c) It helps to release the wine's odor and odor is a major determinant of flavor.

14. Describe the stimulus and receptors for smell.

14-1. The stimuli for the sense of smell are _____ molecules floating in the air. The receptors for smell are hairlike structures located in the nasal passages called _____. If there are any primary odors, they must be (<u>large</u>/small) in number. Human sensitivity to smell (<u>does</u>/does not) compare favorably with that of many other animals, although some animals surpass us in this respect.

Answers: 14-1. chemical, olfactory cilia, large, does.

OUR OTHER SENSES

15. Describe the processes involved in the perception of pressure and pain.

15-1. Answer the following questions concerning the sense of touch.

(a) What four different perceptions are included in the sense of touch?

(b) What three body areas are most sensitive to pressure stimulation?

(c) What is the name of the receiving area in the brain for tactile information?

(d) What similar mechanism does the tactile and visual system use for processing sensory information?

15-2. Pain signals travel to the brain by two slightly different pathways. One pathway sends signals directly and immediately to the cortex and is called the _____ pathway. The other first sends signals through the limbic system and then on to the cortex and is called the _____ pathway. Lingering, less-localized pain is mediated by the _____ pathway.

15-3. Answer the following questions regarding the perception of pain.

(a) What phenomenon did the gate-control theory of pain perception attempt to explain?

(b) What effect do endorphins have with respect to pain?

(c) A descending pathway originating in the midbrain also appears to inhibit the perception of pain. Where might the controls for this pathway originate?

Answers: 15-1. (a) pressure, warmth, cold, and pain (b) fingers, lips, and tongue (c) somatosensory cortex (d) receptive fields **15-2.** fast, slow, slow **15-3.** (a) Why the perception of pain is so subjective (b) An analgesic (pain-relieving) effect (c) In higher brain centers.

16. Describe the perceptual experiences mediated by the kinesthetic and vestibular senses.

16-1. The system that monitors the positions of various parts of the body is called the _____ system. This systems sends information to the brain about body position and movement obtained from receptors located in the joints and _____.

16-2. The system that monitors the body's location in space is called the _____ system. The receptors for the vestibular system are primarily hair cells contained within the _____ canals in the inner ear.

16-3. What point does the text make about the kinesthetic and vestibular systems, and indeed all sensory systems, in carrying out their tasks?

Answers: 16-1. kinesthetic, muscles **16-2.** vestibular, semicircular **16-3.** They integrate information from other senses (in carrying out their tasks).

PUTTING IT IN PERSPECTIVE

17. Explain how this chapter highlighted three of the text's unifying themes.

17-1. The fact that competing theories of both color vision and pitch were eventually reconciled attests to the value of theoretical diversity. Why is this?

17-2. Why must our experience of the world always be highly subjective?

17-3. What do cultural variations in depth perception, taste preferences, and pain tolerance tell us about the physiological basis of perception?

Answers: 17-1. Competing theories drive and guide the resolving research **17-2.** The perceptual processes themselves are inherently subjective **17-3.** That it is subject to cultural influences.

18. **Discuss how the paintings shown in the Application illustrate various principles of visual perception.**

18-1. After reading the Application section in your text, answer the following questions by only looking at the paintings.

(a) Which painting uses the Gestalt principles of perceptual organization to build a total picture out of geometric forms?

(b) Which painting incorporates impossible triangles to achieve its effect?

(c) Which painting makes particular use of pictorial depth cues to enhance the illusion of depth?

(d) Which painting makes use of color mixing to illustrate how different spots of colors can be blended into a picture that is more than the sum of its parts?

(e) Which painting makes use of a reversible figure to enchance a feeling of fantasy?

Answers: 18-1. (a) 4.47 (b) 4.49 (c) 4.45 (d) 4.46 (e) 4.48.

REVIEW OF KEY TERMS

Additive color mixing	Feature detectors	Perceptual set
After image	Fovea	Phi phenomenon
Basilar membrane	Gustatory system	Pictorial depth cues
Binocular depth cues	Impossible figures	Proximal stimuli
Cochlea	Kinesthetic system	Pupil
Color blindness	Lens	Receptive field of a visual cell
Complimentary colors	Light adaptation	Retina
Cones	Monocular cues	Retinal disparity
Convergence	Nearsightedness	Reversible figure
Dark adaptation	Olfactory system	Rods
Depth perception	Optical illusion	Sensation
Distal stimuli	Perception	Sensory adaptation
Farsightedness	Perceptual constancy	Subtractive color mixing
Feature analysis	Perceptual hypothesis	Vestibular system

_____   1. The stimulation of sense organs.

_____   2. The selection, organization, and interpretation of sensory input.

_____   3. Involves a gradual decline in sensitivity to prolonged stimulation.

_____   4. The transparent eye structure that focuses the light rays falling on the retina.

_____   5. The opening in the center of the iris that helps regulate the amount of light passing into the rear chamber of the eye.

_____   6. The neural tissue lining the inside back surface of the eye that absorbs light, processes images, and sends visual information to the brain.

_____   7. Specialized receptors that play a key role in daylight vision and color vision.

_____   8. Specialized receptors that play a key role in night vision and peripheral vision.

_____ 9. A tiny spot in the center of the retina that contains only cones, where visual acuity is greatest.

_____ 10. The process in which the eyes become more sensitive to light in low illumination.

_____ 11. The process in which the eyes become less sensitive to light in high illumination.

_____ 12. A variety of deficiencies in the ability to distinguish among colors.

_____ 13. The retinal area that, when stimulated, affects the firing of a particular cell.

_____ 14. Neurons that respond selectively to very specific features of more complex stimuli.

_____ 15. Works by removing some wavelengths of light, leaving less light than was originally there.

_____ 16. Works by superimposing lights, leaving more light in the mixture than in any one light by itself.

_____ 17. Pairs of colors that can be added together to produce gray tones.

_____ 18. A visual image that persists after a stimulus is removed.

_____ 19. A drawing compatible with two different interpretations that can shift back and forth.

_____ 20. A readiness to perceive a stimulus in a particular way.

_____ 21. A process in which we detect specific elements in visual input and assemble these elements into a more complex form.

_____ 22. An apparently inexplicable discrepancy between the appearance of a visual stimulus and its physical reality.

_____ 23. The illusion of movement created by presenting visual stimuli in rapid succession.

_____ 24. Stimuli that lie in the distance (in the world outside us).

_____ 25. The stimulus energies that impinge directly on our sensory receptors.

_____ 26. An inference about what distal stimuli could be responsible for the proximal stimuli sensed.

_____ 27. Involves our interpretation of visual cues that tell us how near or far away objects are.

_____ 28. Clues about distance that are obtained by comparing the differing views of the two eyes.

_____ 29. Clues about distance that are obtained from the image in either eye alone.

_____ 30. A tendency to experience a stable perception in the face of constantly changing sensory input.

_____ 31. A fluid-filled, coiled tunnel that makes up the largest part of the inner ear.

_____ 32. A membrane running the length of the cochlea that holds the actual auditory receptors, called hair cells.

_____ 33. Involves sensing the eyes converging toward each other as they focus on closer objects.

_____ 34. Our sense of taste.

_____ 35. Our sense of smell.

_____ 36. Objects that can be represented in two-dimensional figures but cannot exist in three-dimensional space.

_____ 37. The sense that monitors the positions of the various parts of the body.

_____ 38. The system that provides the sense of balance.

_____ 39. A condition in which close objects are seen clearly but distant objects appear blury.

_____ 40. A condition in which distant objects are seen clearly but close objects appear blury.

_____ 41. Refers to the fact that objects within 25 feet project images to slightly different locations on the right and left retinas, so the right and left eyes see slightly different views of the object.

_____ 42. Cues about distance that can be given in a flat picture.

Answers: 1. sensation **2.** perception **3.** sensory adaptation **4.** lens **5.** pupil **6.** retina **7.** cones **8.** rods **9.** fovea **10.** dark adaptation **11.** light adaptation **12.** color blindness **13.** receptive field of a visual cell **14.** feature detectors **15.** subtractive color mixing **16.** additive color mixing **17.** complementary colors **18.** afterimage **19.** reversible figure **20.** perceptual set **21.** feature analysis **22.** optical illusions **23.** phi phenomenon **24.** distal stimuli **25.** proximal stimuli **26.** perceptual hypothesis **27.** depth perception **28.** binocular cues **29.** monocular cues **30.** perceptual constancy **31.** cochlea **32.** basilar membrane **33.** convergence **34.** gustatory system **35.** olfactory system **36.** impossible figures **37.** kinesthetic sense **38.** vestibular system **39.** nearsightedness **40.** farsightedness **41.** retinal disparity **42.** pictorial depth cues.

REVIEW OF KEY PEOPLE

Linda Bartoshuk   David Hubel and Torston Weisel   Max Wertheimer
Herman von Helmholtz   Ronald Melzack and Patrick Wall

_____ 1. These two men won the Nobel Prize for their discovery of feature detector cells in the retina.

_____ 2. One of the originators of the trichromatic theory of color vision.

_____ 3. Made use of the phi phenomenon to illustrate some of the basic principles of Gestalt psychology.

_____ 4. A leading authority on taste research.

_____ 5. Proposed a gate-control theory of pain.

Answers: 1. Hubel and Weisel **2.** Helmholtz **3.** Wertheimer **4.** Bartoshuk **5.** Melzack and Wall.

SELF-QUIZ

1. Averting your gaze slightly away from an object you are trying to see under darkened conditions improves your ability to see it. Why is this?
   a. It causes the pupils to open wider.
   b. It allows for stimulation of more cones.
   c. It allows for stimulation of more rods.
   d. It causes the lens to focus more sharply.

2. Information from the right visual field is sent to:
   a. the right side of the visual cortex
   b. the left side of the visual cortex
   c. to both the right and left sides of the visual cortex.

3. The major difference between a green light and a blue light is the:
   a. wave amplitude
   b. wave purity
   c. wavelength
   d. wave saturation

4. If the eye is compared to a camera, the role of the retina would most closely resemble the role of the:
   a. lens
   b. film
   c. shutter
   d. flash cube

5. Which theory of color vision best explains why the color of an afterimage is the complement of the original color?
   a. the trichromatic theory
   b. the opponent process theory
   c. both theories explain this phenomenon equally well
   d. neither theory adequately explains this phenomenon

6. When watching a wild car chase scene in a movie we can be thankful for:
   a. chunking
   b. lateral processing
   c. bottom-up processing
   d. the phi phenomenon

7. Which of the following is one of the binocular distance cues?
   a. convergence
   b. linear perspective
   c. relative height
   d. texture gradients

8. Which of the following is an example of what is meant by perceptual constancy?
   a. moths are always attracted to light
   b. a round pie tin always appears to us as round
   c. proximal and distal stimuli are always identical
   d. distal stimuli never change

9. The fact that the words on this page tend to stand out from the paper it is printed on illustrates the Gestalt principle of:
   a. figure and ground
   b. simplicity
   c. proximity
   d. closure

10. Middle C sounded on a piano sounds different than middle C on a violin because of the difference in:
    a. wavelengths
    b. purity
    c. amplitude
    d. frequency

11. Research has shown that the perception of pitch depends on:
    a. the area stimulated on the basilar membrane
    b. the frequency at which the basilar membrane vibrates
    c. both the area stimulated on the basilar membrane and the frequency at which the basilar membrane vibrates
    d. unknown factors

12. Which of the following is not considered to be one of the four fundamental tastes?
    a. sour
    b. sweet
    c. burnt
    d. bitter

13. Receptive fields and feature detectors are found in:
    a. the visual system
    b. the touch system
    c. the balance system
    d. the visual and touch systems

14. Our sense of balance depends upon:
    a. the semicircular canals
    b. the kinesthetic senses
    c. visual cues
    d. the semicircular canals, the kinesthetic senses, and visual cues

15. The gate-control theory is an attempt to explain:
    a. light and dark adaptation
    b. the transformation from sensation to perception
    c. the adaptation to strong odors
    d. the subjective nature of pain

16. Which of the following terms perhaps best describes human perception?
    a. accurate
    b. objective
    c. subjective
    d. unknowable

Answers: 1. c **2.** b **3.** c **4.** b **5.** b **6.** d **7.** a **8.** b **9.** a **10.** b **11.** c **12.** c **13.** d **14.** d **15.** d **16.** c.

VARIATIONS IN CONSCIOUSNESS

REVIEW OF KEY IDEAS

ON THE NATURE OF CONSCIOUSNESS

1. Discuss the nature of consciousness, including its relation to brain activity.

1-1. The personal awareness of internal and external events is how psychologists define _____. Consciousness is like a moving stream in that it is constantly _____.

1-2. Not only is consciousness constantly changing, but it also may exist at different levels. Freud believed that at its deepest level we would find the _____. For a long time it was believed that the conscious states experienced while under anesthesia or during sleep were very different from the waking state, but recently some theorists have argued that the differences are (less/greater) than originally thought.

1-3. EEG recordings reveal that there (is/is not) some relationship between brain waves and levels of consciousness. There are four principal bands of brain wave activity, based on the frequency of the wave patterns; these are *alpha, beta, delta*, and *theta*. Identify these wave patterns from their descriptions given below.

_____ (a) alert (13-24 cps)   _____ (c) deep sleep (4-7 cps)

_____ (b) drowsy (8-12 cps)   _____ (d) deepest sleep (1-3 cps)

Answers: 1-1. consciousness, changing **1-2.** unconscious, less **1-3.** (a) beta (b) alpha (c) theta (d) delta.

BIOLOGICAL RHYTHMS AND SLEEP

2. Summarize what is known about our biological clocks and the relationship of circadian rhythms to sleep.

2-1. Like most living organisms, human beings experience periodic fluctuations in physiological functioning, which are called _____ rhythms. This means that we must have internal "biological _____" that can monitor the passage of time.

2-2.   The daily, or 24-hour, circadian rhythm is responsible for the regulation of sleep and wakefulness. This is accomplished through the regulation of several bodily processes, including body temperature. Describe below what happens to body temperature when we:

(a) begin to fall asleep.

(b) begin to awaken.

2-3.   There is evidence that exposure to _____ is responsible for regulating the 24-hour circadian clock. Sunlight affects the suprachiasmatic nucleus in the hypothalamus, which in turn signals the _____ gland. The pineal gland then secretes the hormone melatonin, which is a major player in adjusting biological clocks. There is also evidence that most persons tend to drift from a 24-hour cycle to a _____-hour cycle.

Answers: **2-1.** biological, clocks **2-2.** (a) temperature decreases (b) temperature begins to increase **2-3.** sunlight, pineal, 25.

3. Discuss the significance of ignoring circadian rhythms and the value of melatonin for resetting biological clocks.

3-1.   Getting out of time with the circadian rhythms can greatly affect the quality of _____ . This is commonly found among persons suffering from jet lag. Research on jet lag has shown that since there already seems to be a natural tendency to shift to a 25-hour circadian rhythm, most people find it is easier to readjust when they have flown in (an easterly/a westerly) direction.

3-2.   While melatonin has been shown to be helpful in treating sleep problems, other claims of health benefits (have/have not) been proven. Moreover, researchers worry that many people may take too (much/little) of the drug to achieve sleep-related effects. As of now there is no research to show the consequences of ingesting large concentrations of melatonin.

Answers: **3-1.** sleep, a westerly **3-2.** have not, much.

THE SLEEP AND WAKING CYCLE

4. Compare and contrast REM sleep and NREM sleep.

4-1.   The four stages of sleep that do not involve rapid eye movement (REM) are collectively called _____ sleep. During NREM sleep one first descends into stage _____ sleep and then continues to descend into stages 2, 3, and 4. Each descent is accompanied by (slower/faster) brain wave activity, along with declines in body temperature, heart rate, respiration rate, and muscle tension.

4-2.   What particularly differentiates NREM sleep from rapid eye movement sleep, or _____ sleep, is that during REM sleep the brain wave pattern resembles that of a person who is wide _____. However, REM sleep is actually a deep stage of sleep in which the muscle tone is extremely relaxed and the sleeper is virtually _____. It is also during REM sleep that _____ is most likely to occur.

Answers: **4-1.** NREM, 1, slower **4-2.** REM, awake, paralyzed, dreaming.

5. **Describe how sleep patterns evolve through the night and how sleep patterns are related to age and culture.**

5-1. The sleep cycle is repeated approximately four times during an average night of sleep. NREM sleep dominates the early part of the sleep period, but _____ sleep and dreaming dominate the later stages of sleep. As one progresses though the night the depth of NREM sleep tends to progressively (<u>increase/decrease</u>).

5-2. Not only do newborns sleep more frequently and for more total hours during a day than do adults, but they also spend a greater proportion of time in _____ sleep. As they grow older, the children move toward longer but (<u>more/less</u>) frequent sleep periods and the total proportion of REM sleep declines from about 50 percent to the adolescent level of about _____ percent. During adulthood there is a gradual shift toward the (<u>lighter/deeper</u>) stages of sleep.

5-3. Answer the following questions regarding sleeping patterns across cultures.

(a) Which pattern, children sleeping with their parents (co-sleeping) or children sleeping alone, is the most widely practiced?

(b) Where are the "siesta cultures" generally located?

(c) What is the effect of industrialization on the practice of siestas?

Answers: 5-1. REM, decrease **5-2.** REM, less, 20, lighter **5-3.** (a) co-sleeping (b) tropical regions (c) The practice declines.

6. **Summarize evidence on the effects of complete, partial, and selective sleep deprivation.**

6-1. Answer the following questions regarding the effects of different kinds of sleep deprivation.

(a) What is the major effect of both complete and partial sleep deprivation?

(b) While research results show rather benign effects from sleep deprivation, what might be a serious problem when attention lapses due to sleep deprivation?

(c) How would you describe the time of the recovery period from both complete and partial sleep deprivation?

6-2. Studies in which subjects were selectively deprived of REM sleep, leaving NREM sleep undisturbed, found (<u>substantial/little</u>) negative effects from REM deprivation. One curious effect that has been noted from selective REM deprivation is that subjects tend to increase their amount of (<u>NREM/REM</u>) sleep when given the first opportunity to do so. This same rebound effect has also been found with stage 4 or

_____-_____ sleep.

7. Explain restorative and circadian theories of sleep and describe Borbely's integration of these views.

7-1.   Some theories as to why we sleep believe the purpose is to recharge the body. These are known as

_____ theories. Other theories propose that sleep is an aspect of _____ rhythms

regulated by neural mechanisms that are a result of evolution.

7-2.   Borbely has proposed that both kinds of theories are correct. In his view:

(a) What kind of sleep do circadian theories explain?

(b) What kind of sleep do restorative theories explain?

8. Discuss the prevalence, causes, and treatments of insomnia.

8-1.   While practically everybody will suffer from occasional bouts of insomnia, it is estimated that chronic

problems with insomnia occur in about _____ percent of all adults and another

_____ percent complain of occasional insomnia. There are three basic types of insomnia, which are

easily remembered because one type occurs at the beginning of sleep, one type during sleep, and the third type

at the end of sleep. Thus, one type involves difficulty in _____ asleep; one type involves difficulty

in _____ asleep; and one type involves persistent _____ awakening.

8-2.   There are a number of different causes of insomnia, but perhaps the most common one results from events and

problems that generate excessive _____ . Another frequent cause results from pain or difficulty in

breathing due to _____. Certain drugs are also implicated in insomnia.

8-3.   Since there are many different causes of insomnia, it seems reasonable that there (<u>is/is not</u>) a single form of

treatment. However, researchers agree that the most commonly used form of treatment, using sedatives, or

_____ pills, is not the treatment of choice. Evidence shows that while sleeping pills do promote

sleep, they also interfere with both the slow-wave and _____ part of the sleep cycle.

THE WORLD OF DREAMS

9. Discuss the nature of dreams.

9-1.   Which of the following statements is/are correct with respect to the changing scientific view with respect to dreams?

(a) Dreams are not as bizzare as was widely assumed.

(b) Dreams are not the exclusive property of REM sleep.

(c) Non-REM dreams appear to be less vivid and storylike than REM dreams.

Answers: 9-1. All are correct.

10. **Summarize Hall's findings on dream content and discuss how dreams are affected by real-world events.**

    10-1.   Calvin Hall, who analyzed the contents of more than 10,000 dreams, concluded that the content of most dreams is (<u>exotic/mundane</u>). Moreover, he found that dreams seldom involve events that are not centered around _____. Hall also found that dreams tend to be like soap operas in that they revolve around such common themes as misfortune, _____, and _____.

    10-2.   What did Freud mean when he stated that our dreams reflect day residue?

    10-3.   What other factor has an inconsistent effect on our dreams?

Answers: 10-1. mundane, ourselves, sex, aggression **10-2.** Dream content is influenced by what happens to us in our daily lives **10-3.** External stimuli (dripping water, ringing phones, etc.).

11. **Describe the three theories of dreaming covered in the chapter.**

    11-1.   The text mentions three theories as to why we need to dream. Tell what cognitive purpose, if any, each of these theories proposes as to the purpose of dreaming.

        (a) Sigmund Freud's theory about the need to dream.

        (b) The theory proposed by Rosalind Cartwright is cognizant of the fact that dreams are not restricted by logic or reality.

        (c) The activation-synthesis theory of Hobson and McCarley proposes that dreams occur as side effects of neural activation of the cortex by lower brain centers.

Answers: 11-1. (a) Dreams serve the purpose of wish fulfillment (b) Dreams allow for creative problem solving (c) Dreams serve no cognitive purpose.

HYPNOSIS: ALTERED CONSCIOUSNESS OR ROLE PLAYING?

12. **Discuss hypnotic susceptibility, list some prominent effects of hypnosis, and explain the role-playing and altered-state theories of hypnosis.**

12-1. While there are many different hypnotic induction techniques, a common factor among all of them is that they all lead to a heightened state of _____. Research shows that individuals (do/do not) vary in their susceptibility to hypnotic induction. In fact, approximately _____ percent of the population does not respond at all and approximately _____ percent are highly susceptible to hypnotic induction.

12-2. The text lists several of the more prominent effects that can be produced by hypnosis. Identify these effects from their descriptions given below.

(a) Reducing awareness of pain. _____

(b) Engaging in acts one would not ordinarily do. _____

(c) Perceiving things that do not exist or failing to perceive things that do exist. _____

(d) Claiming that sour foods taste sweet. _____

(e) Carrying out suggestions following the hypnotic induction session. _____ _____

(f) Claiming to forget what occurred during the induction session. _____

12-3. A theory of hypnosis proposed by Barber and Orne is that hypnosis is really a form of acting or role playing in which the subjects are simply playing as if they are hypnotized. What two lines of evidence support this theory?

12-4. A theory of hypnosis proposed by Hilgard is that hypnosis does in fact result in an altered state of consciousness. This theory holds that hypnosis results in a dissociation or _____ of consciousness into two parts. One half of the divided consciousness communicates with the hypnotist while the other half remains _____, even from the hypnotized subject. In this case, pain perceived by the "hidden" part of the consciousness (is/is not) reported to the "aware" part of consciousness. The divided state of consciousness proposed by Hilgard (is/is not) a common experience in everyday life. One such example of this commonly experienced state is appropriately called "highway _____."

Answers: 12-1. suggestibility, do, 10, 10 **12-2.** (a) anesthetic (b) disinhibition (c) hallucinations (d) sensory distortions (e) posthypnotic suggestions (f) amnesia **12-3.** Nonhypnotized subjects can duplicate the feats of hypnotized subjects and it has been shown that hypnotized subjects are merely carrying out their expectations of how hypnotized subjects should act **12-4.** splitting or dividing, hidden, is not, is, hypnosis.

MEDITATION: PURE CONSCIOUSNESS OR RELAXATION?

13. **Summarize the evidence on the short-term and long-term effect of meditation.**

13-1. Certain short-term physiological changes may occur during meditation. One of the most prominent of these changes is that EEG brain waves change from the rapid beta waves to the slower _____ and theta waves. This change to slower waves is accompanied by (an increase/a decrease) in metabolic activity, such as heart rate, oxygen consumption, etc. All of these physiological changes are characteristic of a normal state of _____. This state of relaxation (is/is not) unique to meditation.

13-2. The claims made for the long-term effects of meditation may have some merit in that studies have shown that subjects have shown improved mood and lessened anxiety and fatigue, as well as better physical health and increased longevity. These changes can (<u>also</u>/not) be induced by other commonly used methods for inducing relaxation. Moreover, the claim that meditation can produce a unique state of pure consciousness (has/<u>has not</u>) been supported by scientific research.

Answers: **13-1.** alpha, a decrease, relaxation, is not **13-2.** also, has not.

ALTERING CONSCIOUSNESS WITH DRUGS

14. **List and describe the major types of abused drugs and their effects.**

   14-1. The text list six different categories of psychoactive drugs; identify these drugs from the descriptions given below.

   (a) This drug is the most widely used, and abused, of all psychoactive drugs and produces a relaxed euphoria that temporarily boosts self-esteem. Wine and beer are both examples of the drug _____.

   (b) While this class of drugs derived from opium is effective at relieving pain, it can also produce a state of euphoria, which is the principal reason that opiates, or _____, are attractive to recreational users.

   (c) The drugs in this class, such as LSD, mescaline, and psilocybin, are known for their ability to distort sensory and perceptual experiences, which is why they are given the collective name of _____.

   (d) The drugs in this class include marijuana, hashish, and THC. Although they vary in potency each of them can produce a mild and an easy-going state of euphoria along with enhanced sensory awareness and a distorted sense of time. This class of drugs gets its name from the hemp plant _____ from which they are all derived.

   (e) This class of drugs is known for its sleep-inducing (sedation) and behavioral depression effects, resulting in tension reduction and a relaxed state of intoxication. While there are several different drugs in this class, the barbiturates are the most widely abused. Commonly known as "downers," they are more properly called _____.

   (f) This class of drugs produces arousal in the central nervous system and ranges from mildly arousing drugs like caffeine and nicotine, to strongly arousing drugs like cocaine and the amphetamines. Known for their ability to produce an energetic euphoria, the drugs in this class go by the name of _____.

   Answers: **14-1.** (a) alcohol (b) narcotics (c) hallucinogens (d) cannabis (e) sedatives (f) stimulants.

15. **Explain why drug effects vary and how psychoactive drugs exert their effects in the brain.**

   15-1. Taking a specific drug (<u>will</u>/<u>will not</u>) always have the same effect on the same person. This is because drug effects have _____ causation; individual, environmental, and drug factors can combine in many ways to produce the final effect. For example, one's expectations can strongly affect reactions to a drug. This is known as the _____ effect. Moreover, as one continues to take a specific drug, it requires a greater amount of the drug to achieve the same effect. This phenomenon is called drug _____.

15-2. Psychoactive drugs affect the CNS by selectively influencing _____ systems in a variety of ways. The action takes place at the juncture between neurons called the _____. For example, norepinesphrine and dopamine activity is influenced in a variety of ways by the action of _____. Both sedatives and alcohol exert their key effects at GABA synapses. When these two drugs are taken together their combined depressive effect on the CNS may be greater than the sum of their individual effects. Drugs having this effect are said to be _____.

Answers: **15-1.** will not, multifactorial, placebo, tolerance **15-2.** neurotransmitter, synapse, amphetamines, synergistic.

16. Summarize which drugs carry the greatest risk of tolerance, physical dependence, and psychological dependence.

16-1. When a person must continue taking a drug to avoid withdrawal illness, addiction, or _____ <u>dependence</u> is said to occur. When a person must continue taking a drug to satisfy intense emotional craving for the drug, then _____ <u>dependence</u> is said to occur. As can be seen in Table 5.4 in the text, the three riskiest drugs in terms of tolerance and physical and psychological dependence are the _____, _____, and _____.

16-2. How are both physical and psychological dependence established?

Answers: **16-1.** physical, psychological, narcotics/opiates, sedatives, stimulants **16-2.** Gradually with repeated use of the drug.

17. Summarize evidence on the major physical health risks associated with drug abuse.

17-1. There are three major ways in which drugs may affect physical health. The most dramatic is when a person takes too much of a drug, or drugs, and dies of an _____. Another way is when drug usage directly damages bodily tissue; this is referred to as a _____ effect. The third way is when drug usage results in accidents, improper eating and sleeping habits, infections, etc. These effects are collectively called _____ effects.

Answers: **17-1.** overdose, direct, indirect.

PUTTING IT IN PERSPECTIVE

18. Explain how the chapter highlighted four of the unifying themes.

18-1. Identify which of the underlying themes (psychology evolves in a sociohistorical context, experience is subjective, cultures mold some aspects of behavior, and psychology is theoretically diverse) is illustrated by the following statements.

(a) Psychologists have followed many different approaches and developed many different theories in their attempt to understand consciousness.

(b) The study of consciousness by psychologists followed rather than preceded renewed public interest in this topic.

(c) There are striking individual differences in the way people respond to hypnosis, meditation, and drugs.

(d) The significance given to dreams and sleep patterns can be influenced by this factor.

Answers: 18-1. (a) Psychology is theoretically diverse (b) Psychology evolves in a sociohistorical context (c) Experience is subjective (d) Culture molds some aspects of behavior.

APPLICATION: ADDRESSING PRACTICAL QUESTIONS ABOUT SLEEP AND DREAMS

19. **Summarize evidence on common questions about sleep and dreams as discussed in the Application.**

   19-1. Answer the following questions about sleep and napping.

   (a) How much sleep do we require?

   (b) While napping can be refreshing for most people, in what way can it prove inefficient?

   (c) What does evidence show about the effectiveness of attempting to learn complex material, such as a foreign language, during deep sleep?

   19-2. Temporary problems in going to sleep (do/do not) indicate that one is becoming an insomniac. These temporary problems often correct themselves. There are numerous methods for facilitating going to sleep, but a common feature in all of them is that they generate a feeling of _____. Some methods generate a feeling of boredom, which is akin to relaxation. The important point here is that one (does/does not) concentrate on the heavy events in life when attempting to go to sleep.

   19-3. While there are some persons who claim they never dream, what is really happening is that they cannot _____ their dreams. Dreams are best recalled when waking occurs during or immediately following the dream. Determination and practice (can/cannot) improve one's ability to recall dreams.

   19-4. Freud believed that dreams do require interpretation because their true meaning, which he called the _____ content, is symbolically encoded in the obvious plot of the dream, which he called the _____ content. Freud's theory that dreams carry hidden symbolic meaning would mean that dream interpretation (is/is not) a very complicated affair. Many researchers now believe that dreams are (more/less) complicated than Freud believed. Calvin Hall makes the point that dreams require some interpretation simply because they are mostly (visual/verbal).

Answers: 19-1. (a) It varies across individuals (b) Insufficient time is spent in the deeper stages of sleep (c) It is very ineffective **19-2.** do not, relaxation or calmness, does not **19-3.** remember (or recall), can **19-4.** latent, manifest, is, less, visual.

REVIEW OF KEY TERMS

Alcohol
Biological rhythms
Cannabis
Circadian rhythms
Consciousness
Dissociation
Electrocardiograph (EKG)
Electroencephalograph (EEG)

Electromyograph (EMG)
Electro-oculograph (EOG)
Hallucinogens
Hypnosis
Insomnia
Meditation
Narcotis or opiates
Non-REM sleep

Physical dependence
Psychoactive drugs
Psychological dependence
REM sleep
Sedatives
Slow-wave sleep
Stimulants
Tolerance

_____ 1. Our awareness of internal and external stimuli.

_____ 2. A device that records muscle activity and tension.

_____ 3. A device that monitors the electrical activity of the brain.

_____ 4. A device that records the contractions of the heart.

_____ 5. A device that records eye movements.

_____ 6. Periodic fluctuations in physiological functioning.

_____ 7. The 24-hour biological cycles found in humans and many other species.

_____ 8. Sleep involving rapid eye movements.

_____ 9. Sleep stages 1 through 4, which are marked by an absence of rapid eye movements.

_____ 10. Drugs derived from opium that are capable of relieving pain.

_____ 11. Involves chronic problems in getting adequate sleep.

_____ 12. A condition that exists when a person must continue to take a drug to satisfy mental and emotional craving for the drug.

_____ 13. A systematic procedure that typically produces a heightened state of suggestibility.

_____ 14. Involves a splitting off of mental processes into two separate, simultaneous streams of awareness.

_____ 15. A family of mental exercises in which a conscious attempt is made to focus attention in a nonanalytical way.

_____ 16. Chemical substances that modify mental, emotional, or behavioral functioning.

_____ 17. Sleep stages 3 and 4 in which low-frequency delta waves become prominent in EEG recordings.

_____ 18. Drugs that have sleep-inducing and behavioral depression effects.

_____ 19. Drugs that tend to increase central nervous system activation and behavioral activity.

_____ 20. A diverse group of drugs that have powerful effects on mental and emotional functioning, marked most prominently by distortions in sensory and perceptual experience.

_____ 21. The hemp plant from which marijuana, hashish, and THC are derived.

_____ 22. A variety of beverages containing ethyl alcohol.

_____ 23. A progressive decrease in a person's responsiveness to a drug.

_____ 24. A condition that exists when a person must continue to take a drug to avoid withdrawal illness.

REVIEW OF KEY PEOPLE

William Dement   Calvin Hall   J. Allan Hobson
Sigmund Freud   Ernest Hilgard

_____   **1.**   Argued for the existence of the unconscious and the hidden meaning of
                                  dreams.

_____   **2.**   As one of the pioneers in early sleep research, he coined the term REM sleep.

_____   **3.**   After analyzing thousands of dreams, he concluded that their contents are
                                  generally quite mundane.

_____   **4.**   A proponent of the altered state (divided consciousness) theory of hypnosis.

_____   **5.**   His activation-synthesis model proposes that dreams are only side effects of
                                  neural activation.

Answers: 1. Freud **2.** Dement **3.** Hall **4.** Hilgard **5.** Hobson.

SELF-QUIZ

1. The slowest brain wave activity is found with:
   a. alpha waves
   b. beta waves
   c. theta waves
   d. delta waves

2. The circadian rhythm operates around a:
   a. 1-year cycle
   b. 28-day cycle
   c. 24-hour cycle
   d. 90-minute cycle

3. Dreaming only occurs during REM sleep. This statement is:
   a. true
   b. false

4. The circadian rhythm appears to be regulated by:
   a. sunlight
   b. exercise
   c. diet
   d. temperature

5. Which of the following is likely to be found among persons deprived of sleep for a long period of time?
   a. slower reaction times
   b. slurred speech
   d. weariness

6. It has now been concluded that deprivation of REM sleep is more debilitating than deprivation of NREM sleep. This statement is:
   a. true
   b. false

7. According to Borbely's theory of sleep, the need for slow-wave sleep is due to:
   a. the need to recharge the body
   b. circadian rhythms
   c. the need to consolidate information in the memory store
   d. the need to regulate body temperature

8. The content of most dreams is usually:
   a. mundane
   b. exotic
   c. exciting
   d. both exotic and exciting

9. Persons can be made to act as if they are hypnotized even without the use of hypnotic induction. This statement is:
   a. true
   b. false

10. Which of the following physiological changes is unique to meditation?
    a. increased alpha rhythms
    b. increased heart rate
    c. increased oxygen consumption
    d. there are no physiological changes unique to meditation

11. Psychoactive drugs exert their effect on the brain by:
    a. decreasing blood supply to the brain
    b. altering neurotransmitter activity
    c. breaking down essential brain amino acids
    d. penetrating the nucleus of the neurons

12. The most widely abused drug in the United States is:
    a. alcohol
    b. cocaine
    c. heroin
    d. hallucinogens

13. Which of the following is likely to produce highly subjective events?
    a. hypnosis
    b. meditation
    c. psychoactive drugs
    d. hypnosis, meditation, and psychoactive drugs

14. Research has shown that one can learn complex material, such as a foreign language, while sleeping. This statement is:
    a. true
    b. false

15. Dreams might require some interpretation for the simple reason that they:
    a. arise solely from unconscious forces
    b. are predominantly verbal
    c. are predominantly visual
    d. involve such exotic material

Answers: 1. d **2.** c **3.** b **4.** a **5.** d **6.** b **7.** a **8.** a **9.** a **10.** d **11.** b **12.** a **13.** d **14.** b **15.** c.

6 LEARNING THROUGH CONDITIONING

REVIEW OF KEY IDEAS

CLASSICAL CONDITIONING

1. **Describe Pavlov's demonstration of classical conditioning and the key elements in this form of learning.**

   1-1. Classical conditioning is a type of learning that occurs when two stimuli are paired or associated closely in time. In Pavlov's initial demonstration, the two stimuli were a bell and _____.

   1-2. The response to one of the two stimuli occurs naturally and does not have to be learned or acquired through conditioning. This "unlearned" stimulus, in this case the food, is technically known as the _____ stimulus.

   1-3. The other stimulus is said to be neutral in the sense that it does not initially produce a response. When a response to this neutral stimulus is *acquired* or *learned*, the technical name for it is the _____ stimulus. In Pavlov's initial study the conditioned stimulus was the sound of a _____.

   1-4. The unconditioned stimulus in Pavlov's original study was the _____ and the conditioned stimulus was the _____. Salivation to the meat powder is known as the _____ response; salivation to the bell is termed the _____ response.

   1-5. Label the parts of the classical conditioning sequence. Place the commonly used abbreviations for these terms in the parentheses.

   (a) meat: _____ (   )

   (b) salivation to meat: _____ (   )

   (c) bell: _____ (   )

   (d) salivation to bell: _____ (   )

Answers: 1-1. meat powder (food) **1-2.** unconditioned **1-3.** conditioned, bell **1-4.** meat powder, bell, unconditioned, conditioned **1-5.** (a) unconditioned stimulus (UCS) (b) unconditioned response (UCR) (c) conditioned stimulus (CS) (d) conditioned response (CR).

2. Discuss how classical conditioning may shape phobias, other emotional responses.

2-1. The kids in the neighborhood where I (R. S.) grew up used to dig tunnels in a neighbor's backyard. One day a boy got stuck in the tunnel and couldn't get out. Eventually he got out, but after that he didn't want to play in tunnels again. To this day that person still has an intense fear–not only of tunnels but of closed-in spaces in general. Label the parts of the classical conditioning process involved in the acquisition of the phobia of closed-in spaces. (Hint: Even though "getting stuck" certainly involves a behavior or response, it also has stimulus components.)

(a) Getting stuck:

(b) Fear produced by getting stuck:

(c) Tunnels and closed-in spaces:

(d) Fear of tunnels and closed-in spaces:

2-2. The individual described above had developed an intense fear or phobia, acquired in part through the process of _____ conditioning. Other emotions can be conditioned as well. For example, the smell of smoke and Beemans gum described in your text, the playing of "our song," and the sight of one's home after a long absence could all produce a pleasant emotional response (or perhaps a slightly weepy, sentimental feeling). Such smells, sounds, or sights would be considered _____ stimuli.

2-3. Similarly, certain physiological responses can be conditioned. Label the parts of the conditioning process in the study on immunosuppression in rats described in the text. (Use the abbreviations CS, CR, UCS, and UCR.)

_____ The immunosuppressive drug:

_____ Unusual taste:

_____ Decreased antibody production produced by the drug:

_____ Decreased antibody production produced by the taste:

Answers: 2-1. (a) unconditioned stimulus (UCS) (b) unconditioned response (UCR) (c) conditioned stimulus (CS) (d) conditioned response (CR) **2-2.** classical, conditioned **2-3.** UCS, CS, UCR, CR.

3. Describe the classical conditioning phenomena of acquisition, extinction, spontaneous recovery, and higher-order conditioning.

3-1. *Acquisition* of a conditioned response occurs when the CS and UCS are contiguous, or paired. Not all pairings result in conditioning, however. What characteristics of the CS are more likely to produce acquisition of a CR?

3-2. Acquisition refers to the formation of a conditioned response. What is the term that refers to the weakening or disappearance of a CR? _____

3-3. Describe the procedure that results in extinction of a CR.

3-4. After CRs are extinguished they may reappear, even without further conditioning.

(a) For example, after being completely extinguished, a dog may again show the conditioned response (e.g., salivation to a bell) when returned to the apparatus in which it was originally conditioned. What is the name of this type of "reappearance" of the CR?

(b) When, or under what circumstance, is spontaneous recovery likely to occur?

(c) In addition, if an animal is extinguished in a different environment from the one in which conditioning took place, it is likely to again show a CR when returned to the original environment. What is the name of this effect?

3-5. Suppose a bell and meat powder are paired, as in the original Pavlovian study, until a conditioned salivary response occurs to the bell alone. Suppose that the bell is then paired in a series of new trials with a clicking sound. Assuming that the stimuli are potent enough, that the timing is right, and so on:

(a) Will a CR now occur to the clicking sound?

(b) What is the name of this conditioning procedure?

(c) Which stimulus acts as the UCS under this new arrangement?

Answers: 3-1. A novel or particularly intense CS is more likely to produce conditioning **3-2.** extinction **3-3.** The CS is presented for a series of trials alone, without the UCS **3-4.** (a) spontaneous recovery (b) after extinction, following a period of nonexposure to the CS (c) the renewal effect **3-5.** (a) yes (b) higher-order conditioning (c) The bell, the previous CS, now acts as a UCS.

4. Describe the processes of stimulus generalization and discrimination and summarize the classic study of Little Albert.

4-1. With regard to the case of Little Albert:

(a) What was the CS?

(b) The UCS?

4-2. Albert also developed a fear of white dogs and white rabbits, even though he had not been exposed to these stimuli. What is the name of the process that produced these fear responses?

4-3. Why would Albert have been more likely to develop a fear of a white rabbit, say, than a white car or a dark horse?

4-4. The more similar stimuli are to the CS, the more likely the organism will _____ from the CS to the other stimuli. The less similar stimuli are to the CS, the more likely the organism is to _____ them from the CS.

4-5. Casey (R. S.'s cat, now deceased) used to salivate when she heard the sound of food being dumped into her bowl. The process by which she learned to salivate to this particular sound is termed _____ _____. The food is a(an) _____ _____. The sound of the food is a(an) _____ _____. Salivation to the sound is a(an) _____ _____.

4-6. Pets are also likely to salivate when they hear other, similar sounds, like bags rustling in the kitchen or dishes being pulled from the cupboard. Salivation to these other sounds represents stimulus _____.

4-7. With continued training, in which food is paired only with the sound of food entering the bowl and not with the other sounds, the animal will learn to salivate only to the rattling bowl. The process of learning to respond only to one particular stimulus and not to a range of similar stimuli is termed _____.

Answers: **4-1.** (a) a white rat (b) a loud noise **4-2.** stimulus generalization (or just generalization) **4-3.** Because of similarity. The more similar the other stimuli to the CS, the more likely generalization is to occur. **4-4.** generalize, discriminate **4-5.** classical conditioning, unconditioned stimulus, conditioned stimulus, conditioned response **4-6.** generalization **4-7.** discrimination.

OPERANT CONDITIONING

5. Describe Skinner's principle of reinforcement.

5-1. A reinforcer is a stimulus or event that (1) is presented *after* a response and that (2) increases the tendency for the response to be repeated. Apply that definition to this example: Grundoon, a captive monkey, occasionally swings on a bar in his cage. Suppose that at some point Grundoon's trainers decide to give him a spoonful of applesauce whenever he swings. How would they know whether the applesauce is a reinforcer?

5-2. The trainers switch to vinegar. Grundoon, an unusual primate, swings quite frequently when this behavior is followed by vinegar. Is vinegar a reinforcer here? How do you know?

5-3. The trainers try another approach. They present Grundoon with fresh fruit *just before* they think he is likely to jump. It so happens that Grundoon's rate of jumping does increase. Is the fruit a reinforcer here? Why or why not?

Answers: **5-1.** If the animal's rate of swinging increases when followed by applesauce, then applesauce is a reinforcer **5-2.** Yes. Because the vinegar is presented *after the response*, and because the *response rate increases*. (Note that this is an imaginary example to illustrate the point that reinforcement is defined in terms of *consequences*, not by our subjective judgment. I don't know of any monkeys that will respond for vinegar.) **5-3.** No. Reinforcing stimuli, by definition, follow the response. (Again, this is a contrived example just to illustrate the definition.)

6. **Describe the prototype experimental procedures and apparatus used in studies of operant conditioning.**

6-1.   The prototypic apparatus used in operant conditioning studies is the operant chamber, better known as the

_____. On one wall of the chamber is mounted some sort of device that makes for an easily

recorded response. For rats, the device is usually a small _____; for pigeons, the device is a

_____ that the bird learns to peck.

6-2.   A press of the lever or peck at the disk may produce a reinforcer, generally a small bit of food dispensed into

the food cup mounted to one side or below the manipulandum. Each response is recorded on a

_____ _____, a device that creates a graphic record of the number of

responses per unit time.

6-3.   The cumulative recorder records the *rate* of the behavior, that is, the number of _____ made

per unit _____.

6-4.   Below is a highly stylized version of a cumulative record. About how many responses were made during the

first 40 seconds? _____ Which section of the graph (a, b, c, d, or e) has the steepest slope?

_____ Which section of the graph illustrates the fastest rate of responding?

_____ About how many responses were made between the 40th and 70th seconds?

_____

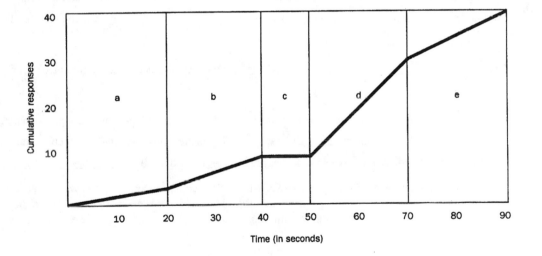

Answers: 6-1. Skinner box, lever (or bar), disk **6-2.** cumulative recorder **6-3.** responses, time **6-4.** 10, d, d, 20.

7. **Describe the operant conditioning phenomena of acquisition, shaping, and extinction.**

7-1.   Acquisition refers to the formation of new responses. In classical conditioning, acquisition occurs through a

simple pairing of the CS and UCS. In operant conditioning, acquisition involves the procedure known as

_____.

7-2.   What is shaping? When is it used?

7-3. Extinction in classical conditioning involves removing the UCS while still presenting the CS.

(a) What is the extinction procedure in operant conditioning?

(b) What is the effect of extinction on behavior (response rate)?

(c) What does the term *resistance to extinction* mean?

Answers 7-1. shaping **7-2.** Shaping involves reinforcing closer and closer approximations to the desired behavior. It is used in the formation of a new response **7-3.** (a) The extinction procedure involves no longer presenting the reinforcers after the response. (b) Response rate decreases and may eventually stop. (c) Animals may continue to respond, for a period of time, even when reinforcers are no longer presented. The extent to which they will *continue to respond during extinction* is referred to as *resistance* to extinction.

8. Explain how stimuli govern operant behavior and how generalization and discrimination occur in operant conditioning.

8-1. Suppose that a rat has been shaped so that when it presses a lever it receives a food pellet. With further training, the rat may respond only when a light (or sound, etc.) in the chamber is on and not when it is off. The food pellet (which follows the response) is a _____. The light (which precedes the response) is a _____ stimulus.

8-2. Reinforcers occur _____ (after/before) the response occurs. Discriminative stimuli occur _____ the response occurs.

8-3. To create a discriminative stimulus, one reinforces a response only in the presence of a particular stimulus and not in its absence. In time that stimulus will gain control of the response: Animals will tend to emit the response only if the discriminative stimulus is (present/absent) and not if it is _____.

8-4. For example, rats can be trained to press a lever when a light comes on and not to press when the light is off. Lever presses that occur when the light is on are followed by a food pellet; those that occur in the dark are not. Label each component of this operant-conditioning process by placing the appropriate letters in the blanks below.

_____ light   a. discriminative stimulus

_____ lever press   b. response

_____ food   c. reinforcer

8-5. "Heel Fido!" says Ralph. Fido runs to Ralph's side. Fido gets a pat on the head. Label the parts of the operant-conditioning sequence by placing the appropriate letters in the blanks. (To avoid confusion, the behavior or response of interest in this example is already labeled.)

_____ "Heel Fido!"   a. discriminative stimulus

_____ Fido gets a pat on the head.   b. response

__b__ Fido runs to Ralph's side.   c. reinforcer

8-6. Phyllis will lend money to Ralph, but only after Ralph promises to pay her back. Ralph is also careful to thank Phyllis for her help. The behavior we are looking at here is Phyllis's lending behavior.

_____"Thank you very much, Phyllis."   a. discriminative stimulus

__b__ Phyllis lends.   b. response

_____"I promise I'll pay you back."   c. reinforcer

8-7. Generalization occurs in operant as well as classical conditioning. For example, when I put dishes in the sink, our cat would *run to her bowl* looking for food. In technical terms, our cat _____ between the sound of food dropping in her bowl and the similar sound of dishes going into the sink. Despite the fact that food does not follow the sound of clattering dishes, our cat did not learn to _____ between the sounds in our kitchen.

Answers: 8-1. reinforcer, discriminative **8-2.** after, before **8-3.** present, absent **8-4.** a, b, c **8-5.** a, c, (b) **8-6.** c, (b), a **8-7.** generalized, discriminate.

9. Discuss the role of delayed reinforcement and conditioned reinforcement in operant conditioning.

9-1. People who smoke like to smoke. Giving up the habit, however, also has its rewards. Given the information about delay of reinforcement, why is the behavior of giving up smoking so difficult to acquire?

9-2. Define the following:

(a) Primary reinforcer:

(b) Secondary or conditioned reinforcer:

Answers: 9-1. Because we, like the rest of the animal kingdom, are more affected by reinforcers that *immediately* follow our behavior than those that follow after a delay. Reinforcement for smoking is immediate; reinforcement for giving up smoking may occur only after a long delay. **9-2.** (a) A primary reinforcer satisfies biological needs, such as needs for food, water, warmth, and sex. (b) A secondary, or conditioned, reinforcer is learned or acquired through association with a primary reinforcer. For humans, common secondary reinforcers include praise, attention, and money.

10. Identify various types of schedules of reinforcement, and discuss their typical effects on responding.

10-1. Schedules of reinforcement are either continuous or intermittent. If reinforcers follow each response, the schedule is referred to as a _____-reinforcement schedule, abbreviated CRF. If reinforcers only follow some responses and not others (e.g., FR, VR), or occur as a function of the passage of time (e.g., FI, VI), the schedule is referred to as a/an _____ schedule.

10-2. Identify the following schedules of reinforcement by placing the appropriate abbreviations in the blanks: continuous reinforcement (CRF), fixed ratio (FR), variable ratio (VR), fixed interval (FI), variable interval (VI).

_____ A pigeon is reinforced whenever it has pecked a disk exactly 200 times.

_____ A pigeon is reinforced for pecking a disk, on the average, 200 times.

_____ A rat is always reinforced for the first response that follows a two-minute interval.

_____ A slot machine delivers a payoff, on the average, after every 10th pull of the lever.

_____ Every time the pigeon pecks a disk, it receives a pellet of food.

_____ A rat is reinforced, on the average, for the first response following a two-minute interval.

_____ A pig is reinforced for the first response after 30 seconds, then for the first response after 42 seconds, then for the first response after 5 seconds, and so on.

_____ Every two weeks Ralph picks up his payroll check at the office.

_____ A rat is reinforced after the 73rd response, then after the 22nd response, then after the 51st response, and so on.

10-3. Resistance to extinction refers to the extent to which responses occur during a period of extinction. What is the general effect of the intermittent schedules of reinforcement on resistance to extinction?

10-4. In terms of the effect on *rate* of responding, what is the general difference between the *ratio* schedules (FR and VR) and the *interval* schedules (FI and VI)?

10-5. In terms of the effect on *pattern* of responding, what is the general difference between *fixed* schedules and *variable* schedules?

Answers: 10-1. continuous, intermittent (or partial) **10-2.** FR, VR, FI, VR, CRF, VI, VI, FI, VR **10-3.** The intermittent schedules increase resistance to extinction. **10-4.** Ratio schedules tend to produce more rapid responding than the interval schedules. **10-5.** Variable schedules tend to produce more regular patterns of responding, without pauses or scalloping, than do their fixed counterparts. They also result in more resistance to extinction.

11. Explain the distinction between positive and negative reinforcement.

11-1. Some Skinner boxes may be set up so that a mild electric shock can be delivered to the feet of the animal through the floor of the box. Suppose that just after the animal presses the bar, the shock is turned *off* for a period of time. Will the lever-pressing behavior be *strengthened* or *weakened*?

11-2. By definition, what effect does reinforcement have on behavior? What is the effect of positive reinforcement on behavior? Negative reinforcement?

11-3. With positive reinforcement, a stimulus is *presented* after the response. What is the procedure with negative reinforcement?

Answers: 11-1. strengthened **11-2.** Reinforcement strengthens (increases the frequency of) behavior. Both positive and negative reinforcement strengthen behavior. **11-3.** The stimulus (an aversive stimulus) is *removed* after the response.

12. Describe and distinguish between escape learning and avoidance learning.

12-1. Review the section on escape and avoidance learning. In escape learning the animal first experiences the aversive stimulus and then makes a response that escapes it. In avoidance learning the animal responds to a cue that permits it to respond *before* the aversive stimulus is delivered, thereby avoiding it altogether. Label the following examples E for escape and A for avoidance.

_____ The weather has changed, and Fred is getting cold. He goes inside.

_____ Little Sandra rapidly removes her hand from the hot stove.

_____ A cue light comes on in the dog's shuttle box. It jumps the hurdle to the other side.

_____ Randolph has been told that he will be mugged if he goes outside, so he stays inside.

_____ Sue has learned some new verbal behavior. If she simply says, "No, I don't want that" shortly after a salesman starts his pitch, the salesman will stop bothering her.

_____ Alice sees Ruppert in the distance. If Ruppert sees her he will ask for her course notes, which she doesn't want to lend him. She heads in the other direction.

12-2. What is the major difference between escape learning and avoidance learning?

Answers: 12-1. E, E, A, A, E, A **12-2.** The major difference is that with escape learning there is no cue stimulus, so that the animal must first experience the aversive stimulus and then *escape* it. In the case of avoidance learning, a cue preceding the aversive stimulus permits the animal to *avoid* the aversive event altogether.

13. Explain the role of negative reinforcement in avoidance behavior.

13-1. In successful avoidance learning, the organism never experiences the aversive stimulus. For example, when a dog in a shuttle box jumps to the other side it never experiences shock. So, why doesn't the jumping response gradually extinguish? One explanation is that the dog isn't just avoiding the shock, it is also escaping something else as well. What stimulus is the dog escaping? _____

13-2. According to Mowrer, the cue stimulus acquires the capacity to elicit fear because it is associated with the shock, the process of _____ conditioning. The jumping behavior, on the other hand, is maintained by escaping the cue stimulus, the process of _____ conditioning. Thus, the type of reinforcement that maintains the jumping is _____ reinforcement.

Answers: 13-1. the cue light (or the conditioned fear of the cue light) **13-2.** classical, operant, negative.

14. Describe punishment and its effects, and list six guidelines for making punishment more effective.

14-1. Punishment involves *weakening* a response by presenting an aversive stimulus after the response has occurred. Review the concepts of reinforcement and punishment by labeling each of the following with one of these terms: positive reinforcement, negative reinforcement, or punishment.

(a) A stimulus is presented after the response; response rate increases:

(b) A stimulus is presented after the response; response rate decreases:

(c) A stimulus is removed after the response; response rate increases:

14-2. Response rate *increases*. Which of the following procedures may have been used?
a. positive reinforcement
b. negative reinforcement
c. punishment
d. either *a* or *b* above

14-3. Response rate *decreases*. Which of the following procedures may have been used?
a. positive reinforcement
b. negative reinforcement
c. punishment
d. either *b* or *c* above

14-4. When a rat presses a bar in an operant chamber, the electric shock stops. Bar pressing increases. What procedure has been used?
a. positive reinforcement
b. negative reinforcement
c. punishment
d. extinction

14-5. When the dog ran after the car, his master immediately threw a bucket of water on him. This sequence of events was repeated only twice, and the dog stopped running after the car. What has occurred?
a. positive reinforcement
b. negative reinforcement
c. punishment
d. extinction

14-6. When Randolph stepped out in his new outfit, everyone stared. If Randolph tends *not* to wear this outfit in the future, what has occurred?
a. positive reinforcement
b. negative reinforcement
c. punishment
d. extinction

14-7.   In the space below list three negative side effects of punishment.

14-8.   Following are five hints that refer to the guidelines for making punishment more effective. Beneath each hint describe the appropriate guideline.

(a) When?

(b) How strong?

(c) How consistently?

(d) What explanations?

(e) Spanking, or withdrawal of privileges?

Answers: 14-1. (a) positive reinforcement (b) punishment (c) negative reinforcement **14-2.** d, because if response rate increases, *either* positive *or* negative reinforcement may be involved **14-3.** c, not d, because negative reinforcement *increases* response rate **14-4.** b **14-5.** c **14-6.** c **14-7.** Punishment may (1) suppress responses in general rather than just the response punished, (2) produce unwanted emotional responses, including fear and anger, and (3) increase aggressive behavior **14-8.** (a) If possible, punishment should be delivered *immediately* after the behavior. (b) Since undesirable side effects increase with the intensity of punishment, it should be *only as strong as needed* to be effective. (c) To be effective punishment should be given *consistently*, after each instance of the behavior. (d) If the *reasons for the punishment* are given to children, the punishment tends to be more effective. (e) In most situations *physical punishment should be avoided* because it tends to increase aggressive behavior in children. In addition, in many cases physical punishment may be less effective than withdrawal of privileges.

NEW DIRECTIONS IN THE STUDY OF CONDITIONING

15.   Discuss the implications of instinctive drift and conditioned taste aversion for traditional views of conditioning and learning.

15-1.   What is instinctive drift?

15-2. Why was the occurrence of instinctive drift surprising to operant psychologists? Discuss this question in terms of the supposed *generality* of the laws of learning.

15-3. What is conditioned taste aversion?

15-4. Why is the occurrence of conditioned taste aversion surprising? Discuss this question in terms of classical conditioning relating to (1) CS-UCS delays and (2) the sense of taste compared with other senses.

Answers: 15-1. It is the tendency for instinctive or innate behavior to interfere with the process of conditioning. **15-2.** Before the 1960s, operant psychologists assumed that any response that animals could emit could readily be conditioned. This turned out not to be true. Animals may exhibit instinctive drift, the tendency to respond with certain innate behaviors that actually interfere with the process of conditioning. **15-3.** It is the fact that if the distinctive taste of a particular food is followed some hours later by sickness (nausea, vomiting, etc.), that taste will become aversive and will also elicit the response of nausea. **15-4.** It is surprising because (1) classical conditioning generally does not occur if there are long CS-UCS delays, and (2) taste is only one of several senses stimulated in this situation. Garcia concluded that animals have an innate tendency to associate taste (rather than sight, sound, etc.) with sickness even though the sickness may occur much later.

16. Explain the evolutionary perspective on learning.

16-1. Psychologists used to believe that there were highly general "laws" of learning. More recently, studies like those just referred to and the emerging field of evolutionary psychology indicate that there probably (are/are not) principles of learning that apply to all species.

16-2. Instead, the new viewpoint emerging among psychologists is that ways of learning have evolved along different paths in different species, so that classical and operant conditioning, for example, are to some extent (universal/species-specific). Finding food, avoiding predators, and reproducing allow a species to survive, but the ways of learning that accomplish these outcomes depend on the _____ value of these processes.

Answers: 16-1. are not **16-2.** species-specific, adaptive (survival, evolutionary).

17. Describe research on signal relations in classical and operant conditioning and explain its theoretical importance.

17-1. In the example of a signal relations study described, the number of conditioning trials in which CS and UCS were paired was the same for two groups. The difference between the two treatment groups was that for one group the (CS/UCS) was also presented *alone* for a series of trials.

17-2. Theorists originally assumed that classical conditioning is an automatic, reflexive process affected only by the number of CS-UCS pairings. If this actually were the case, then what, supposedly, would have been the effect of presenting the UCS alone for a series of trials?
a. Extinction would occur.
b. Conditioning would be weaker.
c. No effect.

17-3. In fact, what did occur in the signal relations studies?
a. Extinction.
b. The UCS trials weakened conditioning.
c. The UCS trials had no effect on conditioning.

17-4. Why were the signal relations studies surprising and of theoretical importance?

17-5. Cognitive processes also seem to be important in operant conditioning. For example, for human beings, responses are more likely to be strengthened if the person *thinks* the response *caused* the favorable outcome. Lower animals (also/do not) seem to show recognition of causal relations between *responses* and *outcomes*. Thus, operant conditioning, like classical conditioning, seems to involve (only automatic/cognitive) processes.

Answers: 17-1. UCS **17-2.** c **17-3.** b **17-4.** These studies indicate that classical conditioning is not just an automatic process but rather depends on some sort of higher mental process, the predictive value that the CS has with regard to the occurrence of the UCS rather than just the number of pairings **17-5.** also, cognitive.

18. Discuss the nature and importance of observational learning.

18-1. In the space below list and define the four processes that Bandura has identified as crucial components of observational learning. The first letter of each concept is listed at the left.

A_____:

R_____:

R_____:

M_____:

18-2. Why is the concept of observational learning so important? For one thing, it represents a third major type of learning besides classical and operant conditioning. We learn not only when we behave but when we _____ the behavior of others.

18-3. In addition, it extends classical and operant conditioning to include not only *direct* experience but _____ or vicarious experience.

18-4. Bandura's theory has helped explain some puzzling aspects of conditioning in human behavior. For example, while punishment by definition (increases/decreases) the behavior it follows, a parent using punishment also serves as a _____ for aggressiveness. In this way events intended to decrease aggression may, through the process of _____ learning, increase aggression in the longer run.

Answers: 18-1. *Attention*: You must pay attention to a model's behavior and its consequences. *Retention*: You must retain or store in memory a mental representation of what you have observed. *Reproduction*: You must have the ability to reproduce the behavior that you observe. *Motivation*: Based on your assessment of the likely payoff, you must have the motivation to reproduce the observed behavior. **18-2.** observe **18-3.** indirect **18-4.** decreases, model, observational.

PUTTING IT IN PERSPECTIVE

19. Explain how this chapter highlighted two of the text's unifying themes.

19-1. Skinner emphasized the importance of *environmental* events (such as reinforcers and punishers and schedules of reinforcement) as the determinants of behavior. As this chapter makes clear, however, environment doesn't act alone—heredity and environment jointly influence our behavior. In support of this theme list the names of two phenomena that show that *biology* has a powerful effect on *conditioning*.

19-2. The second theme well illustrated in this chapter is that psychology evolves in a sociohistorical context. To illustrate this theme, discuss one concept from operant psychology that appears to have influenced our everyday lives.

Answers: 19-1. instinctive drift, conditioned-taste aversion **19-2.** Operant psychology has probably influenced the trend in our society toward relying more on the use of positive reinforcement than punishment in child-rearing, educational settings, and as a management technique in business.

APPLICATION: ACHIEVING SELF-CONTROL THROUGH BEHAVIOR MODIFICATION

20. List and discuss the five steps in a self-modification program.

20-1. In the space below list the five steps of a self-modification program in the order in which they are performed. The letters at the left are the first letters of the key words in each phase.

T: Specify your _____ behavior.

B: Gather _____ data.

D: _____ your program.

EE: _____ and _____ your program.

E: _____ your program.

20-2. What behavior do you want to change? The question sounds simple, but the task of defining a _____ behavior is frequently quite tricky.

20-3. The behavior that you select must be defined in terms of observable events so that you will know if and when it changes. For example, for the problem of anger control, which of the following would be the most *directly observable* definition of "anger"?

a. inner turmoil

b. intense hostility

c. loud voice and clenched fists

20-4. Once you specify the target behavior you must gather _____ data on your behavior prior to the intervention. At this time you should also keep track of events that precede the target behavior, the _____ events, and also the positive and negative reinforcers that follow it, the _____ events.

20-5. To increase a target behavior you would use _____. The reinforcer (<u>can/cannot</u>) be something that you already are receiving. For example, you probably already watch TV, go to movies, or buy things for yourself, so you could make one of these events _____ on an increased frequency of the target behavior.

20-6. You would specify exactly what behavioral goals must be met before you receive the reinforcer; that is, you would arrange the _____. If your goal is to increase studying, you might specify that TV watching for one hour is _____ on having studied for two hours.

20-7. Or, you might specify that for each hour you studied you would earn points that could be "spent" for watching TV, or going to movies, or talking with friends, and so on. This type of arrangement is referred to as a _____ economy.

20-8. In some cases you might want to approach the target response gradually, to reinforce successive approximations to the target behavior using the procedure known as _____.

20-9. To decrease a target behavior you could make some sort of _____ contingent on the behavior. The problem with this approach is that it is difficult to follow through by punishing oneself, so there are two guidelines to keep in mind: (1) Use punishment only in conjunction with _____ reinforcement; and (2) use a relatively _____ punishment that you, or perhaps a third party, will be able to administer.

20-10. For some situations you may be able to identify events that reliably precede the behaviors you are trying to stop. For example, for some people smoking is at least under partial control of certain types of social events. So, one strategy for decreasing a behavior is to identify the (<u>antecedent/consequent</u>) events that may control the behavior.

20-11. Successful execution of the program depends on several factors. To avoid "cheating" try creating a formal written behavioral _____. Or, make an arrangement so that (<u>only you/someone else</u>) delivers the reinforcers and punishments.

20-12. If your program isn't working, some small revision may turn it around. Try increasing the strength of the reinforcer or else try _____ the delay between the behavior and delivery of the reinforcer.

20-13. When does your program end? Generally, you will specify the conditions under which you will stop your program (<u>when you design it/in the middle</u>). You may wish to phase it out by having a gradual reduction in the frequency or potency of reinforcers, although for some successful programs the new behaviors become self-maintaining on their own.

Answers: 20-1. target, baseline, design, execute, evaluate, end **20-2.** target **20-3.** <u>c</u>, although even those behaviors would have to be further described in a behavior modification program. Alternative <u>a</u> is not really observable. Alternative <u>b</u> could be behaviorally defined, but as it stands it is hard to know precisely which behaviors intense hostility refers to. **20-4.** baseline, antecedent, consequences. **20-5.** reinforcement, can, contingent **20-6.** contingency, contingent **20-7.** token **20-8.** shaping **20-9.** punishment, positive, mild **20-10.** antecedent. **20-11.** contract (agreement), someone else **20-12.** decreasing **20-13.** when you design it.

REVIEW OF KEY TERMS

Acquisition
Antecedents
Avoidance learning
Behavioral contract
Behavior modification
Classical conditioning
Conditioned reinforcer
Conditioned response (CR)
Conditioned stimulus (CS)
Continuous reinforcement
Cumulative recorder
Discriminative stimuli
Elicit
Emit
Escape learning

Extinction
Fixed-interval (FI) schedule
Fixed-ratio (FR) schedule
Higher-order conditioning
Intermittent reinforcement
Learning
Negative reinforcement
Observational learning
Operant conditioning
Pavlovian conditioning
Positive reinforcement
Primary reinforcers
Punishment
Reinforcement
Reinforcement contingencies

Resistance to extinction
Schedule of reinforcement
Secondary reinforcers
Shaping
Skinner box
Spontaneous recovery
Stimulus contiguity
Stimulus discrimination
Stimulus generalization
Token economy
Trial
Unconditioned response (UCR)
Unconditioned stimulus (UCS)
Variable-interval (VI) schedule
Variable-ratio (VR) schedule

_____ 1. A relatively durable change in behavior or knowledge that is due to experience.

_____ 2. The most common name of a type of learning in which a neutral stimulus acquires the ability to evoke a response that was originally evoked by another stimulus.

_____ 3. Another name for classical conditioning derived from the name of the person who originally discovered the conditioning phenomenon.

_____ 4. A stimulus that evokes an unconditioned response.

_____ 5. The response to an unconditioned stimulus.

_____ 6. A previously neutral stimulus that has acquired the capacity to evoke a conditioned response.

_____ 7. A learned reaction to a conditioned stimulus that occurs because of previous conditioning.

_____ 8. To draw out or bring forth, as in classical conditioning.

_____ 9. Any presentation of a stimulus or pair of stimuli in classical conditioning.

_____ 10. The formation of a new response tendency.

_____ 11. Occurs when there is a temporal (time) association between two events.

_____ 12. The gradual weakening and disappearance of a conditioned response tendency.

_____ 13. The reappearance of an extinguished response after a period of nonexposure to the conditioned stimulus.

_____ 14. Occurs when an organism responds to new stimuli that are similar to the stimulus used in conditioning.

_____ 15. Occurs when an organism learns not to respond to stimuli that are similar to the stimulus used in conditioning.

_____ 16. Occurs when a conditioned stimulus functions as if it were an unconditioned stimulus.

_____ 17. This term, introduced by Skinner, refers to learning in which voluntary responses come to be controlled by their consequences.

_____ 18. Occurs when an event following a response strengthens the tendency to make that response.

_____ 19. A standard operant chamber in which an animal's responses are controlled and recorded.

_____ 20. Production of voluntary responses in responding in operant conditioning.

_____ 21. The circumstances or rules that determine whether responses lead to presentation of a reinforcer; or, the relationship between a response and positive consequences.

_____ 22. Device that creates a graphic record of operant responding as a function of time.

_____ 23. The reinforcement of closer and closer approximations of the desired response.

_____ 24. Occurs when an organism continues to make a response after the delivery of the reinforcer for it has been terminated.

_____ 25. Cues that precede operant behavior and that influence the behavior by indicating the probable consequences (reinforcement or no reinforcement) of a response.

_____ 26. Stimulus events that are inherently reinforcing because they satisfy biological needs.

_____ 27. Stimulus events that acquire reinforcing qualities by being associated with primary reinforcers.

_____ 28. A specific pattern of presentation of reinforcers over time.

_____ 29. Occurs when every instance of a designated response is reinforced.

_____ 30. The name for all schedules of reinforcement in which a designated response is reinforced only some of the time.

_____ 31. The schedule in which the reinforcer is given after a fixed number of nonreinforced responses.

_____ 32. The schedule in which the reinforcer is given after a variable number of nonreinforced responses.

_____ 33. The schedule in which the reinforcer is given for the first response that occurs after a fixed time interval has elapsed.

_____ 34. The schedule in which the reinforcer is given for the first response that occurs after a variable time interval has elapsed.

_____ 35. Occurs when a response is strengthened because it is followed by the arrival of a rewarding (presumably pleasant) stimulus.

_____ 36. Occurs when a response is strengthened because it is followed by the removal of an aversive ("unpleasant") stimulus.

_____ 37. Occurs when an organism engages in a response that brings aversive stimulation to an end.

_____ 38. Occurs when an organism engages in a response that prevents aversive stimulation from occurring.

_____ 39. Occurs when an event that follows a response weakens or suppresses the tendency to make that response.

_____ 40. Occurs when an organism's responding is influenced by the observation of others, who are called models.

_____ 41. A systematic approach to changing behavior through the application of the principles of conditioning.

_____ 42. Events that typically precede your target behavior and may play a major role in governing your target response; also, another term for discriminative stimuli.

_____ 43. A system for distributing symbolic reinforcers that are exchanged later for a variety of genuine reinforcers.

_____ 44. A written agreement outlining a promise to adhere to the contingencies of a behavior modification program.

_____ 45. Another name for secondary reinforcer.

Answers: 1. learning **2.** classical conditioning **3.** Pavlovian conditioning **4.** unconditioned stimulus (UCS) **5.** unconditioned response (UCR) **6.** conditioned stimulus (CS) **7.** conditioned response (CR) **8.** elicit **9.** trial **10.** acquisition **11.** stimulus contiguity **12.** extinction **13.** spontaneous recovery **14.** stimulus generalization **15.** stimulus discrimination **16.** higher-order conditioning **17.** operant conditioning **18.** reinforcement **19.** Skinner box **20.** emit **21.** reinforcement contingencies **22.** cumulative recorder **23.** shaping **24.** resistance to extinction **25.** discriminative stimuli **26.** primary reinforcers **27.** secondary reinforcers **28.** schedule of reinforcement **29.** continuous reinforcement **30.** intermittent reinforcement **31.** fixed-ratio (FR) schedule **32.** variable-ratio (VR) schedule **33.** fixed-interval (FI) schedule **34.** variable-interval (VI) schedule **35.** positive reinforcement **36.** negative reinforcement **37.** escape learning **38.** avoidance learning **39.** punishment **40.** observational learning **41.** behavior modification **42.** antecedents **43.** token economy **44.** behavioral contract **45.** conditioned reinforcer.

REVIEW OF KEY PEOPLE

Albert Bandura   Robert Rescorla   John B. Watson
Ivan Pavlov   B. F. Skinner

_____ 1. The first to describe the process of classical conditioning.

_____ 2. Founded behaviorism; examined the generalization of conditioned fear in a boy known as "Little Albert."

_____ 3. Elaborated the learning process known as operant conditioning; investigated schedules of reinforcement.

_____ 4. Asserted that environmental stimuli serve as signals and that some stimuli in classical conditioning are better signals than others.

_____ 5. Described and extensively investigated the process of observational learning.

Answers: 1. Pavlov **2.** Watson **3.** Skinner **4.** Rescorla **5.** Bandura.

SELF-QUIZ

1. In Pavlov's original demonstration of classical conditioning, salivation to the bell was the
   a. conditioned stimulus
   b. conditioned response
   c. unconditioned stimulus
   d. unconditioned response

2. Sally developed a fear of balconies after almost falling from a balcony on a couple of occasions. What was the conditioned response?
   a. the balcony
   b. fear of the balcony
   c. almost falling
   d. fear resulting from almost falling

3. When the UCS is removed and the CS is presented alone for a period of time, what will occur?
   a. classical conditioning
   b. generalization
   c. acquisition
   d. extinction

4. Sally developed a fear of balconies from almost falling. Although she has had no dangerous experiences on bridges, cliffs, and the view from tall buildings, she now fears these stimuli as well. Which of the following would account for her acquiring a fear of these other stimuli?
   a. instinctive drift
   b. spontaneous recovery
   c. generalization
   d. discrimination

5. A researcher reinforces closer and closer approximations to a target behavior. What is the name of the procedure she is using?
   a. shaping
   b. classical conditioning
   c. discrimination training
   d. extinction

6. The telephone rings. John answers it and is reinforced by the voice on the other end. In operant conditioning terminology, the ringing of the phone is a
   a. discriminative stimulus
   b. response
   c. positive reinforcer
   d. conditioned stimulus (CS)

7. A rat is reinforced for the first lever-pressing response that occurs, *on the average*, after 60 seconds. Which schedule is the rat on?
   a. FR
   b. VR
   c. FI
   d. VI

8. When the rat presses a lever, the mild electric shock on the cage floor is turned off. What procedure is being used?
   a. punishment
   b. escape
   c. discrimination training
   d. avoidance

9. A cue light comes on in the dog's shuttle box. It jumps the hurdle to the other side. What procedure is being used?
   a. punishment
   b. escape
   c. discrimination training
   d. avoidance

10. Suppose that when a response occurs, a stimulus is presented that has the effect of *decreasing* response strength. What procedure is being used?
    a. positive reinforcement
    b. negative reinforcement
    c. punishment
    d. avoidance training

11. In terms of the traditional view of conditioning, research on conditioned taste aversion was surprising because
    a. there was a very long delay between CS and UCS
    b. the dislike of a particular taste was operantly conditioned
    c. conditioning occurred to all stimuli present when the food was consumed
    d. the sense of taste seems to be relatively weak

12. Animal trainers (the Brelands) trained pigs to put coins in a piggy bank for a food reward. The animals learned the response but, instead of depositing the coins immediately in the bank, the pigs began to toss them in the air, drop them, push them on the ground, and so on. What had occurred that interfered with conditioning?
    a. conditioned taste aversion
    b. negative reinforcement
    c. instinctive drift
    d. modeling

13. Which of the following increases resistance to extinction?
    a. continuous reinforcement
    b. intermittent reinforcement
    c. negative reinforcement
    d. discrimination training

14. Earlier learning viewpoints considered classical and operant conditioning to be automatic processes involving only environmental events that did not depend at all on biological or cognitive factors. Research on which of the following concepts cast doubt on this point of view?
    a. signal relations, instinctive drift, and conditioned taste aversion
    b. extinction, discrimination, and generalization
    c. CRF, ratio, and interval schedules
    d. escape, avoidance, and spontaneous recovery

15. In devising your own self-modification procedure, your first step should be to:
    a. gather baseline data
    b. specify your target behavior
    c. design your program
    d. execute and evaluate your program

Answers: 1. b **2.** b **3.** d **4.** c **5.** a **6.** a **7.** d **8.** b **9.** d **10.** c **11.** a **12.** c **13.** b **14.** a **15.** b.

HUMAN MEMORY

REVIEW OF KEY IDEAS

ENCODING: GETTING INFORMATION INTO MEMORY

1. List and describe the three basic human memory processes.

1-1. The three basic human memory processes are:

(a) Putting information in, a process called _____.

(b) Holding onto information, a process called _____.

(c) Getting information back out, a process called _____.

Answers: 1-1. (a) encoding (b) storage (c) retrieval.

2. Discuss the role of attention in memory.

2-1. Attention requires both filtering out irrelevant information and attending to selected information. Thus if you are being introduced to a new person whose name you want to remember, you must _____ attend to her name and _____ out irrevelant sensory input.

2-2. The debate between early and late selection theories of attention is an argument over *where* this filtering takes place, before or after _____ is given to the arriving information.

2-3. Research evidence, as well as casual observations, seem to support (both/neither) arguments and intermediate selection as well. In fact, some theorists believe that the location of the filter is _____ rather than fixed.

Answers: 2-1. selectively, filter **2-2.** meaning **2-3.** both, flexible.

3. Describe the three levels of information processing proposed by Craik and Lockhart (1972) and their relation to memory.

3-1. Craik and Lockhart propose three levels for encoding incoming information, with ever increasing retention as the depth of processing increases. In their order of depth these three levels are:

(a) _____ (b) _____ (c) _____

3-2. Below are three-word sequences. Tell which level of processing each sequence illustrates and why.

(a) cat   IN   tree _____

(b) car   BAR   czar _____

(c) CAN   CAP   CAR _____

3-3. If this theory is correct then we would expect most persons to best remember the sequence in

_____. This is because the words in this sequence have greater _____ than do the other

two sequences. It has been found that processing time (<u>is/is not</u>) a reliable index of depth of processing, and

thus what constitutes "levels" remains vague.

Answers: 3-1. (a) structural (b) phonemic (c) semantic **3-2.** (a) Semantic because we immediately give meaning to the words (b) Phonemic because the words sound alike (c) Structural because the words look alike **3-3.** cat in tree, meaning, is not.

4. Discuss two techniques for enriching the encoding process.

4-1. Identify which of the following situations illustrates either elaboration or visual imagery as techniques for enriching the encoding process.

(a) A cat owner who hears about a new drug for treating cats is more likely to remember the name of the drug than a person without a cat.

(b) It is easier to remember the word APPLE rather than the word PREVAIL.

4-2. According to Paivio's dual-coding theory, why is it easier to remember the word APPLE rather than the word PREVAIL?

Answers: 4-1. (a) elaboration (b) visual imagery **4-2.** Because it is easier to form a visual image of the word APPLE thus allowing for storage of both the word and image.

STORAGE: MAINTAINING INFORMATION IN MEMORY

5. Describe the role of the sensory store in memory.

5-1. Sensory memory allows for retention of a very (<u>large/ small</u>) amount of information for a very (<u>brief/long</u>)

period of time. The retention time for vision is less than _____, although for other senses it may last

more than a second. In other words, sensory memory allows us to retain almost all incoming information long

enough to allow for further processing.

Answers: 5-1. large, brief, one second.

## CHAPTER SEVEN

6. **Describe the characteristics of short-term memory and contrast them with long-term memory.**

   6-1. Indicate whether the following statements apply to short-term memory (STM) or long-term memory (LTM).

   _____ (a) Has a virtually unlimited storage capacity.

   _____ (b) Has a storage capacity of seven, plus or minus two, items.

   _____ (c) Requires continuous rehearsal to maintain information in store for more than 20 or 30 seconds.

   _____ (d) Stores information more or less permanently.

   _____ (e) Chunking can help to increase the capacity of this system.

   _____ (f) Alan Baddeley has proposed three components of this memory system that make it a "working memory."

   Answers: 6-1. (a) LTM (b) STM (c) STM (d) LTM (e) STM (f) STM.

7. **Summarize the evidence on the hypothesis that all memories are stored permanently in long-term memory (LTM).**

   7-1. There are two views regarding the durability of information in LTM. One is that no information is ever lost and the other is that _____. Those who favor the "no-loss" view explain forgetting as a failure of _____. The information is still there, we just cannot get it out.

   7-2. How do the some-loss proponents counter the following three lines of evidence cited by the no-loss proponents?

   (a) Flashbulb memories of previous events?

   (b) The remarkable recall of hypnotized subjects?

   Answers: 7-1. some information is lost, retrieval **7-2.** (a) They often tend to be inaccurate and less detailed with the passage of time (b) Their recall of information is often found to be incorrect.

8. **Describe how verbal rehearsal relates to LTM storage and discuss the likely causes of the serial position effect.**

   8-1. Perhaps the major way in which information is transferred from STM to LTM is through the use of _____. The longer information is retained in STM through verbal rehearsal, the (less/more) likely it is to be transferred to LTM.

   8-2. Roughly sketch the serial position effect onto the figure below. Then label the area on the sketch with a P that shows the primacy effect and with an R that shows the recency effect.

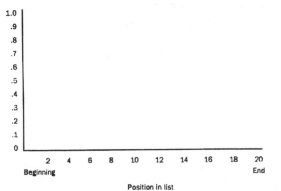

8-3. What appears to account for the primacy effect?

8-4. What appears to account for the recency effect?

Answers: 8-1. rehearsal, more **8-2.** The curve you drew should be in the shape of a U. The primacy effect should be at the beginning (upper left side) and the recency effect at the end (upper right side) **8-3.** Words at the beginning get rehearsed more often **8-4.** Words at the end still remain in STM.

9. **Describe the use of various organizational frameworks in long-term memory.**

   9-1.   Group the following words into two groups or categories:

   rose   dog   grass   cat   tree   rat

   You probably grouped the words into plants and animals, which is the general idea behind _____ networks. If you understand the idea behind semantic networks and its related idea of spreading activation, you should be able to answer the questions below.

   Person A attends an urban university and frequently studies while riding a bus to and from school.

   Person B attends a university located in a rural area and frequently studies outside in one of the many park-like areas surrounding the school.

   (a)   When asked to think of words associated with the word STUDY, which of the above persons is most likely to think of the word GRASS? _____

   (b)   Which person is most likely to think of the word TRAFFIC? _____

   (c)   Which person is most likely to think of the word PEACEFUL? _____

   9-2.   Finally, it appears that LTM also stores information in organized clusters of knowledge about a particular object or sequence of events, such as a professor's office. Clusters of this nature are called

   _____.

   Answers: 9-1. semantic (a) person B (b) person A (c) person B **9-2.** schemas.

RETRIEVAL: GETTING INFORMATION BACK OUT OF MEMORY

10. **Describe how retrieval cues and context cues are related to retrieval.**

   10-1.   In the following examples indicate whether retrieval cues or context cues are being used to retrieve information from long-term memory.

   (a)   In trying to recall the name of a high school classmate, you get the feeling that his first name began with an "L" and begin saying names like Larry, Leroy, Lionel, etc.

   (b)   Or you may attempt to recall the high school classmate by imagining the history class in which he sat in the row next to you.

   Answers: 10-1. (a) retrieval cues (b) context cues.

11. **Summarize evidence demonstrating the reconstructive nature of memory.**

11-1. Since we use schemas to move information in and out of long-term memory, it is not too surprising that retrieved information may be altered by the schema. This is the general idea of the _____ nature of memory.

11-2. For example, Elizabeth Loftus found that subjects were much more likely to falsely recall seeing broken glass on a videotaped scene when they were originally asked, "How fast were the cars going when they (hit/ smashed) into each other?" In this case the word "smashed" resulted in a different _____ than did the word "hit." The distortion of memory by the word "smashed" is an example of the post-event _____ effect.

Answers: **11-1.** reconstructive **11-2.** smashed, schema, misinformation.

12. **Discuss source-monitoring and its implications.**

12-1. While research evidence clearly shows that post-event misinformation does cause alterations in memory, it not so clear about the underlying mechanisms. How do the two explanations below account for the misinformation effect that underlies the reconstructive nature of memory?

(a) The "overwriting" explanation?

(b) Difficulties in source-monitoring?

Answers: **12-1.** (a) The misinformation replaces and destroys the original memory (b) Attributing information to an incorrect source interferes with retrieving the original information.

FORGETTING: WHEN MEMORY LAPSES

13. **Describe the various measures of forgetting.**

13-1. Which of the three different methods of measuring forgetting (recall, recognition, or relearning) is illustrated in each of the following situations?

(a) You are asked to identify a suspect in a police lineup.

(b) You time yourself while learning 20 new French words. After a week you find you have forgotten some of the words, and you again time yourself while learning the list a second time.

(c) You are asked to draw a floor plan of your bedroom from memory.

Answers: **13-1.** (a) recognition (b) relearning (c) recall.

14. **Explain how "forgetting" may be due to ineffective encoding.**

    14-1.   Why are most people unable to recognize the correct penny shown at the beginning of this chapter in the text?

    14-2.   What is another name for information loss due to ineffective coding of this kind?

    14-3.   Why is semantic coding better than phonemic coding for enhancing future recall of written material?

    Answers: 14-1. They never encoded the correct figure in their memories **14-2.** pseudoforgetting **14-3.** Semantic coding will lead to deeper processing and more elaborate associations.

15. **Compare and contrast decay and interference as potential causes of forgetting.**

    15-1.   Two other theories of forgetting propose additional factors that may be involved in retrieval failure. One theory holds that retrieval failure may be due to the impermanence of the memory storage itself. This is the notion behind the _____ theory of forgetting. Decay theory is best able to explain retrieval failure in sensory and _____ memory stores, but there is no evidence that it is involved in retrieval failure in _____ memory.

    15-2.   The other theory attributes retrieval failure to other information already in the memory or to information arriving at a later time. This is the notion behind the _____ theory of forgetting. According to interference theory, the failure may be caused by interference from information already in the memory, a phenomenon called _____ interference, or the failure may be caused by interference occurring after the original memory was stored, a phenomenon called _____ interference. Interference is most likely to occur when the materials being stored are very (similar/different).

    Answers: 15-1. decay, short-term, long-term **15-2.** interference, proactive, retroactive, similar.

16. **Explain how forgetting may be due to factors in the retrieval process.**

    16-1.   Breakdowns in the retrieval process can occur when the encoding specificity principle is violated. This means there has been a mismatch between the _____ cue and the _____ code. A common instance of this violation is seen when one attempts to retrieve a semantically coded word with (semantic/phonetic) retrieval cues.

    16-2.   Sigmund Freud felt that some breakdowns in the retrieval process could be attributed to purposeful suppression of information by unconscious forces, a phenomenon called _____ forgetting. Freud called motivated forgetting _____.

    Answers: 16-1. retrieval, memory, phonemic **16-2.** motivated, repression.

17. **Summarize the repressed memories controversy.**

   17-1. How do psychologists regard the authenticity of recovered repressed memories?

   17-2. If indeed the recovered memories are not authentic, what other two factors could explain them? (Hint: One has to do with the patient and the other with the therapist.)

   17-3. Why can't psychologists resolve this issue?

   Answers: **17-1.** They are deeply divided on this issue **17-2.** The suggestibility of the patient and the encouragement of the therapist **17-3.** There is no way to definitely evaluate the authenticity of individual recollections.

IN SEARCH OF THE MEMORY TRACE: THE PHYSIOLOGY OF MEMORY

18. **Distinguish between the two types of amnesia and identify the anatomical structures implicated in memory.**

   18-1. Amnesia cases due to head injury provide clues about the anatomical basis of memory. There are two basic types of head-injury amnesia. When the memory loss is for events prior to the injury, it is called _____ amnesia. When the memory loss is for events following the injury, it is called _____ amnesia.

   18-2. Damage to what three areas in the limbic system have been found to result in amnesia?

   18-3. The limbic system also appears to play a role in the hypothesized consolidation process, which assumes that the consolidation of memories begins in the _____ system. These memories are then stored in the same areas that were originally involved in processing the sensory input in the _____. At this time the complete picture of the physiological basis of memory is _____.

   Answers: **18-1.** anterograde, retrograde **18-2.** amygdala, hippocampus, thalamus **18-3.** limbic, cortex, unknown.

19. **Summarize evidence on the biochemistry and neural circuitry underlying memory.**

   19-1. Research evidence indicates that specific neural circuits related to specific memories (may/may not) exist. So far, however, such a circuit has only been found for the conditioned _____ response of a rabbit.

   19-2. Which of the following biochemical processes have been implicated in the formation of memories?

   (a) Alterations in neurotransmitter secretions at specific sites.

   (b) Synthesis of acetycholine and also hormonal fluctuations.

   (c) Protein synthesis in the brain.

   (d) Changes in RNA in the brain.

   Answers: **19-1.** may, eyeblink **19-2.** a, b, and c are correct.

20. **Distinguish between implicit versus explicit memory and their relationship to declarative versus procedural memory.**

    20-1.   Label the two following situations as to whether they are examples of implicit or explicit memory.

        (a) After studying for your history test, you were able to easily recall the information during the exam.

        _____

        (b) While studying for your history exam, you unexpectedly recall an incident from the previous summer.

        _____

    20-2.   Another division of memory systems has been hypothesized for declarative memory and procedural memory. Identify these two divisions from their descriptions given below.

      _____ (a) This system allows you to drive a car or play a piano with minimal attention to the execution of movements that are required.

      _____ (b) This system allows you to explain how to drive a car or play a piano to a friend.

    20-3.   It has been suggested that there is an apparent relationship between implicit memory and _____ memory and between explicit memory and _____ memory.

    Answers: 20-1. (a) explicit (b) implicit **20-2.** (a) procedural (b) declarative **20-3.** (a) procedural (b) declarative.

21. **Explain the distinctions between episodic versus semantic memory and prospective versus retrospective memory.**

    21-1.   It has also been hypothesized that declarative memory can be further subdivided into semantic and episodic memory. Identify these two kinds of memory from the following descriptions:

      _____ (a) This kind of memory acts like an encyclopedia, storing all of the factual information you possess.

      _____ (b) This kind of memory acts like an autobiography, storing all of your personal experiences.

    21-2.   Still another distinction between types of memory is the division into prospective and retrospective memory. Identify these two types of memory from the following descriptions:

      _____ (a) This kind of memory is at work when you try to recall the name of your algebra teacher in high school or the capitol of Oregon.

      _____ (b) This kind of memory allows you to carry out the tasks you intend to do tomorrow.

    Answers: 21-1. (a) semantic (b) episodic **21-2.** (a) retrospective (b) prospective.

PUTTING IT IN PERSPECTIVE

22. **Explain how this chapter highlighted the subjectivity of experience and the multifactorial causation of behavior.**

    22-1.   The text mentions three major areas in which subjectivity may influence memory. Identify them below.

    (a) We often see what we want, or are conditioned, to see and thus our _____ is selective.

    (b) Every time we tell about a particular experience, details are added or subtracted because of the _____ nature of memory.

    (c) Particularly painful personal events may lead to _____ forgetting.

22-2. Since the memory of a specific event can be influenced by many factors, operating in each of the three memory stores, it is obvious that memory, like most behavior, has _____ _____.

Answers: 22-1. (a) attention (b) reconstructive (c) motivated **22-2.** multifactorial causation.

APPLICATION: IMPROVING EVERYDAY MEMORY

23. Outline strategies discussed in the Application for improving everyday memory.

23-1. The text lists four general strategies for improving everyday memory. Identify which strategy is being employed in the following examples.

(a) Most persons can remember their phone number because of extensive _____.

(b) Willie Nurd the bookworm always takes breaks between study periods when changing subject matter. Willie must realize the importance of _____.

(c) Ajax never studies any other material besides mathematics on the day of his math exams in order to minimize _____.

(d) Answering questions such as these is much better than simply underlining the same material in the text because it forces you to engage in _____.

23-2. Specific strategies for enhancing memory are called _____ devices. Examples of strategies that do not employ visual images are listed below. See if you can identify which strategy is being employed in each illustration.

(a) Using the phrase "My Very Excellent Mother Just Sells Nuts Under Protest" to remember the names and positions of the planets illustrates the use of an _____ .

(b) International Business Machines is easily identified by its _____ IBM.

(c) Since you are going to the store your roommate asks you to bring her a bar of Ivory soap, a box of Kleenex and a Snickers bar. You then make up a story that begins, "On my way to the Ivory Coast to check on the latest shipment of Kleenex, I . . ." Here you're making use of a _____ method as a mnemonic device.

23-3. Two techniques involving visual imagery, the link method and the method of loci, can also serve as helpful mnemonic devices. Identify them in the examples below.

(a) You want to remember to buy bananas, eggs, milk, and bread. You visualize walking in your front door and triping on a bunch of bananas. Stumbling forward into the hallway you notice broken eggs on the table . . . _____.

(b) You imagine yourself using a banana to break eggs, which you then pour into a bowl of milk and bread. _____.

23-4. Various procedures, such as rearranging material into meaningful groupings, may aid memory because of the improvement in _____.

Answers: 23-1. (a) rehearsal (b) distributed practice (c) interference (d) deep processing **23-2.** mnemonic (a) acrostic (b) acronym (c) narrative **23-3.** (a) method of loci (b) link method **23-4.** organization.

REVIEW OF KEY TERMS

Anterograde amnesia
Attention
Chunk
Consolidation
Decay theory
Declarative memory system
Dual-coding theory
Elaboration
Encoding
Encoding specificity principle
Episodic memory system
Explicit memory
Flashbulb memories
Forgetting curve
Implicit memory
Interference theory

Levels of processing theory
Link method
Long-term memory (LTM)
Method of loci
Mnemonic devices
Nonsense sylables
Overlearning
Primacy effect
Proactive interference
Procedural memory system
Prospective memory
Recall
Recency effect
Recognition
Rehearsal
Relearning

Repression
Retention
Retrieval
Retroactive interference
Retrograde amnesia
Retrospective memory
Schema
Semantic memory system
Semantic network
Sensory memory
Serial-position effect
Short-term memory (STM)
Source monitoring
Source-monitoring error
Storage
Tip-of-the-tongue phenomenon

1. _____ Putting coded information into memory.

2. _____ Maintaining coded information in memory.

3. _____ Recovering information from memory stores.

4. _____ The process of focusing awareness on a narrowed range of stimuli or events.

5. _____ Memory that involves the intentional recollection of previous experiences.

6. _____ A theory that proposes that deeper levels of processing result in longer-lasting memory codes.

7. _____ Involves linking a stimulus to other information at the time of encoding.

8. _____ A theory that memory is enhanced by forming both semantic and visual codes since either can lead to recall.

9. _____ Preserves information in the original sensory form for a very brief time.

10. _____ A limited capacity memory store that can maintain unrehearsed information for 20 to 30 seconds.

11. _____ The process of repetitively verbalizing or thinking about new information.

12. _____ A group of familiar stimuli stored as a single unit.

13. _____ An unlimited capacity memory store that can hold information over lengthy periods of time.

14. _____ Unusually vivid and detailed recollections of momentous events.

15. _____ Occurs when subjects show better recall of items at the beginning and end of a list than for items in the middle.

16. _____ Occurs when items at the beginning of a list are recalled better than other items.

17. _____ Occurs when items at the end of a list are recalled better than other items.

18. _____ Memory for factual information.

19. _____ Memory for actions, skills, and operations.

20. _____ Memory made up of chronological, or temporally dated material.

21. _____ Memory that contains general knowledgew that is not tied to the time when the information was learned.

22. _____ The process of making attributions about the origins of memories.

_____ **23.** These consist of concepts joined together by links that show how the concepts are related.

_____ **24.** An organized cluster of knowledge about a particular object or sequence of events.

_____ **25.** A temporary inability to remember something you know accompanied by the feeling that it's just out of reach.

_____ **26.** Consonant-vowel-consonant letter combinations that do not correspond to words (NOF, KER, etc.).

_____ **27.** A curve graphing retention and forgetting over time.

_____ **28.** The proportion of material remembered.

_____ **29.** The ability to remember information without any cues.

_____ **30.** Requires the selection of previously learned information from an array of options (e.g., multiple-choice tests).

_____ **31.** Requires the memorization of information a second time to determine how much time or effort is saved.

_____ **32.** Attributes forgetting to the impermanence of memory storage.

_____ **33.** Attributes forgetting to competition from other material.

_____ **34.** Occurs when new information impairs the retention of previously learned information.

_____ **35.** Occurs when previously learned information impairs the retention of new information.

_____ **36.** States that the value of a retrieval cue depends on how well it corresponds to the memory code.

_____ **37.** Involves purposeful (motivated) suppression of memories.

_____ **38.** A theoretical process involving the gradual conversion of information into durable memory codes stored in long-term memory.

_____ **39.** The loss of memory for events that occurred prior to a brain injury.

_____ **40.** The loss of memory for events that occur after a brain injury.

_____ **41.** Strategies for enhancing memory.

_____ **42.** The continued rehearsal of material after it has apparently been mastered.

_____ **43.** Involves forming a mental image of items to be remembered in a way that connects them together.

_____ **44.** A mnemonic device that involves taking an imaginary walk along a familiar path.

_____ **45.** Is apparent when retention is exhibited on a task that does not require intentional remembering.

_____ **46.** Occurs when a memory derived from one source is misattributed to another source.

_____ **47.** Involves remembering to perform actions in the future.

_____ **48.** Involves remembering events from the past or previously learned information.

Answers: 1. encoding **2.** storage **3.** retrieval **4.** attention **5.** explicit memory **6.** levels of processing theory **7.** elaboration **8.** dual-coding theory **9.** sensory memory **10.** short-term memory (STM) **11.** rehearsal **12.** chunk **13.** long-term memory (LTM) **14.** flashbulb memories **15.** serial position effect **16.** primacy effect **17.** recency effect **18.** declarative memory system **19.** procedural memory system **20.** episodic memory system **21.** semantic memory system **22.** source monitoring 23. semantic networks 24. schema 25. tip-of-the-tongue phenomenon 26. nonsense syllables 27. forgetting curve 28. retention 29. recall 30. recognition 31. relearning 32. decay theory 33. interference theory 34. retroactive interference 35. proactive interference 36. encoding specificity principle 37. repression 38. consolidation 39. retrograde amnesia 40. anterograde amnesia 41. mnemonic devices 42. overlearning 43. link method 44. method of loci 45. implicit memory 46. source-monitoring error 47. prospective memory 48. retrospective memory.

REVIEW OF KEY PEOPLE

Richard Atkinson & Richard Shiffrin   Herman Ebbinghaus   George Miller
Fergus Craik & Robert Lockhart   Elizabeth Loftus   Endel Tulvig

_____   1.   Proposed three progressively deeper levels for processing incoming information.

_____   2.   Influential in the development of the model of three different kinds of memory stores (sensory, STM and LTM).

_____   3.   Demonstrated that the reconstructive nature of memory can distort eyewitness testimony.

_____   4.   Used nonsense syllables to become famous for his forgetting curve.

_____   5.   One of his many contributions was the encoding specificity principle.

_____   6.   Proposed the concept of chunking for storing information in short-term memory.

Answers: 1. Craik & Lockhart **2.** Atkinson & Shiffrin **3.** Loftus **4.** Ebbinghaus **5.** Tulvig **6.** Miller.

SELF-QUIZ

1. Which of the following is not one of the three basic human memory processes?
   a. storage
   b. retrieval
   c. decoding
   d. encoding

2. Which one of the three levels of processing would probably be employed when attempting to memorize the following three-letter sequences WAB WAC WAD?
   a. structural
   b. semantic
   c. phonemic
   d. chunking

3. Retrieval from long-term memory is usually best when the information has been stored at which level of processing?
   a. structural
   b. semantic
   c. phonemic
   d. chunking

4. According to Paivio's dual-coding theory:
   a. words are easier to encode than images
   b. abstract words are easier to remember than concrete words
   c. visual imagery may hinder the retrieval of words
   d. concrete words are easier to remember than abstract words

5. Which of the memory stores can store the least amount of information?
   a. sensory store
   b. short-term memory
   c. long-term memory

6. Which of the following statements is the most accurate evaluation as to the authenticity of the recall of repressed memories?
   a. Research confirms that they are authentic.
   b. Research confirms that they are not authentic.
   c. Researchers cannot confirm or deny their authenticity.

7. Information is primarily transferred from short-term memory to long-term memory through the process of:
   a. elaboration
   b. rehearsal
   c. clustering
   d. sensory coding

8. In learning a list of 20 new Spanish words you are likely to experience:
   a. a primacy effect
   b. a recency effect
   c. a serial position effect
   d. all of the above

9. Which of these appear to be intimately related?
   a. implicit and procedural memory
   b. implicit and semantic memory
   c. explicit and procedural memory
   d. implicit and declarative memory

10. When you attempt to recall the name of a high school classmate by imagining yourself back in the English class with her, you are making use of:
    a. retrieval cues
    b. context cues
    c. schemas
    d. recognition cues

11. Taking this particular self-test measures your:
    a. constructive errors
    b. reconstructive errors
    c. recall
    d. recognition

12. Ineffective encoding of information may result in:
    a. the primacy effect
    b. the recency effect
    c. pseudoforgetting
    d. chunking

13. Decay theory is best able to explain the loss of memory in:
    a. sensory store
    b. long-term memory
    c. short-term memory
    d. both sensory store and short-term memory

14. When you violate the encoding specificity principle, you are likely to experience an inability to:
    a. encode information
    b. store information
    c. retrieve information
    d. connect the verbal and visual images of an experience

15. The exact neural and chemical mechanisms responsible for the storage of memory are well understood. This statement is:
    a. true
    b. false

16. It is very easy to recall the name of your high school because it has been subjected to extensive:
    a. deep processing
    b. clustering
    c. chunking
    d. overlearning

    Answers: 1. c **2.** a **3.** b **4.** d **5.** b **6.** c **7.** b **8.** d **9.** a **10.** b **11.** d **12.** c **13.** d **14.** c **15.** b **16.** d.

8 LANGUAGE AND THOUGHT

REVIEW OF KEY IDEAS

THE COGNITIVE REVOLUTION IN PSYCHOLOGY

1. Describe the "cognitive revolution" in psychology.

    1-1.   Answer the following questions regarding the cognitive revolution in psychology.

        (a) In what decade did this revolution get underway?

        (b) Why were earlier cognitive approaches abandoned?

        (c) What theoretical school openly opposed the cognitive approach?

    Answers: 1-1. (a) The 1950s (b) They were too subjective (as opposed to being empirical or objective) (c) behaviorism.

LANGUAGE: TURNING THOUGHTS INTO WORDS

2. Outline the key properties of language.

    2-1.   Language is characterized by four properties: its symbolic, semantic, generative, and structured. Identify each of these properties in the following statements.

        (a) Applying rules to arrange words into phrases and sentences illustrates the _____ property of language.

        (b) Using words or geomentric forms to represent objects, actions, or events illustrates the _____ property of language.

        (c) Making different words out of the same letters, such as NOW and WON, illustrates the _____ property of language.

(d) Giving the same meaning to different words, such as chat, katz, and cat, illustrates the _____ property of language.

Answers: 2-1. (a) structured (b) symbolic (c) generative (d) semantic.

3. Describe the hierarchial structure of language.

3-1. Arrange the following parts of language into their correct hierarchial structure:

SENTENCES - SOUNDS - WORDS - MEANINGFUL UNITS - PHRASES

3-2. Identify the following parts (units) of language.

(a) With around 40 of these basic sounds you can say all of the words in the English language. _____

(b) Phonemes are combined into these smallest units of meaning in a language, which may include root words as well as prefixes and suffixes. _____

(c) These rules specify how words can be combined into phrases and sentences. _____

Answers: 3-1. sounds - meaningful units - words - phrases - sentences **3-2.** (a) phonemes (b) morphemes (c) syntax.

4. Outline the development of human language during the first year.

4-1. Answer the following question regarding the development of language during the first year of life.

(a) What are a child's three major vocalizations during the first 6 months of life?

(b) What two gradual changes occur with respect to the sounds being made during the babbling stage of language development?

(c) What is the range in months for the babbling stage of language development?

Answers: 4-1. (a) Crying, laughing, and cooing (b) They become more complex and they increasingly resemble spoken language (c) 6 to 18 months.

5. Describe children's early use of single words and word combinations.

5-1. What does the text mean when it states that the receptive vocabulary of toddlers is much larger than their productive vocabulary?

5-2. Identify the following phenomenon observed in children's early use of language.

(a) What phenomenon is illustrated when a child calls all four-legged creatures "doggie"?

(b) What phenomenon is illustrated when a child puns, "I love your I's"?

(c) Solve the following anagram that best describes how children acquire language skills.? FWSYLIT

Answers: **5-1.** They can understand more spoken words than they can reproduce themselves **5-2.** (a) overextensions (b) metalinguistic awareness (c) swiftly.

6. Discuss the possible evolutionary bases of language.

6-1. While it seems apparent that the ability to communicate has adaptive value, what must be demonstrated to show that evolutionary factors are at work?

Answers: **6-1.** It must increase reproductive fitness (perhaps by decreasing mortality rates in a population).

7. Compare and contrast the behaviorist, nativist, and interactionist perspectives on the development of language.

7-1. Identify the following perspectives on the development of language.

(a) This perspective places great emphasis on the role of reinforcement and imitation.

(b) This perspective assumes that children make use of an innate language acquisition device (LAD) that biologically equips them to acquire language skills.

(c) This interactionist perspective argues that language development is tied to progress in thinking and general cognitive development.

(d) This interactionist perspective argues that language development is directed to some extent by the social benefits children derive from interaction with mature language users.

7-2. Which perspective places greatest emphasis on:

(a) nurture _____

(b) nature _____

(c) nature interacting with nurture _____

8. Discuss culture and language and the status of the linguistic relativity hypothesis.

8-1.　According to Benjamin Whorf's linguistic relativity hypothesis, does thought determine language or does language determine thought?

8-2.　What did Eleanor Rosch's experiment show when she compared the color recognition ability of English-speaking people and Dani people, who have only two words for "color"?

8-3.　While language does not appear to invariably determine thought, it does appear to exert some influence over the way we approach an idea. In other words, one's language may make it either _____ or more _____ to think along certain lines.

PROBLEM SOLVING: IN SEARCH OF SOLUTIONS

9. List and describe the three types of problems proposed by Greeno.

9-1.　Greeno has proposed three types of problems (arrangement, inducing structure, and transformation). Identify each of these types from their descriptions given below.

(a) This type of problem requires the problem solver to discover the relations among the parts of the problem.

(b) This type of problem requires the problem solver to place the parts in a way that satisfies some specific criterion.

(c) This type of problem requires the problem solver to carry out a sequence of changes or rearrangements in order to reach a specific goal.

9-2.　Which types of Greeno's problems are represented in the following situations?

(a) What two three-letter English words can be made from the letters TBU?

(b) Fill in the missing word in, "grass is to green as snow is to _____."

(c) You need to take your child to a pediatrician, your dog to the veterinarian, and your mother to the hairdresser all within a limited time period. You think to yourself, "I'll take the kid and the dog and pick up Mom. Mom can stay with the kid at the doctor's office while I take the dog to the vet. Then I'll . . . "

9-3. Which type of problems are often solved in a sudden burst of insight?

Answers: 9-1. (a) arrangement (b) inducing structure (c) transformation **9-2.** (a) inducing structure (b) arrangement (c) transformation **9-3.** arrangement.

10. Describe four common barriers to effective problem solving.

10-1. Which of the barriers to effective problem solving (functional fixedness, unnecessary constraints, mental set, and irrelevant information) are you overcoming when you:

(a) make a financial decision without first consulting your horoscope?

(b) teach an old dog a new trick?

(c) use a page of newspaper as a wedge to keep a door open?

(d) color outside the lines to make a more interesting picture?

Answers: 10-1. (a) irrelevant information (b) mental set (c) functional fixedness (d) unnecessary constraints.

11. List and describe five examples of general problem-solving strategies.

11-1. The text describes five different problem-solving strategies. One of these strategies simply involves sequentially trying every possible solution, a strategy called _____ and _____. However, when there are a large number of potential solutions, then people often turn to a quicker "rule of thumb" approach called a _____. Which of these heuristics (forming subgoals, working backward, searching for analogies, or changing the representation of the problem) would be most applicable for solving the following problems?

(a) While opening your car door you drop the keys. The keys hit your foot and bounce underneath the car, too far to reach. It has stopped raining so you close your umbrella and ponder how to get your keys.

(b) You have accepted the responsibility for chairing the homecoming celebration at your school.

(c) Alone at night in the office you observe that the ribbon is missing from a printer you want to use. After obtaining a new ribbon you can't figure out how to install it correctly. Glancing around you observe a similar printer with the ribbon installed.

(d) You have agreed to become the campaign chairwoman of a friend who wants to run for student body president. Obviously your goal is to make your friend look like a good choice to students, but which heuristic do politicians often employ here?

Answers: **11-1.** trial, error, heuristics (a) search for analogies (the umbrela can be used as a rake) (b) form subgoals (c) work backward (see how the ribbon comes out of the intact printer) (d) change the representation of the problem (make the opponents look like a bad choice).

12. **Discuss the relationship between field independence and problem solving and cultural variations in cognitive style.**

    12-1.   Answer the following true-false questions regarding the distinctions between field dependent and field independent persons and cultures.

        _____ (a) Field dependent persons are more likely to use internal cues to orient themselves in space.

        _____ (b) Field independent persons are more likely to recognize the component parts of a problem rather than just seeing it as a whole.

        _____ (c) Persons living in cultures that depend on hunting and gathering for their subsistence are generally more field dependent than persons living in more stable agricultural societies.

        _____ (d) Persons raised in cultures with lenient child-rearing practices and an emphasis on personal autonomy tend to be more field independent.

    Answers: **12-1.** (a) false (b) true (c) false (d) true.

DECISION MAKING: CHOICES AND CHANCES

13. **Compare the additive and elimination by aspects approaches to selecting an alternative.**

    13-1.   Which of these two approaches to decision making would probably be best when:

        (a) The task is complex and there are numerous alternatives?

        (b) You want to allow attractive attributes to compensate for unattractive attributes?

    Answers: **13-1.** (a) elimination by aspects (b) additive.

14. **Discuss conflict in decision making and the idea that one can think too much about a decision.**

    14-1.   What do persons often do when faced with a conflict in which they can't decide between alternative choices?

    14-2.   Recent studies have shown that thinking too much about a problem (<u>will/may not</u>) lead to a better solution. One reason suggested for this is that gathering more and more information that is less and less important _____ the picture.

    Answers: **14-1.** They delay their decision **14-2.** clutters or confuses.

15. **Explain the factors that individuals typically consider in risky decision making.**

    15-1.   What differentiates risky decision making from other kinds of decision making?

15-2. What is the most you can know when making a risky decision?

15-3. What two things must be known in order to calculate the expected value of making a risky decision when gambling with money?

15-4. How does the concept of subjective utility explain why some persons still engage in risky decision making when the expected value indicates the probability of a loss?

Answers: 15-1. The outcome is uncertain **15-2.** The probability of of a particular outcome **15-3.** The average amount of money you could expect to win or lose with each play and the probability of a win or loss **15-4.** The personal worth of the outcome may outweigh the probability of losing.

16. Describe the availability and representativeness heuristics used to estimate subjective probabilities.

16-1. Estimating the probability of an event on the basis of how often one recalls it has been experienced in the past

is what Tversky and Kahneman call a (an) _____ heuristic.

16-2. When most people are asked if there are more words that begin with N or words that have N as the third letter, they apply the availability heuristic and guess incorrectly. Explain why they do this.

16-3. Estimating the probability of an event on the basis of how similar it is to a particular model or stereotype of

that event is what Tversky and Kahneman call a _____ heuristic.

16-4. "Steve is very shy. He has a high need for structure and likes detail. Is Steve more likely to be a salesperson or a librarian?" When persons are given this problem, they usually guess that he is a librarian even though there are many more salespersons than there are librarians. Explain why they do this.

Answers: 16-1. availability **16-2.** Because they can immediately recall many more words that begin with N than words having N as the third letter **16-3.** representativeness **16-4.** Because they employ the representativess heuristic and Steve fits the stereotype of a librarian.

17. Discuss the effects of framing and anticipatory regret on decision making.

17-1. Asking a person if they would prefer their glass of wine to be half-full or half-empty illustrates the general idea

behind the _____ of questions.

17-2. Are persons more likely to take risky options when the problem is framed so as to obtain gains, or when it is framed so as to cut losses?

17-3. Answer the following questions regarding the effects of anticipatory guilt on decision making.

    (a) How does a high vulnerability to regret affect a person's decision making?

    (b) What appears to be a dominant characteristic of persons who are vulnerable to anticipatory guilt?

Answers: 17-1. framing **17-2.** When it is framed so as to cut losses **17-3.** (a) They tend to make safer decisions (b) low self-esteem.

PUTTING IT IN PERSPECTIVE

18. Explain how this chapter highlighted four of the text's themes.

18-1. Indicate which one of the four unifying themes (the influence of heredity and the environment, similarities and differences across cultures, the empirical nature of psychology, and the subjectivity of experience) are best represented by the following statements.

    (a) Psychologists developed objective measures for higher mental processes thus bringing about the cognitive revolution.

    (b) The manner in which questions are framed can influence cognitive appraisal of the questions.

    (c) Neither pure nativist theories nor pure nurture theories appear to adequately explain the development of language.

    (d) The ecological demands of one's environment appear to somewhat affect one's cognitive style.

Answers: 18-1. (a) the empirical nature of psychology (b) the subjectivity of experience (c) the influence of heredity and the environment (d) similarities and differences across cultures.

UNDERSTANDING PITFALLS IN DECISION MAKING

19. Describe some examples of flawed reasoning in decision making that reflect our use of the representativeness heuristic.

19-1. The text lists four examples of flawed reasoning (the gambler's fallacy, ignoring base rates and the laws of probability, ignoring the law of small numbers, and overestimating the improbable). State which example of flawed use of the representativeness heuristic is being illustrated below.

    (a) The belief that a small sampling of cases can be as valid as a large sampling of cases.

(b) The belief that the odds of a chance event increases if the event hasn't occurred recently.

(c) Inflating the probability of dramatic, vivid, but infrequent events.

(d) Using the representativeness heuristic and guessing that "Steve" is a librarian and not a salesperson.

Answers: 19-1. (a) ignoring the law of small numbers (b) the gambler's fallacy (c) overestimating the improbable (d) ignoring base rates and the laws of probability.

20. **Describe our propensities to overestimate the improbable, seek confirming information, and overrate our confidence.**

   20-1. What heurestic is probably operating when we overestimate the number of persons who die of tornadoes as compared to asthma?

   20-2. What omission leads to the confirmation bias when making decisions?

   20-3. How is this same phenomenon related to belief perseverance?

   20-4. Answer the following true/false questions regarding the overconfidence effect.

   _____ (a) We are much less subject to this effect when making decisions about ourselves as opposed to more worldly matters.

   _____ (b) Scientists are not generally prone to this effect when making decisions about information in their own fields.

   _____ (c) In the study of college students cited by the text it was observed that the gap between personal confidence and actual accuracy of decisions increased as the confidence level increased.

Answers: 20-1. The availability heurestic **20-2.** Failure to seek out disconfirming evidence **20-3.** Disconfirming evidence is subjected to skeptical evaluation **20-4.** (a) false (b) false (c) true.

REVIEW OF KEY TERMS

Availability heuristic	Heuristic	Overextension
Belief perseverance	Holophrase	Overregularization
Cognition	Insight	Phonemes
Confirmation bias	Language	Problem solving
Decision making	Language acquisition device (LAD)	Representativeness heuristic
Fast mapping	Linguistic relativity	Risky decision making
Field dependence-independence	Mean length of utterance (MLU)	Syntax
Framing	Mental set	Telegraphic speech
Functional fixedness	Metalinguistic awareness	Trial and error
Gambler's fallacy	Morphemes	

1. _____ A collection of symbols, and rules for combining those symbols, that can be used to create an infinite variety of messages.

2. _____ The smallest units of sound in a spoken language.

3. _____ The smallest units of meaning in a language.

4. _____ The rules that specify how words can be combined into phrases and sentences.

5. _____ Using a word incorrectly to describe a wider set of objects or actions than it is meant to.

6. _____ Single-word utterances that represent the meaning of several words.

7. _____ Consists mainly of content words with articles, prepositions, and other less-critical words omitted.

8. _____ The ability to reflect on the use of language.

9. _____ Basing the estimated probability of an event on the ease with which relevant instances come to mind.

10. _____ Basing the estimated probability of an event on how similar it is to the typical prototype of that event.

11. _____ The mental processes involved in acquiring knowledge.

12. _____ The tendency to perceive an item only in terms of its most common use.

13. _____ The sudden discovery of a correct solution to a problem following incorrect attempts.

14. _____ A strategy for solving problems.

15. _____ The process by which children map a word on an underlying concept after only one exposure to the word.

16. _____ The average of youngsters' spoken statements (measured in morphemes).

17. _____ Generalizing grammatical rules to irregular cases where they do not apply.

18. _____ Making decisions under conditions of uncertainty.

19. _____ A hypothetical innate mechanism or process that facilitates the learning of language.

20. _____ Persisting in using problem-solving strategies that have worked in the past.

21. _____ The theory that one's language determines one's thoughts.

22. _____ The active efforts to discover what must be done to achieve a goal that is not readily attainable.

23. _____ Trying possible solutions sequentially and discarding those that are in error until one works.

24. _____ Evaluating alternatives and making choices among them.

25. _____ How issues are posed or how choices are structured.

26. _____ The tendency to hang onto beliefs in the face of contradictory evidence.

27. _____ The tendency to seek information that supports one's decisions and beliefs while ignoring disconfirming evidence.

28. _____ Refers to individuals' tendency to rely primarily on external versus internal frames of reference when orienting themselves in space.

29. _____ The belief that the odds of a chance event increase if the event hasn't occurred recently.

REVIEW OF KEY PEOPLE

Noam Chomsky   Herbert Simon   B. F. Skinner
Daniel Kahneman and Amos Tversky

_____   **1.**   Won the Nobel Prize for his research on decision making and artificial intelligence.

_____   **2.**   Proposed that children learn language through the established principles of learning.

_____   **3.**   Proposed that children learn language through a biologically built-in language acquisition device.

_____   **4.**   Performed research that showed people base probability estimates on heurestics that do not always yield reasonable estimates of success.

Answers: 1. Simon **2.** Skinner **3.** Chomsky **4.** Kahneman and Tversky.

SELF-QUIZ

1. Which of the following explanations best explains the success of the cognitive revolution in psychology?
    a. the refining of introspection as a research method
    b. the development of empirical methods
    c. the use of psychotherapy to explore the unconscious
    d. the success in teaching chimps to use language

2. Which of the following represents the bottom of the hierarchy in the structure of language?
    a. meaningful units
    b. phrases
    c. sounds
    d. words

3. The word SLOWLY would be an example of a:
    a. metalinguistic
    b. phoneme
    c. syntactical unit
    d. morpheme

4. Which of the following words best describes the speed at which children acquire language skills?
    a. slowly
    b. swiftly
    c. haltingly

5. When a child says that TUB and BUT are constructed of the same three letters, she is showing an awareness of:
   a. morphemes
   b. phonemes
   c. metalinguistics
   d. syntax

6. The fact that children appear to learn rules, rather than specific word combinations, when acquiring language skills argues most strongly against which theory of language development?
   a. cognitive
   b. behaviorist
   c. nativist

7. Which of the following is not one of the basic properties of language?
   a. generative
   b. symbolic
   c. structured
   d. alphabetical

8. Which of the following heuristics would you probably employ if assigned the task of carrying out a school election?
   a. work backward
   b. representativeness
   c. search for analogies
   d. form subgoals

9. Which one of Greeno's problems is exemplified by the anagram?
   a. arrangement
   b. inducing structure
   c. transformation
   d. chunking

10. People generally prefer a choice that provides an 80 percent chance of success over one that provides a 20 percent chance of failure. This illustrates the effect of:
    a. the availability heuristic
    b. the representativeness heuristic
    c. framing
    d. confirmation bias

11. When faced with having to choose among numerous alternatives, most persons will opt for:
    a. an elimination by aspects approach
    b. an additive approach
    c. a means/end analysis
    d. a subjective-utility model

12. As compared to field dependent persons, field independent persons are more likely to come from cultures that:
    a. discourage lenient child-rearing practices
    b. depend on a stable agricultural base
    c. encourage personal autonomy
    d. encourage group cohesiveness

13. Most persons mistakenly believe that more people die from tornadoes than from asthma. This is because they mistakenly apply:
    a. a means/end analysis
    b. a compensatory decision model
    c. an availability heuristic
    d. a representativeness heuristic

## CHAPTER EIGHT

14. Failure to actively seek out contrary evidence may lead to:
    a. overestimating the improbable
    b. the conjunction fallacy
    c. the gambler's fallacy
    d. confirmation bias

15. Which of the following perhaps best illustrates the interaction effect of both heredity and environment on behavior?
    a. the development of language skills in a child
    b. the development of field independence in nomadic cultures
    c. the development of problem-solving skills in experts
    d. the development of the overconfidence effect in all of us

Answers: 1. b **2.** c **3.** d **4.** b **5.** c **6.** b **7.** d **8.** d **9.** a **10.** c **11.** a **12.** c **13.** c **14.** d **15.** a.

9 INTELLIGENCE AND PSYCHOLOGICAL TESTING

REVIEW OF KEY IDEAS

KEY CONCEPTS IN PSYCHOLOGICAL TESTING

1. **List and describe the principle categories of psychological tests.**

   1-1.   Most psychological tests can be placed into one of two very broad categories. These two categories are:

   _____ tests and _____ tests.

   1-2.   There are three categories of mental abilities tests. Below are examples of each of these categories. Identify them.

   (a) The ACT and SAT tests you may have taken before entering college are examples of _____ tests.

   (b) The exams you frequently take in your introductory psychology class are examples of _____ tests.

   (c) Tests used to demonstrate general intellectual giftedness are examples of _____ tests.

   1-3.   Personality tests allow an individual to compare himself or herself to other persons with respect to particular personality _____. Personality tests generally (do/do not) have right and wrong answers.

   Answers: 1-1. mental ability, personality **1-2.** (a) aptitude (b) achievement (c) intelligence **1-3.** characteristics or traits, do not.

2. **Discuss the concepts of standardization and test norms.**

   2-1.   Developing test norms and uniform procedures for use in the administration and scoring of a test is the general idea behind test _____.

   2-2.   In order to interpret a particular score on a test it is necessary to know how other persons score on this test. This is the purpose of test _____. An easy method for providing comparisons of test scores is to convert the raw scores into _____ scores.

   Answers: 2-1. standardization **2-2.** norms, percentile.

3. **Explain the meaning of test reliability and validity and how they are estimated.**

   3-1.   The ability of a test to produce consistent results across subsequent measurements of the same persons is
   known as its _____. The ability of a test to actually measure what it claims to measure is known as
   its _____.

   3-2.   Readministering the same test to the same group of persons in a week or two following the original testing
   allows one to estimate the _____ of a test. If a test is highly reliable, then a person's scores on the
   two different administrations will be very similar. The amount of similarity can be assessed by means of the
   _____ coefficient.

   3-3.   There are three general kinds of validity. Identify each of these kinds from the descriptions given below.

   (a)   This kind of validity will tend to be high when, for example, scores on the ACT and SAT actually predict
   success in college.

   (b)   This kind of validity will be of particular importance to you when taking your exams for this class. It will
   be high if the exam sticks closely to the explicitly assigned material.

   (c)   This kind of validity is more vague than the other two kinds and refers to the ability of a test to measure
   abstract qualities, such as intelligence.

   3-4.   As with the estimation of reliability, the estimation of validity makes use of the _____.

   Answers: 3-1. reliability, validity **3-2.** reliability, correlation **3-3.** (a) criterion-related validity, (b) content validity,
   (c) construct validity **3-4.** correlation coefficient.

THE EVOLUTION OF INTELLIGENCE TESTING

4. **Summarize the contributions of Galton, Binet, Terman, and Wechsler to the evolution of
   intelligence testing.**

   4-1.   Identify each of the above men from the descriptions of their contributions given below.

   (a)   This man developed the first useful intelligence test. His tests were used to predict success in school, and
   scores were expressed in terms of mental age. _____

   (b)   This man revised Binet's tests to produce the Stanford-Binet Intelligence Scale, the standard for all future
   intelligence tests. _____

   (c)   This man began the quest to measure intelligence. He assumed that intelligence was mainly inherited and
   could be measured by assessing sensory acuity. _____

   (d)   This man developed the first successful test of adult intelligence, the WAIS. He also developed new
   intelligence tests for children. _____

(e) In developing his new intelligence tests, this man added many non-verbal items, which allowed for the separate assessment of both verbal and non-verbal abilities. He also replaced the IQ score with one based on the normal distribution. _____

Answers: 4-1. (a) Binet (b) Terman (c) Galton (d) Wechsler (e) Wechsler.

BASIC QUESTIONS ABOUT INTELLIGENCE TESTING

5. **Explain the meaning of an individual's score on a modern intelligence test.**

   5-1.   Answer the following questions regarding intelligence test scores.

   (a) In what manner is human intelligence assumed to be distributed?

   (b) What percentage of people have an IQ score below 100?

   (c) What percentage of persons would score two or more standard deviations above the mean? (see Fig. 9.6 in the text)

   Answers: 5-1. (a) It forms a normal distribution (bell curve) (b) 50% (c) 2 percent.

6. **Describe the reliability and validity of modern intelligence tests.**

   6-1.   Answer the following questions about the reliability of modern intelligence tests.

   (a) What kind of reliability estimates (correlation coefficients) are found with most modern intelligence tests?

   (b) What might be a problem here with respect to an individual's test score?

   6-2.   Answer the following questions with respect to the validity of modern intelligence tests.

   (a) What is the correlation between IQ tests and grades in school?

   (b) What is the correlation between IQ tests and the number of years of schooling that people complete?

(c) What might be a general problem with assuming intelligence tests are a valid measure of general mental ability?

Answers: 6-1. (a) They are in the low .90's (b) Temporary conditions could lower the score **6-2.** (a) .50 to .60 (b) .60 to .80 (c) They principally focus on academic/verbal intelligence and ignore other kinds of intelligence.

7. Discuss how well IQ scores predict vocational success.

7-1. Is the ability of intelligence tests to predict vocational success much higher or much lower than their ability to predict academic success?

7-2. What two kinds of intelligence proposed by Sternberg, which may be especially important for vocational success, are not assessed by IQ tests?

Answers: 7-1. much lower **7-2.** practical intelligence and social intelligence.

HEREDITY AND ENVIRONMENT AS DETERMINANTS OF INTELLIGENCE

8. Summarize evidence from twin studies and adoption studies on whether heredity affects intelligence and discuss the concept of heritability.

8-1. Below are the mean correlations for the intelligence of three different groups of children: fraternal twins reared together, identical twins reared apart, and identical twins reared together. Match the group with the appropriate correlation.

.86 _____ .60 _____

.72 _____

8-2. What do the above correlations tell us about the role of heredity on intelligence?

8-3. What relationship has been found between the intelligence of children adopted out at birth and their biological parents?

8-4. The consensus estimate of experts is that the heritability ratio for human intelligence hovers around 60 percent. What does this mean?

8-5. Why can you not use a heritability ratio to explain a particular individual's intelligence?

Answers: 8-1. (.86) identical twins reared together (.72) identical twins reared apart (.60) fraternal twins reared together **8-2.** That heredity plays a significant role in intelligence **8-3.** There is a significant correlation in intelligence **8-4.** The variation in intelligence in a particular group is estimated to be 60% due to heredity, leaving 40% for environmental factors **8-5.** It is a group statistic and may give misleading results when applied to particular individuals.

9. **Summarize evidence from research on adoption, environmental deprivation or enrichment, and home environment showing how experience shapes intelligence.**

   9-1. Complete the statements below that list three findings from adoption studies indicating that environment influences intelligence.

   (a) There is (no/some) relationship between the intelligence of adopted children and their foster parents.

   (b) Siblings reared together are more alike than siblings _____.

   (c) Unrelated children reared together show a significant positive relationship with respect to their

   _____.

   9-2. What effects on intelligence have been found among children reared in deprived environments?

   9-3. What effects on intelligence have been found among children moved from deprived environments to more enriched environments?

   9-4. What relationship has been found between the intellectual quality of home environment and the intelligence of children?

   Answers: 9-1. (a) foster parents (b) reared apart (c) intelligence **9-2.** There is a gradual decrease in intelligence across time **9-3.** There is a gradual increase in intelligence across time **9-4.** They are significantly correlated.

10. **Using the concept of reaction range, explain how heredity and the environment interact to affect intelligence.**

    10-1. The notion behind the concept of reaction range is that heredity places an upper and lower _____ on how much an individual can vary with respect to a characteristic such as intelligence. The reaction range for human intelligence is said to be around _____ IQ points.

    10-2. This means that a child with an average IQ of 100 can vary between 90 and 110 IQ points, depending on the kind of _____ he or she experiences.

10-3. The major point here is that the limits for intelligence are determined by _____ factors and the movement within these limits is determined by _____ factors.

Answers: 10-1. limit, 20-25 **10-2.** environment **10-3.** genetic or hereditary, environmental.

11. Discuss proposed explanations for cultural differences in IQ scores.

11-1. Three explanations for the cultural differences in IQ scores are listed below. Tell what each of these explanations means.

(a) Jensen's heritability explanation.

(b) Cultural disadvantage.

(c) Cultural bias in IQ tests.

11-2. Which one of these explanations is best supported by research?

Answers: 11-1. (a) The cultural differences are due to heredity (b) The cultural differences are due to environmental factors. (c) IQ tests are biased in favor of persons from white middle-class backgrounds **11-2.** cultural disadvantage.

NEW DIRECTIONS IN THE ASSESSMENT AND STUDY OF INTELLIGENCE

12. Describe new trends in the assessment and study of intelligence.

12-1. Answer the following questions regarding new trends in the assessment and study of intelligence.

(a) One trend is that two kinds of tests are replacing intelligence tests in many school districts. What kinds of tests are these?

(b) A second trend concerns the search for biological correlates of intelligence. Most work here seeks to find correlations between reaction time and IQ. What have been the results so far?

Answers: 12-1. (a) achievement and aptitude tests (b) The correlations are too low to be of any practical significance.

13. **Describe Sternberg's and Gardner's theories of intelligence.**

13-1.   Sternberg's triarchic theory proposes that intelligence is composed of three basic parts. Match these parts with their individual functions:

_____ Contextual subtheory   (a) Emphasizes the role played by society.

_____ Experiential subtheory   (b) Emphasizes the cognitive processes underlying intelligence.

_____ Componential subtheory   (c) Emphasizes the interplay between intelligence and experience.

13-2.   Sternberg also theorizes that the componential subtheory is composed of three divisions. Match these divisions with their appropriate function:

_____ Metacomponents   (a) Involved in learning and storing information.

_____ Performance components   (b) The executive processes that govern approaches to problems.

_____ Knowledge-acquisition   (c) Carries out the instructions of the metacomponents.
         components

13-3.   Gardner has proposed seven relatively distinct human intelligences. What does his research show with respect to a "g" factor among these separate intelligences?

Answers: 13-1. contextual (a), experiential (c), componential (b) **13-2.** metacomponents (b), performance components (c), knowledge-acquisition components (a) **13-3.** There does not appear to be a "g" factor; rather, people display a mix of strong, weak, and intermediate abilities.

PUTTING IT IN PERSPECTIVE

14. **Discuss how the chapter highlighted three of the text's unifying themes.**

14-1.   Answer the following questions about the three unifying themes (cultural factors shape behavior, heredity and environment jointly influence behavior, and psychology evolves in a sociohistorical content).

(a)   What theme is exemplified by the continuing involvement of psychologists in the debate about the roots of racial and ethnic differences in intelligence?

(b)   What theme is exemplified by the different views about the nature of intelligence held by Western and non-Western cultures.

(c)   What theme is exemplified by the extensive research using twin studies, adoption studies, and family studies?

Answers: 14-1. (a) Psychology evolves in a sociohistorical context. (b) Cultural factors shape behavior. (c) Heredity and environment jointly influence behavior.

15. **Discuss popular ideas about the nature of creativity.**

    15-1.   Popular notions about creativity would have us believe that creative ideas arise from nowhere, occur in a burst of insight, are not related to hard work, and are unrelated to intelligence. What does the text say about these notions?

    Answers: 15-1. They are all false.

16. **Describe creativity tests and summarize how well they predict creative achievement.**

    16-1.   Most tests of creativity attempt to assess (<u>convergent/ divergent</u>) thinking, such as: "List as many uses as you can for a book." Creativity scores are based on the _____ of alternatives generated and the originality and _____ of the suggested alternatives.

    16-2.   Creativity tests are rather (<u>good/mediocre</u>) predictors of creativity in the real world. One reason for this is that they attempt to treat creativity as a (<u>specific/general</u>) trait while research evidence seems to show it is related to quite _____ domains.

    Answers: 16-1. divergent, number, usefulness (utility) **16-2.** mediocre, general, specific.

17. **Discuss associations between creativity and personality, intelligence, and mental illness.**

    17-1.   What four personality characteristics are rather consistently found to be related to creativity?

    17-2.   What is the intelligence level of most highly creative people?

    17-3.   What form of mental illness appears to be associated with creative achievement?

    Answers: 17-1. autonomy, independence, self-confidence, nonconformity **17-2.** Average to above average **17-3.** mood disorders.

REVIEW OF KEY TERMS

Achievement tests
Aptitude tests
Construct validity
Content validity
Covergent thinking
Correlation coefficient
Creativity
Criterion-related validity
Deviation IQ scores

Divergent thinking
Heritability ratio
Intelligence quotient (IQ)
Intelligence tests
Mental age
Normal distribution
Percentile score
Personality tests

Psychological test
Reaction range
Reliability
Standardization
Test norms
Test-retest reliability
Validity

_____ 1. A standardized measure of a sample of a person's behavior.

_____ 2. Tests that measure general mental ability.

_____ 3. Tests that measure various personality traits.

_____ 4. Tests that assess talent for specific kinds of learning.

_____ 5. Tests that gauge the mastery and knowldege of various subject areas.

_____ 6. The development of uniform procedures for administering and scoring tests, including the development of test norms.

_____ 7. Data that provides information about the relative standing of a particular test score.

_____ 8. Number indicating the percentage of people who score above or below a particular test score.

_____ 9. The measurement consistency of a test.

_____ 10. Estimated by comparing subjects' scores on two administrations of the same test.

_____ 11. The ability of a test to measure what it was designed to measure.

_____ 12. The degree to which the content of a test is representative of the domain it is supposed to measure.

_____ 13. The degree to which the scores on a particular test correlate with scores on an independent criterion (test).

_____ 14. The degree to which there is evidence that a test measures a hypothetical construct.

_____ 15. A score indicating the mental ability typical of a chronological age group.

_____ 16. Mental age divided by chronological age and multiplied by 100.

_____ 17. A symmetrical, bell-shaped curve that describes the distribution of many physical and psychological attributes.

_____ 18. Scores that translate raw scores into a precise location in the normal distribution.

_____ 19. An estimate of the percentage of variation in a trait determined by genetic inheritance.

_____ 20. Genetically determined limits on intelligence.

_____ 21. The generation of ideas that are original, novel, and useful.

_____ 22. Thinking that attempts to narrow down a list of alternatives to a single best solution.

	23.	Thinking that attempts to expand the range of alternatives by generating many possible solutions.
	24.	A numerical index of the degree of relationship between two variables.

Answers: 1. psychological tests **2.** intelligence tests **3.** personality tests **4.** aptitude tests **5.** achievement tests **6.** standardization **7.** test norms **8.** percentile score **9.** reliability **10.** test-retest reliability **11.** validity **12.** content validity **13.** criterion-related validity **14.** construct validity **15.** mental age **16.** intelligence quotient (IQ) **17.** normal distribution **18.** deviation IQ scores **19.** heritability ratio **20.** reaction range **21.** creativity **22.** convergent thinking **23.** divergent thinking **24.** correlation coefficient.

REVIEW OF KEY PEOPLE

Alfred Binet
Sir Francis Galton
Arthur Jensen

Sandra Scarr
Robert Sternberg

Lewis Terman
David Wechsler

	1.	Developed the Standford-Binet Intelligence Scale.
	2.	Developed the first successful test of adult intelligence.
	3.	Postulated a cognitive triarchic theory of intelligence.
	4.	Proposed a reaction range model for human intelligence.
	5.	Developed the first useful intelligence test.
	6.	Postulated a heritability explanation for cultural differences in intelligence.
	7.	Began the quest to measure intelligence.

Answers: 1. Terman **2.** Wechsler **3.** Sternberg **4.** Scarr **5.** Binet **6.** Jensen **7.** Galton.

SELF-QUIZ

1. This self-test you are now taking is an example of:
   a. an aptitude test
   b. an achievement test
   c. an intelligence test
   d. a criterion-related test

2. Which of the following statistics is generally used to estimate reliability and validity?
   a. the correlation coefficient
   b. the standard deviation
   c. the percentile score
   d. the median

3. What kind of validity do tests such as the SAT and ACT particularly strive for?
   a. content validity
   b. construct validty
   c. absolute validity
   d. criterion-related validity

4. If a psychologist readministers the same test to the same individuals following a two-week interval, she is probably interested in the test's:
   a. reliability
   b. standardization
   c. validity
   d. norms

5. With respect to modern intelligence tests:
   a. reliability is generally higher than validity
   b. validity is generally higher than reliability
   c. reliability and validity are about the same
   d. I have no idea what you are talking about

6. If the heritability ratio for intelligence is 80%, this means that for you as an individual 80% of your intelligence is determined by heredity and 20% is determined by your environment. This statement is:
   a. true
   b. false

7. Perhaps the strongest evidence for a heredity factor for intelligence comes from studies of:
   a. unrelated children reared together
   b. deprived home environments
   c. enriched home environments
   d. identical twins reared apart

8. If the reaction range concept of human intelligence is correct, then a child with exactly normal intelligence will probably not exceed an IQ of:
   a. 100
   b. 110
   c. 120
   d. 130

9. IQ tests are fairly good predictors of:
   a. academic success
   b. vocational success
   c. creativity
   d. social success

10. What effect has been found among children moved from deprived to enriched environments?
    a. they abruptly increase in intelligence
    b. they gradually increase in intelligence
    c. they show no change in intelligence
    d. they gradually decrease in intelligence

11. Which of the following groups shows the highest correlation with respect to intelligence?
    a. fraternal twins reared together
    b. fraternal twins reared apart
    c. identical twins reared apart
    d. both a and c

12. The search for biological correlates of intelligence are beginning to prove quite fruitful. This statement is:
    a. true
    b. false

13. What is the role of metacomponents in Sternberg's triarchic theory of intelligence?
    a. learning and storing information
    b. carrying out instructions
    c. giving instructions
    d. all of the above

14. What form of mental illness has been frequently found to be associated with outstanding creative ability?
    a. anxiety disorders
    b. mood disorders
    c. schizophrenia
    d. antisocial personality

15. Most tests of creativity emphasize:
    a. convergent thinking
    b. divergent thinking
    c. social intelligence
    d. practical intelligence

Answers: 1. b **2.** a **3.** d **4.** a **5.** a **6.** b **7.** d **8.** b **9.** a **10.** b **11.** c **12.** b **13.** c **14.** b **15.** b.

10 MOTIVATION AND EMOTION

REVIEW OF KEY IDEAS

MOTIVATIONAL THEORIES AND CONCEPTS

1. **Explain the key elements of evolutionary theory and how it accounts for specific gender differences in mating behavior.**

   1-1. Human motives include drives relating to hunger, sex, need for achievement, need for affiliation, and so on. According to evolutionary theorists, the various forms of motivation, like other human and animal characteristics, occur because they have _____ value.

   1-2. Do males seek more or fewer sexual partners than females? In many mammalian species, including humans, the answer is that _____ tend to seek more partners. Evolution favors mechanisms that increase the probability of passing genes on to the next generation, and for males that likelihood is enhanced by mating with (few/many) members of the opposite sex.

   1-3. For females, on the other hand, who are limited in terms of the number of offspring that they can produce in a breeding season, there is no evolutionary advantage in mating with many males. So, females tend to be (less/more) selective of mates than males and to seek (fewer/more) sexual partners.

   1-4. Buss also provides an evolutionary explanation of sex differences in *jealousy*. Since the mother gives birth to the child, she knows that the child is hers. Paternity—who the father is—(is/is not) certain, however.

   1-5. Thus, for males to increase the likelihood that they pass on their genes, they must guard against (sexual/emotional) infidelity. For females, on the other hand, survival of their offspring depends to a greater extent on the commitment of the male, and his resources, to the relationship. According to this explanation, the more important factor for females is (sexual/emotional) fidelity.

   Answers: **1-1.** adaptive (survival) **1-2.** males, many **1-3.** more, fewer **1-4.** is not **1-5.** sexual, emotional.

2. **Compare and contrast the drive and incentive theoretical perspectives on motivation.**

   2-1. Review the sections on drive and incentive motivational theories. Then check your understanding by placing the name of the type of theory (drive or incentive) in the blanks below.

   _____ Cannot easily account for behavior that *increases* tension.

_____ Motivation to pursue a goal or object depends on the *value* of the object and one's *expectancy* of success at obtaining it.

_____ Emphasizes homeostasis, the pressure to return to a state of equilibrium.

_____ Emphasizes environmental factors in motivation.

_____ Actions result from attempts to reduce internal states of tension.

_____ Emphasizes "pull" from the environment (as opposed to "push" from internal states).

Answers: 2-1. drive, incentive, drive, incentive, drive, incentive.

3. Distinguish between biological and social needs and describe the hierarchy of needs proposed by Maslow.

3-1. Most theories distinguish between _____ _____ needs, such as hunger and thirst, and _____ needs, which are acquired through _____ or the process of socialization. Most biological needs are required for the _____ of the group or individual.

3-2. While there are relatively few _____ needs, an individual may theoretically acquire an unlimited number of _____ needs.

3-3. Note that while aggression is listed in Figure 10.4 as a biological need, some theorists consider aggression to be largely acquired or social. Thus, the distinction between biological and social needs is a useful one but (<u>is/is not</u>) always clear cut.

3-4. Write the names of Maslow's hierarchical levels of needs in the blanks at the right of the pyramid. Start with (a) at the lowest level.

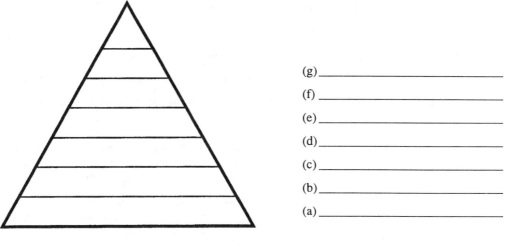

(g) _____

(f) _____

(e) _____

(d) _____

(c) _____

(b) _____

(a) _____

3-5. When or in what circumstance, according to Maslow, does a higher level of need become activated?

3-6. How do needs toward the top of the pyramid differ from those near the bottom?

3-7. Maslow asserted that our highest growth need is our need for self-actualization. What is the need for self-actualization?

Answers: 3-1. biological, social, learning, survival **3-2.** biological, social **3-3.** is not **3-4.** (a) physiological needs (b) safety and security needs (c) belongingness and love needs (d) esteem needs (e) cognitive needs (f) aesthetic needs (g) need for self-actualization **3-5.** A higher level is activated only when a lower level is fairly well satisfied. For example, needs for achievement and recognition are generally activated only after needs for love and belongingness are satisfied. **3-6.** The closer a need is to the top of the pyramid, the more it is socially based; the closer to the bottom, the more it is biologically based **3-7.** the need to express one's full potential.

THE MOTIVATION OF HUNGER AND EATING

4. Summarize evidence on the areas of the brain implicated in the regulation of hunger.

4-1. One of the major parts of the brain involved in eating behavior is the structure known as the

_____. Two main areas of the hypothalamus associated with hunger level are the

_____ hypothalamus (LH) and the _____ nucleus of the hypothalamus

(VMH).

4-2. Different things happen when these two areas are electrically stimulated as opposed to when they are destroyed or lesioned. When the lateral hypothalamus is electrically stimulated, animals tend to (start/stop) eating. When the LH is lesioned, however, the animals (start/stop) eating.

4-3. Summarize the effects on eating that result from either stimulating or lesioning the hypothalamus by writing either "start" or "stop" in the blanks at the right.

Lateral, electrical stimulation: _____

Lateral, lesioning: _____

Ventromedial nucleus, electrical stimulation: _____

Ventromedial nucleus, lesioning: _____

4-4. Starvation is likely to occur for rats with a lesioned _____ hypothalamus, while obesity

results when rats have their _____ hypothalamus destroyed.

4-5. Several recent findings cast doubt on the simple "stop-start" model of eating behavior. For one thing, the neurochemical changes are more complicated than previously thought; for another, there appears to be (only two/more than two) areas of the hypothalamus important for eating behavior. While the ventromedial and lateral parts of the hypothalamus are still regarded as important determinants of eating, the idea of an on-off mechanism in the brain is now regarded as (too simplistic/still correct).

Answers: 4-1. hypothalamus, lateral, ventromedial **4-2.** start, stop **4-3.** start, stop, stop, start **4-4.** lateral (LH), ventromedial (VMH) **4-5.** more than two, too simplistic.

5. Summarize evidence on how fluctuations in blood glucose and insulin affect hunger.

5-1. Much of the food we consume is converted into _____, a simple sugar that is an important source of energy. Manipulations that lower glucose tend to _____ hunger; raising glucose levels generally decreases hunger. Based on this evidence, Mayer proposed that neurons called _____ monitor glucose levels and contribute to the experience of hunger. (While glucostats were originally thought to be exclusively in the brain, their location and exact nature remain obscure.)

5-2. For cells to extract glucose from the blood, the hormone insulin must be present. Injections of insulin (in nondiabetics) will produce a (an) _____ in the level of sugar in the blood, with the result that the person experiences a (an) _____ in the sensation of hunger. In addition to insulin, some investigators have suggested that another hormone, abbreviated CCK, is related to (increasing/decreasing) the experience of hunger.

Answers: 5-1. glucose, increase, brain (hypothalamus), glucostats, liver **5-2.** decrease, increase, decreasing.

6. Summarize evidence how culture, learning, food cues, and stress influence hunger.

6-1. Although we have some innate taste preferences, it is also clear that _____ affects our food choices. For example, taste preferences and aversions may be learned by pairing a taste with pleasant or unpleasant experiences, the process of _____ conditioning.

6-2. In addition, we learn eating habits and food preferences simply by observing the behavior of others, such as parents or friends, the process known as _____ learning.

6-3. Some people may experience hunger when the clock says it's time to eat. These food-related _____ in our environment—the taste of food, the availability or sight of food, and the _____ of day—may influence food consumption.

6-4. Besides affecting eating habits and providing cues to eating, the environment may also provide unpleasant or frustrating events that produce emotional _____, a factor that may also trigger eating in many people. Although stress and increased eating are linked, recent evidence suggests that the important factor may be heightened physiological _____ produced by stress rather than the stress itself.

Answers: 6-1. learning (the environment), classical **6-2.** observational **6-3.** cues, time **6-4.** stress, arousal.

SEXUAL MOTIVATION: THE MYSTERY OF SEXUAL ORIENTATION

7. Summarize evidence on the determinants of sexual orientation.

7-1. What factors determine sexual orientation? Psychoanalysts looked for the answer in the parent-child relationship. Behaviorists assumed that conditioning was involved, that homosexuality resulted from the association of same-sex stimuli and sexual arousal. Thus, both psychoanalytic theorists and the behavioral theorists proposed (environmental/biological) explanations of homosexuality.

7-2. Research on the personal histories of homosexuals has (supported/not supported) the idea that homosexuality is caused primarily by environmental factors.

7-3. Recent studies have produced persuasive evidence indicating that homosexuality is in part genetic. Which of the following types of studies have supported this conclusion? (Place a Y or N in each blank, Y if this type of study has supported the genetic inference and N if it has not.)

(a) _____ Studies of hormonal differences between heterosexuals and homosexuals adults.

(b) _____ Studies of twins and adopted children.

(c) _____ Research on the anterior hypothalamus.

7-4. Subjects in one of the studies described were gay men who had either an identical twin brother, a fraternal twin brother, or an adopted brother. For each of the categories, what percent of the brothers of the subjects were also gay? Place the appropriate percents in the blanks.

(a) _____ Identical twins   22%

(b) _____ Fraternal twins   11%

(c) _____ Adopted brothers   52%

7-5. LeVay (1991) has reported that a cluster of neurons in the anterior _____ is (smaller/larger) in gay men than in straight men. Since all of the gay men in this study had died of AIDS, which itself could produce changes in brain structure, these findings should be interpreted with caution. Nonetheless, these data are consistent with the idea that there are (environmental/biological) factors that are related to sexual orientation.

Answers: 7-1. environmental **7-2.** not supported **7-3.** (a) N (b) Y (c) Y **7-4.** (a) 52% (b) 22% (c) 11% **7-5.** hypothalamus, smaller, biological.

ACHIEVEMENT: IN SEARCH OF EXCELLENCE

8. Describe the achievement motive and discuss how individual differences in the need for achievement influence behavior.

8-1. People with high achievement motivation have a need to:

a. master difficult challenges

b. outperform others

c. excel and compete

d. all of the above

8-2. What is the relationship between estimates of achievement motive in a country and the economic growth of that country?

8-3. The procedure used for measuring need for achievement is the same as that used to measure need for affiliation: subjects tell stories about pictures shown in the _____.

8-4. How do people who score high on need for affiliation differ from those who score low?

Answers: 8-1. d **8-2.** Countries with estimated high achievement motivation have higher economic growth (and greater productivity in general) **8-3.** TAT **8-4.** They tend to work hard, compete, be persistent, delay gratification, and be successful in their careers.

9. **Explain how situational factors and fear of failure affect achievement strivings.**

9-1.   According to Atkinson's elaboration of McClelland's views, achievement-oriented behavior is determined not only by (1) achievement motivation but by (2) the _____ that success will occur and (3) the _____ _____ of success.

9-2.   As the difficulty of a task increases, the _____ of success at the task decreases. At the same time, success at harder tasks may be more satisfying, so the _____ value of the task is likely to increase. Thus, when both the incentive value and probability of success are weighed together, people with a high need for achievement would tend to select tasks of (extreme/moderate) difficulty.

9-3.   In addition to success, Atkinson has included fear of failure in the equation. Thus, Atkinson proposes that there are six factors that affect pursuit of achievement: a motivation to achieve (to be successful) and a motivation to avoid _____; perceived *probability* of _____ and the perceived probability of _____; and the *incentive values* of both _____ and _____.

Answers: 9-1. probability, incentive value **9-2.** probability, incentive, moderate **9-3.** failure, success, failure; success, failure.

THE ELEMENTS OF EMOTIONAL EXPERIENCE

10. **Describe the cognitive component of emotion.**

10-1.   The word *cognition* refers to thoughts, beliefs, or conscious experience. When faced with an ugly-looking insect (or, for some people, being on the edge of a cliff or having to make a speech in public), you might say to yourself, "This is terrifying (or maybe disgusting)." This thought or cognition has an *evaluative* aspect: we assess our emotions as pleasant or unpleasant. Thus, one component of emotion is the _____ component, which includes _____ in terms of pleasantness-unpleasantness.

Answers: 10-1. cognitive, evaluation.

11. **Describe the physiological underpinnings of emotion.**

11-1.   The second component of emotion is the _____ component, which includes actions of the *autonomic* nervous system. Your encounter with a cockroach might be accompanied by changes in heart rate, breathing, or blood pressure—or by increased electrical conductivity of the skin known as the _____ skin response (GSR).

11-2.   Lie detectors don't actually detect lies, they detect bodily changes that reflect the _____ component of emotion, changes, for example, in heart rate, blood pressure, and the GSR. One can't be certain that the emotion reflected in "lie detectors" involves lying. Research has found that lie detectors are inaccurate about _____ of the time.

11-3.   Physiological arousal associated with emotion reflects mainly activity of the _____ nervous system, which regulates glands, smooth muscles, and blood vessels.

Answers: 11-1. physiological, galvanic **11-2.** physiological (autonomic arousal), one-fourth to one-third (i.e., about one-third of the innocent suspects were judged guilty by the polygraph, and about one-fourth of the guilty suspects were judged innocent by the polygraph) **11-3.** autonomic.

12. Discuss the body language of emotions and the facial feedback hypothesis.

12-1. We communicate emotions not only verbally but _____, through our postures and gestures and, especially, in our facial _____.

12-2. Ekman and Friesen found that there are at least _____ fundamental facial expressions of emotion and perhaps as many as ten. Since children who have been blind since birth show the same expressions as sighted children, it seems reasonable to believe that basic facial expressions are largely (learned/innate).

12-3. According to some researchers facial expressions not only reflect emotions but help create them. This viewpoint, known as the _____ hypothesis, asserts that facial muscles send signals to the brain that help produce the subjective experience of emotion. For example, turning up the corners of your mouth will tend to make you feel _____.

Answers: 12-1. nonverbally (through body language), expressions **12-2.** six, innate **12-3.** facial-feedback, happy.

13. Discuss cross-cultural similarities and variations in emotional experience.

13-1. Ekman and Friesen asked people in different cultures to label the emotion shown on photographs of faces. How did these studies support the idea that facial expressions tend to be universal across cultures?

13-2. Events that increase heart rate (or produce a "lump in the throat," perspiration, tense muscles, etc.) in one culture will tend to do so in other cultures as well. Thus, the _____ reactions to different stimulus events are quite similar across cultures.

13-3. People in different cultures also tend to *think* about emotional events in the same way. In other words, the _____ component of emotion seems to be quite similar cross-culturally.

13-4. While there are similarities in emotional expression across cultures, there are also striking differences. For example, certain word labels for emotion (e.g., sadness, anger, remorse) that exist in some cultures (are/are not) universal across cultures.

13-5. Although people in different cultures show the same basic expressions of emotion, *when* they do so is governed by different cultural norms. What emotions are you "supposed to" show at a funeral, or when watching a sporting event? The unwritten rules that regulate our display of emotion, known as _____ rules, vary considerably across cultures.

Answers: 13-1. People from very different cultures, including cultures that have had virtually no contact with the West, show considerable agreement in labeling photographs of facial expressions with one of approximately six basic emotions. **13-2.** physiological **13-3.** cognitive (thinking) **13-4.** are not **13-5.** display.

14. **Compare and contrast the James-Lange and Cannon-Bard theories of emotion and explain how Schachter reconciled these conflicting views in his two-factor theory.**

14-1.   For each of the following statements indicate the theory being described.

(a) The subjective experience of emotion is caused by different patterns of autonomic arousal.

_____

(b) Emotions cannot be distinguished on the basis of a autonomic arousal; general autonomic arousal causes one to look for an explanation or label. _____

(c) Love is accompanied by a different autonomic pattern from hate. _____

(d) The subjective experience of emotion is caused by two factors, by arousal and by cognition.

_____

(e) Emotions originate in subcortical brain structures; different emotions produce almost identical patterns of autonomic arousal. _____

(f) Ralph observes that his heart pounds and that he becomes a little out of breath at times. He also notices that these signs of arousal occur whenever Mary is around, so he figures that he must be in love.

_____

14-2.   In what sense does Schachter's theory reconcile the James-Lange and Cannon-Bard theories?

Answers: 14-1. (a) James-Lange (b) Schachter's two-factor (c) Schachter's two-factor (d) James-Lange (e) Cannon-Bard (f) Schachter's two-factor **14-2.** Schachter's view is similar to the James-Lange theory in that arousal is thought to precede the conscious experience of emotion; it is similar to the Cannon-Bard theory in that there is assumed to be just one general physiological arousal response rather than a different visceral response for each emotion. Since arousal is in large part the same regardless of the emotion, Schachter proposed that we feel different emotions as a result of inferences we make from events in the environment.

15. **Summarize the evolutionary perspective on emotion.**

15-1.   By preparing an organism for aggression and defense, the emotion of anger helps an organism survive. The emotions of fear, surprise, and interest have similar functions. From an evolutionary perspective, all emotions developed because of the _____ value they have for a species.

15-2.   Evolutionary theorists view emotions primarily as a group of (<u>innate/learned</u>) reactions that have been passed on because of their survival value. They also believe that emotions originate in subcortical areas, parts of the brain that evolved before the cortical structures associated with higher mental processes. In the view of the evolutionary theorists, emotion evolved before thought and is largely (<u>dependent on/independent of</u>) thought.

15-3.   How many basic, inherited emotions are there? The evolutionary writers assume that the wide range of emotions we experience are blends or different levels of approximately _____ innate or prewired primary emotions.

PUTTING IT IN PERSPECTIVE

16. **Explain how this chapter highlighted five of the text's unifying themes.**

   16-1.　Five of the text's organizing themes were prominent in this chapter. Indicate which themes fit the following examples by writing the appropriate abbreviations in the blanks below: C for cultural contexts, SH for sociohistorical context, T for theoretical diversity, HE for heredity and environment, and MC for multiple causation.

   (a) Achievement behavior is affected by achievement motivation, the likelihood of success, the likelihood of failure, and so on. ____

   (b) Display rules in a culture tell us when and where to express an emotion. ____

   (c) Changing attitudes about homosexuality have produced more research on sexual orientation; in turn, data from the research has affected societal attitudes. ____

   (d) Body weight seems to be influenced by set point, blood glucose, and inherited metabolism. It is also affected by eating habits and acquired tastes, which vary across cultures. ____, ____, and ____

   (e) The James-Lange theory proposed that different emotions reflected different patterns of physiological arousal; Cannon-Bard theory assumed that emotions originate in subcortical structures; Schachter viewed emotion as a combination of physiological arousal and cognition. ____

   Answers: **16-1.** (a) MC (b) C (c) SH (d) HE, MC, C (e) T.

APPLICATION: UNDERSTANDING THE ROOTS OF WEIGHT PROBLEMS

17. **Discuss the contribution of oversensitivity to external cues, genetic predisposition, dietary restraint, and set point to obesity.**

   17-1.　External cues, such as the time of day and the attractiveness and smell of food, all influence hunger. Schachter proposed that _____ people are especially sensitive to *external* cues and not very sensitive to *internal*, physiological cues that relate to hunger. According to Schachter, normal-weight people eat as a function of internal cues while obese people are controlled to a greater extent by _____ cues.

   17-2.　Judith Rodin, one of Schachter's students, found that people sensitive to external food cues tend to secrete insulin, which may reduce blood _____ and increase _____. Rodin's research has blurred the distinction between internal and external cues: Since insulin produces an *internal* signal, it is difficult to argue that the eating occurs simply because of _____ cues.

   17-3.　Rodin has found that many obese people are not especially responsive to external cues and that many thin or normal-weight people are responsive to such cues. Thus, Rodin has concluded that the link between obesity and sensitivity to external cues is (stronger/weaker) than Schachter had proposed.

   17-4.　It is by now clear that some of the factors that influence body weight are genetic. What did Stunkard and his associates (1986, 1990) find in their studies of adopted children and in their comparisons of identical and fraternal twins? Indicate *true* or *false* next to the statements below.

   _____ Adopted children were found to be quite similar to their biological parents in body weight.

   _____ Adopted children were found to be quite similar to their adoptive parents in body weight.

   _____ Identical twins reared apart are far more similar in weight than were fraternal twins reared together.

17-5. The concept of set point may help explain why body weight remains so stable. The theory proposes that each individual has a "natural" body weight determined in large part by the *number* of _____ that an individual happens to have. Although the number of fat cells in the body may increase through persistent overeating, the number is usually (<u>very stable/highly variable</u>) throughout one's lifetime.

17-6. The larger the (<u>number/size</u>) of fat cells, the higher the set point. Dieting or weight gain produces a change in the _____ of the fat cells but not, in most cases, the _____ of fat cells.

17-7. In other words, the number of fat cells, and possibly set point, (<u>remain the same/vary</u>) despite changes in one's weight. Thus, maintenance of body weight below one's "natural" weight or _____ tends to be quite difficult.

Answers: 17-1. obese, external **17-2.** glucose (sugar), hunger, external **17-3.** weaker **17-4.** True, False, True **17-5.** fat cells, very stable **17-6.** number, size, number **17-7.** remain the same, set point.

REVIEW OF KEY TERMS

Achievement motive
Bisexuals
Display rules
Drive
Emotion
Galvanic skin response (GSR)
Glucose

Glucostats
Heterosexuals
Hierarchy of needs
Homeostasis
Homosexuals
Incentive
Insulin

— Lie detector
Motivation
Need for self-actualization
— Polygraph
Set point
Sexual orientation

_____ **1.** Goal-directed behavior that may be affected by needs, wants, interests, desires, and incentives.

_____ **2.** A state of physiological equilibrium or balance.

_____ **3.** An internal state of tension that motivates the organism to reduce the tension and return to homeostasis.

_____ **4.** An external goal that motivates behavior.

_____ **5.** A systematic arrangement of needs according to priority.

_____ **6.** The need to fulfill one's potential.

_____ **7.** Blood sugar.

_____ **8.** Neurons that are sensitive to glucose.

_____ **9.** A hormone secreted by the pancreas needed for extracting glucose from the blood.

_____ **10.** The theoretical natural point of stability in body weight.

_____ **11.** Whether a person prefers emotional-sexual relationships with members of the same sex, the other sex, or either sex.

_____ **12.** People who seek emotional-sexual relationships with members of the same sex.

_____ **13.** People who seek emotional-sexual relationships with members of the other sex.

_____ 14. People who seek emotional-sexual relationships with members of either sex.

_____ 15. The need to master difficult challenges and to excel in competition with others.

_____ 16. An increase in the electrical conductivity of the skin related to an increase in sweat gland activity.

_____ 17. A reaction that includes cognitive, physiological, and behavioral components.

_____ 18. The technical name for the "lie detector."

_____ 19. The informal name for polygraph, an apparatus that monitors physiological aspects of arousal (e.g., heart rate, GSR).

_____ 20. Cultural norms that regulate the expression of emotions.

Answers: 1. motivation **2.** homeostasis **3.** drive **4.** incentive **5.** hierarchy of needs **6.** need for self-actualization **7.** glucose **8.** glucostats **9.** insulin **10.** set point **11.** sexual orientation **12.** homosexuals **13.** heterosexuals **14.** bisexuals **15.** achievement motive **16.** galvanic skin response (GSR) **17.** emotion **18.** polygraph **19.** lie detector **20.** display rules.

REVIEW OF KEY PEOPLE

Walter Cannon
William James
Abraham Maslow

David McClelland
Henry Murray

Stanley Schachter
Judith Rodin

_____ 1. Proposed that emotions arise in subcortical areas of the brain.

_____ 2. Compiled an influential catalogue of common social needs; also devised the TAT.

_____ 3. Developed a theory of motivation involving a hierarchy of needs; stressed the need for self-actualization.

_____ 4. Proposed that eating on the part of obese people is controlled by external cues; devised the two-factor theory of emotion.

_____ 5. Found that external cues may elicit insulin secretions and that the obese are not especially sensitive to external cues.

_____ 6. Is responsible for most of the early research on achievement motivation.

_____ 7. Thought that emotion arises from perception of different patterns of autonomic arousal.

Answers: 1. Cannon **2.** Murray **3.** Maslow **4.** Schachter **5.** Rodin **6.** McClelland **7.** James.

SELF-QUIZ

1. Which of the following is unlearned, uniform in expression, and universal within a particular species?
   a. incentive
   b. drive
   c. instinct
   d. motivation

2. In Maslow's hierarchy of needs, which of the following needs would be activated only after all other levels of needs have been satisfied?
   a. physiological needs
   b. safety and security needs
   c. esteem needs
   d. need for self-actualization

3. What happens when a rat's lateral hypothalamus is lesioned?
   a. It starts eating.
   b. It looks for a sexual partner.
   c. It stops eating.
   d. It loses bladder and bowel control.

4. What is the effect of insulin on blood glucose?
   a. Glucose level increases.
   b. Glucose level decreases.
   c. Glucose changes to free fatty acids.
   d. CCK increases.

5. Which of the following is thought to be a major determinant of set point?
   a. number of fat cells
   b. size of fat cells
   c. amount of exercise
   d. skill at tennis

6. Which data from twin studies provide *the most convincing* evidence of the influence of heredity on human behavior?
   a. Identical twins reared together are more similar than fraternal twins reared together.
   b. Identical twins reared together are more similar than fraternal twins reared apart.
   c. Identical twins reared apart are more similar than fraternal twins reared apart.
   d. Identical twins reared apart are more similar than fraternal twins reared together.

7. Polygraphs or lie detectors detect
   a. lies
   b. unconscious processes
   c. body language
   d. physiological arousal

8. The need for self-actualization is the need to
   a. achieve intimacy
   b. avoid failure and achieve success
   c. compensate for inferiority
   d. fulfill one's potential

9. The evolutionary theories of emotion assert that emotions
   a. are to a large extent learned
   b. have survival value
   c. are primarily social motives
   d. are produced through classical conditioning

10. Which of the following theories proposes that emotion arises from perception of different patterns of autonomic arousal?
    a. Schachter's two-factor theory
    b. Cannon-Bard
    c. James-Lange
    d. evolutionary theory

11. What test is generally used to measure need for achievement?
    a. the TAT
    b. the GSR
    c. the Rorschach
    d. the MMPI

12. Evidence regarding facial expression in different cultures and observation of the blind suggests that
    a. Schachter's two-factor theory is correct.
    b. Facial expression of emotion is in large part innate.
    c. Emotions originate in the cortex.
    d. Learning is the major factor in explaining basic facial expressions.
13. According to Schachter's theory of emotion
    a. Different emotions are represented by different autonomic reactions.
    b. Emotions originate in subcortical brain structures.
    c. Fear produces a desire to avoid affiliation.
    d. Both arousal and cognition are needed to produce emotion.
14. There appear to be between six and ten basic facial expressions of emotion. Cross-cultural studies suggest that these facial expressions:
    a. are to a large extent produced by family interactions
    b. are to a large extent biologically determined
    c. are primarily social in origin
    d. have no evolutionary significance
15. Stunkard found that adopted children's body weights tended to resemble the body weights of the children's
    a. biological parents
    b. adoptive parents
    c. nonbiological siblings
    d. mothers and maternal aunts

Answers: 1. c 2. d 3. c 4. b 5. a 6. d 7. d 8. d 9. b 10. c 11. a 12. b 13. d 14.c 15. a.

11 HUMAN DEVELOPMENT ACROSS THE LIFE SPAN

REVIEW OF KEY IDEAS

PROGRESS BEFORE BIRTH: PRENATAL DEVELOPMENT

1. Outline the major events of the three phases of prenatal development.

1-1. Each box below represents one month in the typical pregnancy; each short line at the top of the boxes represents one week. Indicate the beginning and end of each phase of prenatal development by placing the appropriate capital letters from the diagram in the blanks below.

```
A    B    C         D         E              F                                G
     | | | | | | | |
┌────┬─────────┬──────┬──────┬──────┬──────┬──────┬──────┬──────┬──────┬──────┐
│    │         │      │      │      │      │      │      │      │      │      │
└────┴─────────┴──────┴──────┴──────┴──────┴──────┴──────┴──────┴──────┴──────┘
```

(a) The germinal stage begins at birth, represented by point _____ in the diagram, and ends at point _____.

(b) The embryonic stage begins at point _____ and ends at point _____.

(c) The fetal stage begins at point _____ and ends at point _____.

1-2. List the names of the three phases of prenatal development in the order in which they occur. In the parentheses at the right indicate the age ranges encompassed by each stage.

(a) _____ (   )

(b) _____ (   )

(c) _____ (   )

1-3. Match the letter identifying each stage in the previous question with the descriptions below.

_____ The placenta begins to form.

_____ At the end of this stage the organism begins to have a human appearance; it is about an inch in length.

_____ The zygote begins to implant in the uterine wall; about one in five are rejected.

_____ Muscles and bones develop and physical movements occur.

_____ Most major birth defects probably have their origins in this stage.

_____ The age of viability (about 22 to 26 weeks after conception) occurs during this stage.

Answers: 1-1. (a) A, B (b) B, D (c) D, G **1-2.** (a) germinal (birth to two weeks) (b) embryonic (two weeks to two months) (c) fetal (two months to nine months) **1-3.** a, b, a, c, b, c.

2. Summarize the impact of environmental factors, including prenatal health care, on prenatal development.

2-1. Indicate whether the following statements concerning environmental factors and fetal development are true (T) or false (F).

_____ Severe malnutrition increases the risk of birth complications and neurological deficits.

_____ Studies consistently indicate that moderate malnutrition does not have a harmful effect on infant development.

_____ Few if any drugs consumed by a pregnant woman are able to pass through the placental barrier.

_____ Relative to its affluence the U.S. has a high infant mortality rate.

_____ Recent studies indicate that moderate drinking during pregnancy produces no risk for the developing fetus.

_____ Heavy drinking of alcohol by a pregnant woman may produce microencephaly, heart defects, and retardation in her child.

_____ Smoking during pregnancy is related to increased risk of miscarriage and other birth complications.

_____ The placenta screens out many but not all infectious diseases.

_____ Genital herpes is usually transmitted during the birth process, when newborns come into contact with their mothers' lesions.

_____ AIDS is transmitted primarily during the birth process, when newborns come into contact with their mothers' blood cells.

_____ Good-quality prenatal care is associated with fewer premature births and higher infant survival rates.

Answers: 2-1. T, F, F, T, F, T, T, T, T, T, T.

THE WONDROUS YEARS OF CHILDHOOD

3. Describe general trends and cultural variations in motor development

3-1. In the space below, list and describe the two basic trends in motor development described in the text.

Cephalocaudal trend:

Proximodistal trend:

3-2. The average ages at which children display various behaviors and abilities are referred to as developmental _____. While these averages provide useful information they don't reflect variability, and the age at which children display certain behaviors or abilities varies (<u>enormously/very little</u>) across children.

3-3.   Thus, with regard to the behavior of walking up steps, for example, which of the following is true?

        a. children walk up steps at approximately the same age.

        b. many normal children don't walk up steps until well after or well before the average age indicated.

3-4.   The process that underlies the developmental norms is *maturation*. What is maturation? (Be specific with regard to the factors of hereditary and environment.)

3-5.   Cross-cultural research has revealed a considerable degree of consistency between cultures in terms of when and in what order motor skills appear. In general, early motor development is much more dependent on (maturation/culture) than is later motor development. As children in a culture grow older, however, the motor skills that they acquire depend to a greater extent on (maturation/culture).

Answers: 3-1. Head to foot: children tend to gain motor control of the upper body before the lower body. Center outward: the tendency to gain control of the torso before the limbs **3-2.** norms, enormously **3-3.** b **3-4.** Maturation refers to developmental changes that occur in an organism as a result of *genetic*, as opposed to environmental, factors **3-5.** maturation, culture.

4. Summarize the findings of Thomas and Chess's longitudinal study of infant temperament.

4-1.   Identify the following designs by placing the appropriate names in the blanks: longitudinal, cross-sectional, sequential.

        (a) _____ In this experimental design researchers compare groups of subjects of differing ages at a single point in time.

        (b) _____ This design measures a single group of subjects over a period of time.

4-2.   Thomas and Chess identified three basic temperaments, described below. Place the names of these temperamental styles in the appropriate blanks.

        (a) _____ Happy, regular in sleep and eating, adaptable, not readily upset.

        (b) _____ Less cheery, less regular in sleep and eating, slower in adapting to change, more wary of new experiences, moderate in reactivity.

        (c) _____ Glum, erratic in sleep and eating, resistant to change, irritable.

4-3.   (a) Approximately what percentage of the children are easy? _____

        (b) Slow-to-warm-up? _____

        (c) Difficult? _____

        (d) About what percentage is a mixture of the three basic categories? _____

4-4.   What is the major conclusion from the Thomas and Chess study?

Answers: 4-1. (a) cross-sectional (b) longitudinal **4-2.** (a) easy (b) slow-to-warm-up (c) difficult
4-3. (a) 40% (b) 15% (c) 10% (d) 35% **4-4.** A child's temperament at 3 months tended to be a fair predictor of his or her temperament at 10 years of age. This stability over time suggests that temperament has a strong biological basis.

5. Summarize research on infant-mother attachment, including cultural variations.

5-1.   Newborn babies do not form attachments to their mothers immediately. They begin to show a strong preference for their mothers, often crying when they are separated, beginning at about _____ months of age.

5-2.   The emotional distress that occurs when some infants are separated from their caregivers is called _____ anxiety. This distress peaks at about _____ months of age and then begins to decline.

5-3.   Research by Ainsworth and her colleagues indicates that attachments between mothers and their infants tend to fall into three categories. While most children develop *secure* attachments, some develop *anxious-ambivalent* attachments, characterized by a high degree of _____ when separation from the mother occurs. Still others are not distressed when the mother leaves and tend to avoid contact with her, a pattern referred to as _____ attachment. These patterns of attachment may have important consequences for later social development.

5-4.   Is infant-mother "bonding" during the first few hours after birth important? Research thus far indicates that:
a. Skin-to-skin contact between infants and mothers tends to produce stronger attachments later.
b. Bonding immediately after birth produces very clear benefits.
c. There is no convincing evidence that this type of contact leads to healthier attachments in the long run.

5-5.   Does day care affect infant-mother attachment? Belsky has found that day care for more than 20 hours per week increases the likelihood that a/an (insecure/secure) attachment will form between mother and infant.

5-6.   Belsky's findings must be put in perspective, however. Which of the following statements are/is true (T) or false (F)?

_____   The proportion of insecure attachments found in the Belsky studies is only slightly higher than the U.S. norm.

_____   Some studies have found that day care can have beneficial effects on children's intellectual and social development.

_____   Negative effects of day care are slight or nonexistent in spacious, adequately staffed and equipped facilities.

5-7.   Separation anxiety occurs at roughly the same ages across different cultures. There are some interesting cross-cultural differences, however, shown in Table 11.1 in your text.

(a) Which cultural sample (USA, Germany, or Japan) showed the highest proportion of *avoidant* attachments?
_____

(b) Which cultural sample evidenced *no avoidant attachments* at all? _____

(c) Which sample showed the highest levels of *anxious/ambivalent* attachments?
_____

(d) Which two countries had the highest proportion of *secure* attachments? _____ and
_____

Answers: 5-1. 6 to 8 **5-2.** separation, 14 to 18 **5-3.** anxiety, avoidant **5-4.** c. **5-5.** insecure **5-6.** true, true, true
5-7. (a) Germany (b) Japan (c) Japan (d) USA, Japan.

6. Outline Erikson's stages of childhood personality development and critique Erikson's theory.

6-1.   Erikson's theory is clearly derived from Freudian psychoanalytic theory. Freud asserted that there are five childhood stages that determine the adult's personality. In contrast, Erikson proposed that there are _____ stages that influence personality across an individual's (childhood/entire lifespan).

6-2. Erikson described four childhood stages and four adult stages. In the spaces below write the names of the crises that mark the four *childhood* stages, and indicate in the parentheses the approximate ages at which the crises are supposed to occur.

(a) _____ vs. _____   (   )

(b) _____ vs. _____   (   )

(c) _____ vs. _____   (   )

(d) _____ vs. _____   (   )

6-3. Below are descriptions of several individuals. In what childhood stage would they have acquired the characteristics described, according to Erikson? Use the letters from the question above to indicate the stages.

_____ Jack has trouble functioning effectively in the world outside his family; he is unproductive, and he lacks a sense of competence.

_____ Kristi is insecure and suspicious of everyone.

_____ Larry was torn between being independent of his family and avoiding conflict; as an adult he feels guilty and lacks self-esteem.

_____ From an early age Maureen's parents never seemed satisfied with what she did. Maureen is plagued by a sense of shame and self-doubt.

6-4. As you may have noted in responding to the previous item, a weakness of Erikson's theory is that it attempts to account for very (few/many) aspects of personality. Thus, the theory cannot explain the enormous individual _____ between people.

Answers: 6-1. 8, entire lifespan **6-2.** (a) trust vs. mistrust (first year) (b) autonomy vs. shame and doubt (second year) (c) initiative vs. guilt (ages 3 to 6) (d) industry vs. inferiority (age 6 through puberty) **6-3.** d, a, c, b **6-4.** few, differences.

7. Outline Piaget's stages of cognitive development and critique Piaget's theory.

7-1. The diagram below represents Piaget's four main stages of development. Write the names of the stages in the appropriate blanks.

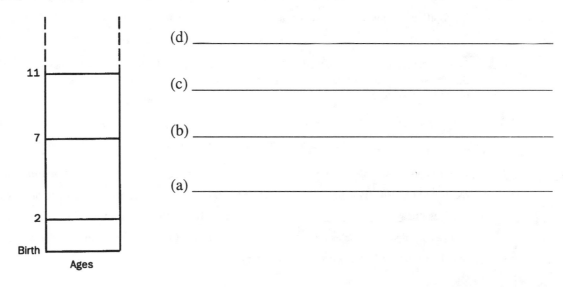

(d) _____

(c) _____

(b) _____

(a) _____

7-2. Following is a list of characteristics of children's thinking during various stages. Identify the stage by placing the correct letter (from the diagram above) in the blanks.

_____ At the end of this stage the child is beginning to develop the capacity for symbolic thought (to think terms of mental images).

_____ At the beginning of this stage the child's behavior is dominated by reflexes and the ability to coordinate sensory input and movement.

_____ The child understands conservation and can handle hierarchical classification but tends not to use abstractions.

_____ The child's thought processes are abstract and systematic.

_____ Object permanence occurs toward the end of this stage.

_____ During the first part of this stage, "out of sight, out of mind" might describe the child's reaction to hidden objects.

_____ When water is poured from a wide beaker into a taller beaker, children say there is now more water in the taller beaker.

_____ The child demonstrates a lack of understanding of conservation.

_____ The child shows the shortcomings of centration, irreversibility, egocentrism, and animism.

_____ For the first time the child in this stage is mentally able to undo an action and also is able to focus on more than one feature of a problem at the same time.

7-3. When my (R. S.) daughter Vanessa was about 5, I placed two rows of stones on the grass, as illustrated below. Each row contained the same number of stones.

Row A: • • • • • • •

Row B: • • • • • • •

I then spread out one row so that it took up more space:

Row A: • • • • • • •

Row B: • • • • • • •

(a) I then asked Vanessa to point to the row that now had more stones. If Vanessa behaved like other *preoperational* children, which row would she point to? _____

(b) The preoperational child has not yet mastered the principle that physical quantities remain constant in spite of changes in their shape or, in this case, arrangement. What is the name of this principle?

_____

7-4. Some research has demonstrated that certain aspects of Piaget's theory may be incorrect in detail. For example, there is some evidence that object permanence and some aspects of conservation may develop (earlier/later) than Piaget had thought.

7-5. Piaget also had little to say about individual _____ in development or about so-called

_____ of stages in which elements of an earlier stage may appear in a later one.

7-6. Piaget thought that people of all cultures would pass through the stages at the same time; subsequent research has found that this (is/is not) the case. While the *sequence* of stages appears to be relatively invariant across cultures, the _____ that children follow in passing through these stages varies considerably across cultures. Nonetheless, Piaget's brilliance, the novelty of his approach, and the wealth of research that his theory inspired assure his place in history.

8. Outline Kohlberg's stages of moral development and critique Kohlberg's theory.

8-1. Kohlberg's theory includes three moral levels, each with two stages for a total of six stages. Indicate which of the three moral levels is described in each of the following statements.

(a) Acts are considered wrong because they are punished or right because they lead to positive consequences. _____

(b) Individuals at this level conform very strictly to society's rules, which they accept as absolute and inviolable. _____

(c) This level is characterized by situational or conditional morality, such that stealing might be considered wrong in one circumstance but permissible in another. _____

8-2. The central ideas of Kohlberg's theory have received a fair amount of support. Research has found that children (<u>do/do not</u>) tend to progress through Kohlberg's stages in the order that he indicated. As children get older, stages 1 and 2 reasoning tend to decrease while stages 3 and 4 reasoning tend to _____.

8-3. There have also been several criticisms of Kohlberg's theory. First, individuals may show characteristics of several different stages at the same time. In other words, as was true of other stage theories, there tends to be a "_____" of stages.

8-4. Second, some critics assert that Kohlberg's theory reflects the liberal, individualistic values that characterize modern _____ societies rather than human beings in general. In other words, Kohlberg's theory (<u>does/does not</u>) address disparities in moral development that exist across cultures.

8-5. Third, Gilligan (1982) has asserted that Kohlberg's theory reflects a masculine view of morality, with an emphasis on _____ , as opposed to a more feminine emphasis on caring and self-sacrifice. While some evidence supports Gilligan's idea about gender differences in interpretation of the moral dilemmas, research thus far (<u>has/has not</u>) found gender differences in the *ages* at which children go through Kohlberg's stages.

THE TRANSITION OF ADOLESCENCE

9. Describe the major events of puberty.

9-1. Read over the section on <u>Puberty and the Growth Spurt</u> in your text. Then fill in the blanks below with the appropriate terms.

(a) _____ The approximately two-year span preceding puberty that is marked by rapid growth in height and weight.

(b) _____ The period of time during which secondary sex characteristics appear.

(c) _____ Physical features that distinguish one sex from another but that are not essential for reproduction (e.g., facial hair in males, breasts in females).

(d) _____ The stage during which sexual functions essential for reproduction reach maturity.

(e) _____ The stage that includes menarche in females and the production of sperm in males.

(f) _____ The first occurrence of menstruation.

(g) _____ The transitional period between childhood and adulthood that includes early physical changes (puberty) and later cognitive and social changes.

Answers: 9-1. (a) pubescence (b) pubescence (c) secondary sex characteristics (d) puberty (e) puberty (f) menarche (g) adolescence

10. Evaluate the assertion that adolescence is a time of turmoil in light of current evidence on adolescent suicide.

10-1. How tumultuous is adolescence? With regard to suicide and other indicants of stress, current data indicate that: (Mark T or F for each of the following statements.)

_____ Suicide rates among adolescents is higher than for any other age group.

_____ The ratio of attempted to completed suicides is much higher for adolescents than for any other age group.

_____ In general, adolescents encounter no more turmoil than people do in other periods of life.

Answers: 10-1. F, T, T.

11. Explain why the struggle for a sense of identity is particularly intense during adolescence and discuss some common patterns of identity formation.

11-1. Adolescence is a period of change, so it is readily understandable that adolescents tend to focus on the struggle for _____, the question of "Who am I?"

11-2. Recall that Erik Erikson described four crises that mark childhood. What is the crisis that marks adolescence, according to Erikson? _____ vs. _____

11-3. Marcia (1966, 1980) has described four orientations that people may adopt in attempting to resolve the identity crisis. These are not stages that people pass through in an orderly manner but statuses that they may adopt on either a relatively permanent or temporary basis. One possible status is simply to take on the values and roles prescribed by one's parents; this is termed _____. While this may temporarily resolve the crisis, in the long run the individual may not be comfortable with the adopted identity. A second orientation involves a period of experimentation with various ideologies and careers and a delay in commitment to any one; this is termed _____. If the experimentation and lack of commitment become permanent, the individual is said to be in a status of _____ _____. On the other hand, if the consideration of alternatives leads to conviction about a sense of self, one takes on the status referred to as _____ _____.

Answers: 11-1. identity **11-2.** identity vs. confusion **11-3.** foreclosure, moratorium, identity diffusion, identity achievement.

12. Summarize evidence on the stability of personality and the prevalence of the mid-life crisis and outline Erikson's stages of development in adulthood.

12-1. Do people's personalities change throughout their lifetimes? Research evidence supports the conclusion that:
a. personality is stable across one's lifetime
b. personality changes across one's lifetime
c. both of the above are true
d. neither of the above is true

12-2. Explain how it is possible that personality appears both to stay the same and to change dramatically over time.

12-3. Two influential studies conducted in the 1970s asserted that people experience a period of emotional turmoil sometime between ages 35 and 45, a transitional phase known as the _____ _____.

12-4. The midlife crisis, described as a period of reappraisal and assessment of time left, was thought by the original writers (Gould and Levinson) to be a transitional phase that affected (<u>a minority/most</u>) adults. More recent research has found that this is not the case.

12-5. The disparity between the conclusions of Gould and of Levinson and those of the more recent researchers (e.g., McCrae & Costa) may have to do with the difference in methods used. Explain.

12-6. In the spaces below write the names of the crises that mark Erikson's three stages of adulthood. In the parentheses indicate the approximate period of adulthood during which the crises are supposed to occur.

(a)_____ vs. _____   (   )

(b)_____ vs. _____   (   )

(c)_____ vs. _____   (   )

12-7. Following are descriptions of the crises occurring in each of the above stages. Indicate the stages by placing the appropriate letters (from the previous question) in the blanks.

_____ Concern for helping future generations versus a self-indulgent concern for meeting one's own desires.

_____ Concern to find meaning in the remainder of one's life versus a preoccupation with earlier failures and eventual death.

_____ Concern for developing a capacity for intimacy with others versus a strategy in which others are manipulated as a means to an end.

Answers: 12-1. c **12-2.** Some personality traits (e.g., extroversion-introversion) appear to be quite stable; others (e.g., masculinity-femininity) tend to change as people grow older **12-3.** midlife crisis **12-4.** most **12-5.** Gould and Levinson used interview and case study methods, methods which are less objective than those used in the more recent research by McCrae and Costa and others **12-6.** (a) intimacy vs. isolation (early adulthood) (b) generativity vs. self-absorption (middle adulthood) (c) integrity vs. despair (aging years) **12-7.** b, c, a.

13. Describe typical transitions in family relations during the adult years.

13-1. In part as a result of economic factors and in part due to an increased emphasis on personal autonomy, remaining single or postponing marriage is a much more acceptable option today than it was a few decades ago. Nonetheless, people emerge from families and most ultimately form new families. Over _____ percent of adults eventually marry.

13-2. While the first few years of married life tend to be quite happy, an early source of tension concerns different expectations in an era of changing gender roles. According to a recent survey, men and women have different views about the meaning of *equality*. What do *men* mean by equality in marriage? How do *women* define this concept? What is the evidence about task sharing?

13-3. What event in the family cycle tends to cause the first drop in marital satisfaction? When does marital satisfaction tend to start climbing back?

Answers: 13-1. 90 **13-2.** In one recent survey, half the men were unable to define equality in marriage at all; the other half defined it in psychological terms. Women defined it more concretely—in terms of sharing tasks and responsibilities. The evidence indicates that women are still doing the bulk of the housework in America even when employed outside the home. **13-3.** Although most couples rate parenthood as a very positive experience, marital satisfaction tends to drop at the birth of the first child. Marital satisfaction tends to increase when children leave home. The "empty nest" seems to have little lasting negative impact.

14. Describe the physical and cognitive changes associated with aging.

14-1. As we age, our physical and cognitive characteristics change. Indicate which of the following physical traits increase and which decrease by placing checkmarks in the appropriate blanks.

	INCREASES	DECREASES
Physical changes		
Proportion of body fat:	_____	_____
Overall weight:	_____	_____
Number of neurons in the brain:	_____	_____
Visual acuity:	_____	_____
Ability to see close:	_____	_____
Hearing:	_____	_____

14-2. An abnormal condition marked my memory loss and loss of other cognitive abilities is termed a

_____. Dimentia occurs in approximately _____% of individuals over age 65.

14-3. With regard to changes in *general intelligence* and in *memory* that may accompany aging, which of the following is/are true? (Mark T or F.)

_____ Average test scores in cognitive ability show some decline after age 60.

_____ For the majority of people the decline in cognitive ability that occurs in later years may not be significant.

_____ The memory loss that accompanies aging is relatively severe.

_____ The type of memory loss is thought to involve working memory or processing speed.

14-4. Despite the decline in physical and cognitive capacities, aging is not so bad as it may at first seem. With regard to loss of brain cells, it's not so much a matter of "Who needs 'em?" as that the gradual loss appears to have (little/a strong) effect on functioning.

14-5. Intellectual performance and memory decline modestly with advancing age and are not universal. Speed of problem solving generally (does/does not) decrease with age, but problem solving ability (is/is not) impaired if time is not a factor.

Answers: 14-1. Body fat and overall weight increase (except that overall weight may decrease somewhat after the mid-50s); the rest decrease **14-2.** dementia, 15% **4-3.** T, T, F, T **4-4.** little **4-5.** does, is not.

PUTTING IT IN PERSPECTIVE

15. Explain how this chapter highlighted the text's unifying theme about the joint influence of heredity and environment.

15-1. The behavior of a child is the result of the child's genetic inheritance and its environment, which includes the

behavior of the child's parents. In turn, the behavior of the parents toward the child is affected both by their

inherited characteristics and by the behavior of the child. Thus, behavior is the result, not of heredity or

environment operating separately, but of an _____ between the two factors.

15-2. To understand the concept of *interaction* consider this problem: There is a form of mental retardation that results from phenylketonuria, an inherited inability to metabolize a common amino acid in milk. When fed milk, children born with phenylketonuria become mentally retarded. Is this type of retardation an inherited disorder?
a. Yes, it's genetic.
b. No, it's caused by the environment.
c. A certain proportion of the causal factors are hereditary and the remainder due to the environment.
d. The disorder results from heredity and environment operating jointly.

15-3. This chapter has been concerned with changes in human behavior across the life span. The theme being stressed here is that these changes result from an *interaction* of heredity and environment. In your own words, explain how the interaction operates.

Answers: 15-1. interaction **15-2.** d. (This disorder might at first seem to be inherited, since there is a genetic trait involved. But the retardation does not occur if the infant is not fed milk products, which involves the environment. The point is that this disorder, like behavior in general, cannot be attributed solely to nature or to nurture or even to relative weights of each: It is a function of an *interaction* between the two.) **15-3.** The interaction of heredity and environment refers to the fact that we are a product of both factors. It means more than that, however. Heredity and environment don't operate separately. Interaction means that the genetic factors affect the operation of the environment and that environmental factors affect genetic predispositions. The influence of one factor *depends on* the effects of the other.

APPLICATION: UNDERSTANDING GENDER DIFFERENCES

16. **Summarize evidence on gender differences in behavior and discuss the significance of these differences.**

    16-1. Which gender tends to show more of (score higher on tests of) the following traits or abilities? Check the appropriate column.

    Cognitive

verbal skills	MALES	FEMALES	NEITHER
mathematical skills	MALES	FEMALES	NEITHER
visual-spatial skills	MALES	FEMALES	NEITHER

    Social

aggression	MALES	FEMALES	NEITHER
sensitivity to nonverbal cues	MALES	FEMALES	NEITHER
susceptibility to influence	MALES	FEMALES	NEITHER
sexual permissiveness	MALES	FEMALES	NEITHER

    16-2. There is an enormous overlap between the genders with regard to these traits. There are, of course, many females who are more aggressive than the average male and many males who are more sensitive to nonverbal cues than the average female. Thus, it is important to note that the differences referred to in this section are differences between group _____ and that the size of the differences is relatively

    _____ .

    Answers: 16-1. cognitive: females, males, males; social: males, females, females, males **16-2.** averages (means), small.

17. **Explain how biological and environmental factors contribute to existing gender differences.**

    17-1. For evolutionary theorists, the relative invariance of gender differences found across cultures reflects natural selection. Males seek (<u>few/many</u>) sexual partners because this evolutionary strategy has had adaptive value. Greater aggressiveness has survival value for males as well because it enhances their ability to acquire material _____ sought by females selecting a mate.

    17-2. Evolutionary theorists also assert that ability differences between the genders reflect the division of labor in our ancestral past. Males were primarily the hunters and females the gatherers, and the adaptive demands of hunting may have produced males' superiority at most _____ tasks.

    17-3. While the evolutionary view of gender is a plausible explanation of the remarkable similarity in gender differences across cultures, there are reasonable alternative explanations. In addition, evolutionary hypotheses are (<u>difficult/easy</u>) to test empirically.

17-4. Several studies suggest that *hormones* are a major factor in shaping gender differences. For example, females exposed prenatally to high levels of an _____-like drug given their mothers during pregnancy tend to show more male-typical behavior than do other females.

17-5. While some research findings support the role of hormones in gender development, the data are not conclusive. For one thing, these studies are based on small samples of people who have abnormal conditions. For another, most of the research is by necessity (experimental/correlational), and there are plausible alternative explanations for the findings.

17-6. Other biological evidence suggests that males depend more heavily on the left hemisphere for verbal processing and the right for spatial processing than is the case with females. In other words, males may tend to exhibit more cerebral _____ than females. Results on this topic have been mixed, however. In addition, it would be difficult to see how gender differences in *specialization* could account for gender differences in *ability*, that is, the superiority of males on spatial tasks and the superiority of females on _____ tasks.

17-7. Research on the role of biology in determining gender is intriguing but still open to dispute. The effect of environmental factors on gender roles is less controversial. Children learn as a result of the consequences for their behavior, the rewards and punishments that they receive in the process of _____ conditioning.

17-8. Children also acquire information by seeing what others do, the process of _____ learning. While children imitate both males and females, they are more likely to imitate the behavior of (same-sex/ opposite-sex) models.

17-9. In addition to operant conditioning and observational learning, children are active participants in their own gender-role socialization, the process referred to as _____-socialization. First, once they discover (at age 5 or 6) that being a boy or girl is a permanent condition, they will then _____ themselves as boys or girls. Second, following classification in terms of gender, children will _____ characteristics and behaviors associated with their gender. Third, they will bring their _____ in line with their values by engaging in "sex-appropriate" behaviors.

17-10. Whether through operant conditioning, observational learning, or self-socialization, the major forces for gender-role socialization occur in three main aspects of the child's environment: in their _____, in _____, and in the _____.

Answers: 17-1. many, resources **17-2.** spatial (visual-spatial) **17-3.** controversial, difficult **17-4.** androgen, spatial (visual-spatial) **17-5.** correlational **17-6.** specialization, verbal **17-7.** operant **17-8.** observational (modeling), same-sex **17-9.** self, classify (categorize), value, behavior **17-10.** families, schools, media.

REVIEW OF KEY TERMS

Age of viability
Aggression
Attachment
Centration
Cephalocaudal trend
Cognitive development
Conservation
Cross-sectional design
Development
Developmental norms
Dementia
Egocentrism
Embryonic stage
Fetal alcohol syndrome

Fetal stage
Gender
Gender differences
Gender roles
Gender stereotypes
Germinal stage
Infant mortality
Irreversibility
Longitudinal study
Maturation
Menarche
Motor development
Object permanence
Placenta

Prenatal period
Primary sex characteristics
Proximodistal trend
Puberty
Pubescence
Secondary sex characteristics
Separation anxiety
Sex
Social clock
Stage
Temperament
Zygote

1. The sequence of age-related changes that occurs as a person progresses from conception to death.

2. The period of pregnancy, extending from conception to birth.

3. The first two weeks after conception.

4. The structure that connects the circulation of the fetus and the mother but that blocks passage of blood cells.

5. The second stage of prenatal development, lasting from two weeks after conception until the end of the second month.

6. The third stage of prenatal development, lasting from two months after conception through birth.

7. The age at which the baby can first survive in the event of a premature birth.

8. A collection of congenital problems associated with a mother's excessive use of alcohol during pregnancy.

9. The death rate in the first year of life per 1000 births.

10. Developmental changes in muscular coordination required for physical movement.

11. The head-to-foot direction of motor development.

12. The center-outward direction of motor development.

13. The average ages at which people display certain behaviors and abilities.

14. Characteristic mood, energy level, and reactivity.

15. One group of subjects is observed over a long period of time.

16. Investigators compare groups of subjects of differing ages at a single point in time.

17. Emotional distress displayed by an infant when separated from a person with whom it has formed an attachment.

18. Culturally constructed distinctions between femininity and masculinity.

19. Widely held beliefs about females' and males' abilities, personality traits, and social behavior.

20. Development of thinking, reasoning, remembering, and problem solving.

21. A mental capacity that involves recognizing that objects continue to exist even when they are no longer visible.

_____ **22.** Piaget's term for the awareness that physical quantities remain constant in spite of changes in their shape or appearance.

_____ **23.** The Piagetian term for the tendency to focus on just one feature of a problem and neglect other important features.

_____ **24.** The inability to cognitively visualize reversing an action.

_____ **25.** Thinking characterized by a limited ability to share another person's viewpoint.

_____ **26.** The attribution of lifelike qualities to inanimate objects.

_____ **27.** A developmental period during which certain behaviors and capacities occur.

_____ **28.** The biologically based categories of male and female.

_____ **29.** Expectations concerning what the appropriate behavior is for each sex.

_____ **30.** An abnormal deterioration in mental faculties that accompanies aging in about 15 percent of people over age 65.

_____ **31.** A close, emotional bond of affection between an infant and its caregiver.

_____ **32.** Physical features associated with gender that are not directly needed for reproduction.

_____ **33.** The physical structures necessary for reproduction.

_____ **34.** The two-year span preceding puberty marked by the appearance of secondary sex characteristics and by rapid growth.

_____ **35.** The first occurrence of menstruation.

_____ **36.** The stage during which reproductive functions reach maturity.

_____ **37.** A person's notion of a developmental schedule that specifies what he or she should have accomplished by certain points in life.

_____ **38.** Developmental changes that reflect one's genetic blueprint rather than environment.

_____ **39.** A one-celled organism created by the process of fertilization, the union of sperm and egg.

_____ **40.** Behavioral differences between females and males.

Answers: 1. development **2.** prenatal period **3.** germinal stage **4.** placenta **5.** embryonic stage **6.** fetal stage **7.** age of viability **8.** fetal alcohol syndrome **9.** infant mortality **10.** motor development **11.** cephalocaudal trend **12.** proximodistal trend **13.** developmental norms **14.** temperament **15.** longitudinal design **16.** cross-sectional design **17.** separation anxiety **18.** gender **19.** gender stereotypes **20.** cognitive development **21.** object permanence **22.** conservation **23.** centration **24.** irreversibility **25.** egocentrism **26.** animism **27.** stage **28.** sex **29.** gender roles **30.** dementia **31.** attachment **32.** secondary sex characteristics **33.** primary sex characteristics **34.** pubescence **35.** menarche **36.** puberty **37.** social clock **38.** maturation **39.** zygote **40.** gender differences.

REVIEW OF KEY PEOPLE

Mary Ainsworth   Lawrence Kohlberg   Alexander Thomas & Stella Chess
Erik Erikson   Jean Piaget

_____ **1.** Conducted a major longitudinal study that identified three basic styles of children's temperament.

_____ **2.** Partitioned the life span into eight stages, each accompanied by a psychosocial crisis.

_____ **3.** Pioneered the study of children's cognitive development.

_____ **4.** Developed a stage theory of moral development.

_____ **5.** Described three categories of infant-mother attachment.

Answers: 1. Thomas & Chess **2.** Erikson **3.** Piaget **4.** Kohlberg **5.** Ainsworth.

SELF-QUIZ

1. Which prenatal period begins at the second week and ends at the second month of pregnancy?
   a. germinal stage
   b. embryonic stage
   c. fetal stage
   d. seminal stage

2. In which prenatal stage do most major birth defects probably have their origins?
   a. germinal stage
   b. embryonic stage
   c. fetal stage
   d. seminal stage

3. The cephalo-caudal trend is the tendency for infants to gain control of the:
   a. upper body before the lower body
   b. torso before the limbs
   c. brain before bowel
   d. mind before matter

4. Maturation refers to developmental changes that occur in an organism as a result of:
   a. centration and animism
   b. genetic factors
   c. environmental factors
   d. parental and peer pressures

5. What is the major conclusion from Thomas and Chess's longitudinal study of temperament?
   a. Children's temperaments tend to go through predictable stages.
   b. The temperament of the child is not a good predictor of the temperament of the adult.
   c. Opposites attract.
   d. Children's temperaments tend to be consistent over the years.

6. The crisis occurring in the first year, according to Erikson, is one involving:
   a. trust versus mistrust
   b. initiative versus guilt
   c. industry versus inferiority
   d. identity versus conformity

7. During which stage in Piaget's system is the child first able to handle conservation problems and hierarchical classification problems?
   a. sensorimotor
   b. preoperational
   c. concrete operations
   d. formal operations

8. A child in the early sensorimotor period is shown a ball, which she watches intensely. The ball is then hidden under a pillow. What will the child do?
   a. ask, "Where is the pillow?"
   b. stare at the pillow but not pick it up
   c. move the pillow and pick up the ball
   d. ignore the pillow, as if the ball didn't exist

9. Who developed a stage theory of moral development?
   a. Piaget
   b. Kohlberg
   c. Gould
   d. Bowlby

10. Which of the following cognitive capacities is most likely to decline as a function of aging?
    a. speed of processing
    b. crystallized intelligence
    c. problem-solving ability
    d. specialized intelligence

11. Suicide in the 15–23 age group (adolescents and young adults) occurs:
    a. more frequently than in all other age groups
    b. more frequently than in the 25-44 age groups
    c. more frequently than in the 65-73 age group
    d. at about the same rate as or less frequently than other age groups

12. Which of the following factors tends to be accompanied by a drop in ratings of marital satisfaction?
    a. childlessness during early married life
    b. the birth of the first child
    c. the first child's departure for college
    d. when the last child leaves home

13. Females tend to score slightly higher than males on tests of:
    a. verbal ability
    b. mathematical ability
    c. visual-spatial ability
    d. specialized ability

14. Females exposed to high levels of _____ during prenatal development tend to have masculine interests and preferences for male playmates.
    a. estrogen
    b. androgen
    c. lithium chloride
    d. insulin

15. Once children discover that their gender is permanent, they are likely to want to engage in behavior that is "sex appropriate" as defined by the culture. This process is referred to as:
    a. operant conditioning
    b. observational learning
    c. self-socialization
    d. classical conditioning

Answers: 1. b **2.** b **3.** a **4.** b **5.** d **6.** a **7.** c **8.** d **9.** b **10.** a **11.** d **12.** b **13.** a **14.** b **15.** c.

12 PERSONALITY: THEORY, RESEARCH, AND ASSESSMENT

REVIEW OF KEY IDEAS

THE NATURE OF PERSONALITY

1. Define the construct of personality in terms of consistency and distinctiveness.

1-1. I can always tell when my colleague across the hall has finished for the day because I hear squeaking as he carefully moves his computer table under his bookcase. And I know what follows: He closes and reshelves his books, sorts the papers on his desk into two piles, and slides the pens and pencils into his desk drawer bin. The fact that my colleague engages in the *same behaviors* almost every day illustrates the feature of personality termed _____.

1-2. When I'm done, on the other hand, I usually just stand up and walk out, leaving my somewhat (some would say very) messy desk behind. The fact that my colleague and I *differ* with respect to office neatness illustrates the feature of personality termed _____.

Answers: **1-1.** consistency (stability) **1-2.** distinctiveness (behavioral differences).

2. Explain what is meant by a personality trait and describe proposed systems for organizing traits.

2-1. A consistent or durable disposition to behave in particular way is referred to as a personality _____. Personality trait descriptions frequently consist of a series of _____, such as anxious, excitable, shy, aggressive, and so on.

2-2. There are an enormous number of trait words that could be used to describe people. For example, Gordon Allport came up with a system that included 4500 personality traits. Raymond Cattell reduced Allport's list to just _____ traits, and more recently McCrae and Costa have described yet a simpler model involving only _____ traits.

Answers: **2-1.** traits, adjectives **2-2.** 16, five.

3. **List and describe the three components into which Freud divided personality and his three levels of awareness.**

   3-1. Below is a schematic illustration of the three Freudian structures of personality. Label each.

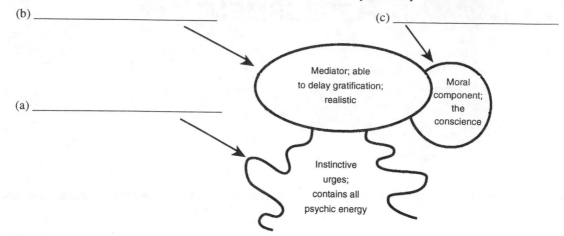

(b) _____

(c) _____

(a) _____

Mediator; able to delay gratification; realistic

Moral component; the conscience

Instinctive urges; contains all psychic energy

   3-2. Freud superimposed the levels of consciousness on the psychic structures. The following illustration makes clear that two of the structures exist at all three levels while one is entirely unconscious. Label the levels.

(a) _____

(b) _____

(c) _____

Answers: **3-1.** (a) id (b) ego (c) superego **3-2.** (a) conscious (b) preconscious (c) unconscious. (The diagram shows that the ego emerges from the id and that the superego grows out of the ego.)

4. **Explain the preeminence of sexual and aggressive conflicts in Freud's theory and describe the operation of defense mechanisms.**

   4-1. Freud believed that most of our conflicts arise from _____ and _____ urges. Conflicts relating to these areas were preeminent in his mind because (1) they are subject to subtle social _____ and, for that reason, are a source of confusion; and (2) they are more apt to be _____ than other urges.

4-2. Following is a list of the defense mechanisms. Match each with the correct description by placing the appropriate letters in the blanks.

A. rationalization   E. reaction formation

B. repression   F. regression

C. projection   G. identification

D. displacement

_____ A return to an earlier, less mature stage of development.

_____ Forming an imaginary or real alliance with a person or group; becoming like them.

_____ Creating false but reasonable-sounding excuses.

_____ Pushing distressing thoughts into the unconscious.

_____ Attributing ones own thoughts, feelings, or conflicts to another.

_____ Expressing an emotion that is the exact opposite of the way one really, but unconsciously, feels.

_____ Diverting emotional feelings from their original source to a substitute target.

4-3. Using the letters from the previous question, match the defense mechanisms with the following examples.

_____ After John and Marsha break up, John says he hates Marsha; this statement helps him defend against his real feelings of affection.

_____ "Society is filled with perverts," says the preacher; but later evidence suggests that he is the one with the sexual conflicts.

_____ In reaction to the stress of entering college, Alice started acting like a grade-school kid.

_____ Bruce acts like John Wayne, and he owns tapes of all the Duke's movies.

_____ Mary is angry at her mother, so she kicks her baby brother.

Answers: 4-1. sexual, aggressive, norms (rules, controls), frustrated (thwarted, unfulfilled) **4-2.** F, G, A, B, C, E, D
4-3. E, C, F, G, D.

5. Outline Freud's psychosexual stages of development and their theorized relations to adult personality.

5-1. List Freud's stages of psychosexual development, in the order in which they are supposed to occur, in the blanks below. Place the approximate ages (Table 12.3) in the parentheses.

(a) _____ (　　　　)

(b) _____ (　　　　)

(c) _____ (　　　　)

(d) _____ (　　　　)

(e) _____ (　　　　)

5-2. The following behaviors or personality characteristics were thought to result from fixation at a particular psychosexual stage. Place the names of the correct stages in the blanks.

(a) She has problems with anger control, is hostile toward people in authority, and defies any attempt at regulation of her behavior. _____

(b) He eats too much, drinks too much, and smokes. _____

(c) He has occasional outbursts of hostility toward his father that he can't understand. In family arguments he sides with his mother. _____

5-3. The Oedipus complex occurs during the _____ stage, at about age four or five. This complex theoretically involves an erotically tinged attraction toward the (same-sex/opposite-sex) parent and a strong hostility toward the (same-sex/opposite-sex) parent. Resolution of the Oedipus complex involves (increasing/ stopping) both the child's erotic attraction and the child's hostility.

Answers: 5-1. (a) oral (0-1) (b) anal (2-3) (c) phallic (4-5) (d) latency (6-12) (e) genital (puberty on) **5-2.** (a) anal (b) oral (c) phallic **5-3.** phallic, opposite-sex, same-sex, stopping.

6. Summarize the revisions of Freud's theory proposed by Jung and Adler.

6-1. Freud devised the theory and method of treatment termed *psychoanalysis*. To differentiate his approach from Freud's, Jung called his theory _____ _____. Like Freud, Jung emphasized the unconscious determinants of personality. Unlike Freud, he proposed that the unconscious consists of two layers, a _____ unconscious and a _____ unconscious. The personal unconscious is similar to Freud's unconscious. The collective unconscious is a repository of inherited, ancestral memories that Jung termed _____.

6-2. Jung's major contribution to psychology is considered by many to be his description of two major personality types: _____, reserved, contemplative people who tend to be concerned with their own internal world of thoughts; and _____, outgoing people who are more interested in the external world of others.

6-3. For Freud, the driving energy behind the human personality was sexuality; for Jung it may have been the collective unconscious. For Adler, it was striving for _____ and the attempt to overcome childhood feelings of inferiority. Efforts to overcome imagined or real inferiorities involve _____ through development of one's abilities. While Adler considered compensation to be a normal mechanism, he saw _____ as an abnormal attempt to conceal feelings of inferiority.

6-4. Adler is associated with the term _____ _____, an exaggerated feeling of inadequacy supposedly caused by parental pampering or neglect in early childhood. To a greater extent than either Freud or Jung, Adler emphasized the effects of the social context on personality development. For example, he thought that _____ _____ (that is, whether one is an only child, first-born, second-born, etc.) had a major effect on personality. Although the concept created considerable interest, birth order has turned out to be a (weaker/ stronger) and (more/less) consistent factor than he had supposed.

Answers: 6-1. analytical psychology, personal, collective, archetypes **6-2.** introverts, extraverts **6-3.** superiority, compensation, overcompensation **6-4.** inferiority complex, birth order, weaker, less.

7. Summarize the strengths and weaknesses of the psychodynamic approach to personality.

7-1. Psychoanalytic formulations have had a major impact on the field of psychology. List the three contributions discussed in your text.

7-2. Among the criticisms of the psychodynamic formulations are the three points listed in your text. First, psychodynamic concepts are frequently too _____ to permit a scientific test. Second, the scientific studies that have been done have provided _____ support for the psychodynamic theories. Third, the psychodynamic approaches generally provide a _____ point of view (for example, Freud's concept of penis envy).

Answers: 7-1. the discovery that *unconscious forces* can influence behavior, that *internal conflict* may generate psychological distress, and that *early childhood experiences* influence the adult personality **7-2.** vague (unclear), modest (weak, poor), male-centered (sexist).

BEHAVIORAL PERSPECTIVES

8. **Discuss how Skinner's principles of operant conditioning can be applied to the understanding of personality.**

   8-1. Which of the following processes plays an important part in Skinner's ideas about human behavior?
      a. mental conflict
      b. the mind
      c. free will
      d. none of the above

   8-2. According to Skinner, much of our behavior is affected by reinforcement, punishment, or extinction—in other words, by the environmental _____ that follow our behavior. For example, if some individuals behave in a consistently aggressive manner (i.e., have aggressive personality traits), they do so because they have been _____ for behaving aggressively in the past.

   8-3. Skinner recognized that there are differences between people and that people behave relatively consistent over time. This distinctiveness and consistency occur, however, not because of what's going on in an individual's *mind* but because of what has occurred previously in their _____.

   8-4. Thus, for Skinner, personality is not mental, but environmental. People do not change their minds, their environment changes. Skinner makes a strong case for the point of view that our behavior is caused or _____ rather than free and that the determinants are largely _____ rather than genetic.

   Answers: 8-1. d **8-2.** consequences (stimuli, events), reinforced **8-3.** environment **8-4.** determined, environmental.

9. **Describe Bandura's social-learning theory.**

   9-1. In what respect is Bandura's point of view similar to Skinner's?

   9-2. Bandura's major theoretical contribution is his concept of observational learning. What is observational learning?

   9-3. According to Bandura whom do we imitate, and under what circumstances?

9-4.   Explain Bandura's concept of self-efficacy.

Answers: 9-1. It is similar in that Bandura believes that personality is largely shaped through learning. **9-2.** Observational learning is the process through which we learn behaviors by observing someone else's (i.e., a model's) behavior. For example, we learn not only by being reinforced (Skinner) but by observing someone else being reinforced. **9-3.** We tend to imitate models whom we like, consider attractive or powerful, view as similar to ourselves, or see being reinforced. Children tend to imitate same-sex models. **9-4.** Self-efficacy is our belief in our ability to perform certain behaviors in order to obtain certain outcomes. Self-efficacy affects whether we undertake a task and how well we perform it.

10. **Identify Mischel's major contribution to personality theory and indicate why his ideas have generated so much controversy.**

   10-1.   Mischel's major contribution to personality theory is his contention that human behavior is determined to a

           much greater extent by the _____ than by _____.

   10-2.   Why is this such a controversial idea for personality theory?

Answers: 10-1. situation (situational factors), personality (personality traits) **10-2.** The notion is controversial because the very definition of personality involves the word *consistency*. Mischel's findings suggest that behavior is not as consistent as personality theorists may have thought, that it is strongly affected by an ever-changing situation.

11. **Summarize the strengths and weaknesses of the behavioral approach to personality.**

   11-1.   The major strengths of the behavioral approach have been its commitment to empirical

           _____, which keeps it open to new findings and ideas, and its identification of important

           _____ determinants of behavior.

   11-2.   The major weaknesses of the behavioral approach, according to its critics, have been its overdependence on

           research involving _____ subjects, its failure to integrate _____ factors

           into the theories, and its _____ view of personality.

Answers: 11-1. research, environmental (situational). **11-2.** animal, biological (genetic), fragmented.

HUMANISTIC PERSPECTIVES

12. **Explain how humanism was a reaction against both the behavioral and psychodynamic approaches and discuss the assumptions of the humanistic view.**

   12-1.   The humanistic movement reacted against (a) the behavioral approach, because of its mechanistic, fragmented

           view of personality and its emphasis on _____ research, and against (b) the psychoanalytic

           approach, because of its emphasis on _____ drives.

12-2. In addition, humanistic psychology objected to both movements because of their emphasis on

_____, or absolute causation. The humanists also thought that the behaviorists and the Freudians failed to recognize the (<u>unique/common</u>) qualities of human behavior.

12-3. Humanistic psychology emphasizes the (<u>similarities/differences</u>) between human beings and the other animal species; believes we (<u>are controlled by/can rise above</u>) our biological heritage; asserts that we are largely (<u>rational/irrational</u>) creatures; and stresses a (<u>subjective/objective</u>) approach that emphasizes people's impressions over the realities of the situation.

Answers: 12-1. animal, primitive (animalistic) **12-2.** determinism, unique **12-3.** differences, can rise above, rational, subjective.

13. Identify the single structural construct in Rogers's person-centered theory and summarize his view of personality development.

13-1. How would you describe yourself? What are your unique qualities? What is your typical behavior? What are you like? Your answers to these questions are likely to reflect what Rogers called the

_____.

13-2. Although Ralph tends to be a submissive and somewhat lazy person (and that is the way his friends, family, and co-workers describe him), he views himself as hard-working and dynamic, a leader both on the job and at home.

(a) What is Ralph's self-concept?

(b) Is his self-concept congruent or incongruent? _____

(c) According to Rogers, what parental behavior may have led to this incongruence? _____
_____

(d) According to Rogers, what parental behavior would have resulted in Ralph's achieving congruence rather than incongruence? _____ _____

13-3. Define the following Rogerian concepts.

(a) conditional love:

(b) unconditional love:

13-4. What is defensiveness for Rogers?

Answers: 13-1. The self or self-concept. **13-2.** (a) that he is hard-working, dynamic, and a leader (b) incongruent (c) conditional love or acceptance (d) unconditional love or acceptance **13-3.** (a) affection given conditionally, the condition being that the child or adult must live up to another's expectations (b) affection given without conditions, full acceptance of the person that is not dependent on what he or she is or does **13-4.** As with Freud, people defend against anxiety by distorting or denying reality. For Rogers, people's defensiveness arises when people defend their self-concepts against inconsistent experiences. Thus, defensiveness is related to incongruence.

14. Explain what Maslow meant by self-actualization and summarize his findings on self-actualizing people.

14-1. In a few words, what did Maslow mean by self-actualization?

14-2. Suppose a woman had the talent and ambition to be a mathematician but followed the urging of others and became a nurse instead. How would her behavior relate to self-actualization and mental health, according to Maslow?

14-3. Which of the following characteristics did Maslow ascribe to self-actualized people? Place Y in the blank if the description applies, N if it does not.

_____ Spontaneous

_____ Have more profound emotional experiences than others

_____ Uncomfortable being alone

_____ Not dependent on others for approval

_____ Enjoy strong friendships that are few in number

_____ Extreme in personality (e.g., either conforming or rebellious)

Answers: 14-1. the need to fulfill one's potential **14-2.** She would not be self-actualized, so she would not be as healthy as she could be **14-3.** Y, Y, N, Y, Y, N.

15. Summarize the strengths and weaknesses of the humanistic approach to personality.

15-1. Three contributions from humanistic psychology are discussed in the text. First, the humanistic movement called attention to _____ factors, such as beliefs and expectancies. Second, the movement emphasized the notion of the _____, one's view of oneself. Third, it stressed the issue of what constitutes a _____, as opposed to an abnormal, personality.

15-2. Critics have also identified several weaknesses of the humanistic formulations. Match the weaknesses listed below with the statements by placing the appropriate letters in the blanks.

A. poor testability

B. unrealistic view of human nature

C. inadequate evidence

_____ Humanistic psychologists tend to scorn research, so little experimental support for their views has emerged.

_____ Even without research, some of the descriptions, such as of self-actualized personalities, have an idealized, perfectionistic ring.

_____ Humanistic ideas are frequently difficult to define, so research on some concepts is difficult or impossible.

BIOLOGICAL PERSPECTIVES

16. Describe Eysenck's biological theory of personality.

16-1. According to Eysenck, individual differences in personality can be understood in terms of a hierarchy of traits. At the top of the hierarchy are three fundamental traits from which all other traits derive:

_____, _____, and _____.

16-2. Eysenck asserts that a major factor in personality involves the ease with which people can be

_____, either operantly or classically. Eysenck believes that differences in conditionability, like personality differences in general, are to a large extent a function of (<u>environmental/genetic</u>) factors.

16-3. Conditionability, in turn, is related to extraversion-introversion. Eysenck has indicated that (<u>extraverts/introverts</u>) have higher levels of physiological arousal, which make (<u>extraverts/introverts</u>) more readily conditioned.

16-4. Why would it be that people who are more easily conditioned tend to be introverts?

17. Summarize evidence on personality similarity in twins and other research on heritability of personality.

17-1. Which of the following groups were included in the Featured Study?
a. identical twins reared together
b. identical twins reared apart
c. fraternal twins reared together
d. fraternal twins reared apart
e. all of the above

17-2. The most important and conclusive result of this study was the finding that the personalities of ____ were more similar than those of _____.
a. identical twins reared together
b. identical twins reared apart
c. fraternal twins reared together
d. fraternal twins reared apart

17-3. Approximately what percentage of the variance in personality was assumed to be caused by genetic factors?
a. 5 to 10 percent
b. 10 to 22 percent
c. 40 to 58 percent
d. 70 to 76 percent

17-4. How important a determinant of personality was family environment, according to the results of this study?

a. of very little importance

b. of great importance, but not as important as heredity

c. more important than heredity

17-5. The recent twin studies are likely to have a major impact on the way psychologists think about the causes of human behavior. Why are the results so important and so surprising?

Answers: **17-1.** e **17-2.** b, c. This is the most important comparison because: even though the fraternal twins shared the same environment, their common environment did not make them nearly as similar as twins who did not have a common environment *but who shared the same heredity*. **17-3.** c **17-4.** a **17-5.** Theories of development and personality have tended to stress the importance of the environment, especially the family environment; the recent twin studies find heredity to be very important and family environment to be of little importance. Thus, the results are contrary to the expectations of most of us and of much of the theorizing in the field of personality.

18. Discuss the evolutionary analyses of personality.

18-1. For evolutionary theorists the biological basis of personality traits relates to their adaptive significance. Traits evolved that contributed to reproductive fitness of our human ancestors. While the evolutionary position is persuasive, these theorists have not yet confronted the issue, of critical importance for personality theory, of the origins of _____ differences.

Answer: **18-1.** individual.

19. Summarize the strengths and weaknesses of the biological approach to personality.

19-1. Generally, parents are blamed for kids' personalities. I recently asked a friend of mine why she thought a mutual acquaintance of ours was so obnoxious. She said, "Well, raised with such crazy parents, what would you expect?" I said, "Is that an argument for environment or heredity?" That is one of the benefits of the twin studies: They put data in place of speculation. But what are some of the weaknesses of this research? One is that heritability ratios should be regarded only as _____ that will vary depending on sampling procedures. Another is that there is no comprehensive biological _____ of personality.

Answers: **19-1.** estimates, theory.

CULTURE AND PERSONALITY

20. Summarize research on culture and personality.

20-1. For a decade or so after World War II, researchers using the Freudian model attempted to find a modal personality type representative of each culture. This attempt was (<u>successful/not successful</u>).

20-2. With the current increased attention to cultural factors, interest in the relationship between personality and culture has again surfaced, and the new data have revealed both cross-cultural similarities and differences. With regard to similarity, precisely the same "big _____ " personality factors tend to emerge in different cultures.

20-3. With regard to differences, research by Markus and Kitayama clearly indicates that the individualistic orientation characteristic of the West, for example, is not universal across cultures. Thus, while Americans tend to value (<u>independence/connectedness</u>), Asians value (<u>interdependence/uniqueness</u>) among people. While American parents encourage their children to (<u>stand out/blend in</u>), Asian parents emphasize taking pride in the accomplishments of (<u>each individual/the group</u>).

Answers: **20-1.** not successful **20-2.** five **20-3.** independence, interdependence, stand out, the group.

PUTTING IT IN PERSPECTIVE

21. Explain how this chapter highlighted three of the text's unifying themes.

21-1. We've just discussed one of the three themes emphasized in this chapter, that our behavior is influenced by our cultural heritage. Two other themes prominently demonstrated in the area of personality are that the field is theoretically _____ and that psychology evolves in a _____ context.

21-2. Freudian, behavioral, and biological perspectives of personality assume that behavior is determined; the _____ perspective does not. The biological perspective stresses genetic inheritance; the behavioral perspective stresses (<u>heredity/the environment</u>). As these examples illustrate, the study of personality has produced an enormous amount of theoretical _____.

21-3. Concerning sociohistorical context, it is clear that theories of personality have strongly affected our culture. For example, the surrealist art movement, begun in the 1920s, derives directly from _____ psychology, as do other movements in literature and the arts. And the current debate on the effects of media violence is to a large extent a product of research in social _____ theory.

21-4. In turn, culture has affected psychology. For example, it seems quite likely that the sexually repressive climate of Victorian Vienna caused Freud to emphasize the _____ aspects of human behavior; and it is clear, from Freud's own description, that World War I influenced his development of the second Freudian instinct, the _____ instinct. Thus, psychology evolves in a _____ context.

Answers: **21-1.** diverse, sociohistorical **21-2.** humanistic, the environment, diversity **21-3.** psychoanalytic (Freudian, psychodynamic), learning **21-4.** sexual, aggression, sociohistorical.

APPLICATION: UNDERSTANDING PERSONALITY ASSESSMENT

22. Outline the four principal uses of personality tests.

22-1. List the four principal uses of personality tests in the blanks next to the correct descriptions.

(a) Psychological _____: Measuring personality traits in empirical studies.

(b) _____: Advising people on career plans and decisions.

(c) _____ selection: Choosing employees in business and government.

(d) Clinical _____: Assessing psychological disorders.

Answers: **22-1.** (a) research (b) Counseling (c) Personnel (d) diagnosis.

23. Describe the self-report inventories and summarize their strengths and weaknesses.

23-1. The MMPI, 16PF, and NEO personality inventories are (projective/self-report) tests. All three tests are also used to measure (single/multiple) traits.

23-2. Identify which tests (MMPI, 16PF, or NEO) are described by each of the following.

(a) _____ Originally designed to diagnose psychological disorders.

(b) _____, _____ Originally designed to assess the normal personality.

(c) _____ Contains 187 items.

(d) _____ Contains 567 items.

(e) _____ Measures the "big five" personality traits.

(f) _____ Includes four validity scales to help detect deception.

23-3. The major strength of self-report inventories, in comparison with simply asking a person what they are like, is that they provide a more precise and more (objective/personal) measure of personality.

23-4. The major weakness of self-report inventories is that they are subject to several sources of error, including the following: (1) Test-takers may intentionally fake responses, that is, may engage in deliberate _____. (2) While not realizing it, people may answer questions in ways to make themselves "look good," the _____ _____ bias. (3) In addition, some people tend either to agree or to disagree with nearly every statement on a test, a source of error involving _____ sets.

Answers: 23-1. self-report, multiple **23-2.** (a) MMPI (b) 16PF, NEO (c) 16PF (d) MMPI (e) NEO (f) MMPI **23-3.** objective **23-4.** deception (lying), social desirability, response.

24. Describe the projective tests and summarize their strengths and weaknesses.

24-1. If you have ever looked at clouds and described the images you've seen, you've done something similar to taking a projective test. If you thought that the images you saw reflected something about your personality, then you also accepted the *projective hypothesis*. The projective hypothesis is the idea that people will tend to _____ their characteristics onto ambiguous stimuli, so that what they see reveals something about their personalities and problems.

24-2. Two major projective tests are the Rorschach, a series of _____, and the TAT, a series of simple _____.

24-3. The advantages of projective tests are that (1) since the way the tests are interpreted is not at all obvious, it is difficult for people to engage in intentional _____; and (2) projective tests may be sensitive to aspects of personality of which people are _____.

24-4. The major weaknesses of projective tests concerns inadequate evidence that they are _____ (consistent) or that they are _____ (measure what they are intended to measure). Nonetheless, the projective tests are valued by many clinicians and have been useful in some kinds of research.

Answers: 24-1. project **24-2.** inkblots, pictures (scenes) **24-3.** deception, unconscious (unaware) **24-4.** reliable, valid.

REVIEW OF KEY TERMS

Archetypes
Behaviorism
Collective unconscious
Compensation
Conscious
Defense mechanisms
Displacement
Ego
Extraverts
Fixation
Humanism
Id
Identification

Incongruence
Introverts
Model
Need for self-actualization
Observational learning
Oedipal complex
Personality
Personality trait
Pleasure principle
Preconscious
Projection
Projective tests
Psychodynamic theories

Psychosexual stages
Rationalization
Reaction formation
Reality principle
Regression
Repression
Self-actualizing persons
Self-concept
Self-efficacy
Self-report inventories
Striving for superiority
Superego
Unconscious

_____ 1. An individual's unique constellation of consistent behavioral traits.

_____ 2. A characteristic that represents a durable disposition to behave in a particular way in a variety of situations.

_____ 3. Instruments consisting of vague, ambiguous stimuli that people respond to in ways that may reveal people's needs, feelings, and personalities.

_____ 4. All the diverse theories, descended from the work of Sigmund Freud, that focus on unconscious mental forces.

_____ 5. The primitive, instinctive component of personality that operates according to the pleasure principle.

_____ 6. The id's demands for immediate gratification of its urges.

_____ 7. The decision-making component of personality that operates according to the reality principle.

_____ 8. The ego's delay of gratification of the id's urges until appropriate outlets and situations can be found.

_____ 9. The moral component of personality that incorporates social standards about what represents right and wrong.

_____ 10. Consists of whatever you are aware of at a particular point in time.

_____ 11. Contains material just beneath the surface of awareness that can be easily retrieved.

_____ 12. Contains thoughts, memories, and desires that are well below the surface of conscious awareness.

_____ 13. The series of largely unconscious Freudian reactions that protect a person from unpleasant emotions such as anxiety or guilt.

_____ 14. The defense mechanism that pushes distressing thoughts and feelings into the unconscious or keeps them from emerging into consciousness.

_____ 15. Attributing your own thoughts, feelings, or motives to another.

_____ 16. Creating false but plausible excuses to justify unacceptable behavior.

_____ 17. Diverting emotional feelings (usually anger) from their original source to a substitute target.

_____ 18. Behaving in a way that is exactly the opposite of one's true feelings.

_____ 19. Reverting to immature patterns of behavior.

_____ 20. Bolstering self-esteem by forming an imaginary or real alliance with some person or group.

_____ 21. Developmental periods with a characteristic sexual focus that leave their mark on adult personality.

_____ 22. A failure to move forward from one stage to another as expected.

_____ 23. Characterized by erotically tinged desires for one's opposite-sex parent and hostility toward one's same-sex parent.

_____ 24. A storehouse of latent memory traces inherited from our ancestral past.

_____ 25. Emotionally charged images and thought forms that have universal meaning.

_____ 26. People who tend to be preoccupied with the internal world of their own thoughts, feelings, and experiences.

_____ 27. People who tend to be interested in the external world of people and things.

_____ 28. A universal drive to adapt, to improve oneself, and to master life's challenges.

_____ 29. Efforts to overcome imagined or real inferiorities by developing one's abilities.

_____ 30. A theoretical orientation based on the premise that scientific psychology should study only observable behavior.

_____ 31. Learning that occurs when an organism's responding is influenced by the observation of others.

_____ 32. A person whose behavior is observed by another.

_____ 33. Our belief about our ability to perform behaviors that should lead to expected outcomes.

_____ 34. A theoretical orientation that emphasizes the unique qualities of humans, especially their freedom and potential for personal growth.

_____ 35. A collection of beliefs about one's own nature, unique qualities, and typical behavior.

_____ 36. The degree of disparity between one's self-concept and one's actual experience.

_____ 37. The need to fulfill one's potential.

_____ 38. People with exceptionally healthy personalities, marked by continued personal growth.

_____ 39. Personality tests that ask people a series of questions about their characteristic behavior.

Answers: 1. personality **2.** personality trait **3.** projective tests **4.** psychodynamic theories **5.** id **6.** pleasure principle **7.** ego **8.** reality principle **9.** superego **10.** conscious **11.** preconscious **12.** unconscious **13.** defense mechanisms **14.** repression **15.** projection **16.** rationalization **17.** displacement **18.** reaction formation **19.** regression **20.** identification **21.** psychosexual stages **22.** fixation **23.** Oedipal complex **24.** collective unconscious **25.** archetypes **26.** introverts **27.** extraverts **28.** striving for superiority **29.** compensation **30.** behaviorism **31.** observational learning **32.** model **33.** self-efficacy **34.** humanism **35.** self-concept **36.** incongruence **37.** need for self-actualization **38.** self-actualizing persons **39.** self-report inventories.

REVIEW OF KEY PEOPLE

Alfred Adler   Sigmund Freud   Walter Mischel
Albert Bandura   Carl Jung   Carl Rogers
Hans Eysenck   Abraham Maslow   B. F. Skinner

_____ 1. The founder of psychoanalysis.

_____ 2. Developed the theory called analytical psychology and anticipated the humanists' emphasis on personal growth and self-actualization.

_____ **3.** Founder of an approach to personality named individual psychology.

_____ **4.** Modern behaviorism's most prominent theorist, recognized for his theories on operant conditioning.

_____ **5.** A contemporary behavioral theorist who elaborated the concept of observational learning.

_____ **6.** His chief contribution to personality theory has been to focus attention on the extent to which situational factors govern behavior.

_____ **7.** One of the fathers of the human potential movement, he called his approach a person-centered theory.

_____ **8.** The humanist who developed a theory of self-actualization.

_____ **9.** Proposed that conditionability and introversion-extraversion are largely genetically determined.

Answers: 1. Freud **2.** Jung **3.** Adler **4.** Skinner **5.** Bandura **6.** Mischel **7.** Rogers **8.** Maslow **9.** Eysenck.

SELF-QUIZ

1. Personality traits are characterized by:
   a. consistency and distinctiveness
   b. charm and wit
   c. change as a function of the situation
   d. lack of individual differences

2. Someone attributes his thoughts or feelings or conflicts to someone else. For example, although he chronically interrupts people, he thinks that other people interrupt him. What Freudian defense mechanism is illustrated?
   a. rationalization
   b. reaction formation
   c. regression
   d. projection

3. Which of the following is entirely unconscious, according to Freud?
   a. the id
   b. the ego
   c. the superego
   d. the archetype

4. Although Osmo at an unconscious level has great hatred for Cosmo, he believes that he likes Cosmo and, to the outside world, gives all the appearance of liking him. Which defense mechanism is Osmo using?
   a. regression
   b. reaction formation
   c. projection
   d. rationalization

5. The Oedipal complex occurs during the:
   a. oral stage
   b. anal stage
   c. phallic stage
   d. genital stage

6. Which of the following concepts did Carl Jung originate?
   a. id
   b. superego
   c. inferiority complex
   d. introversion-extraversion

7. Which of the following did Adler emphasize in his theory of personality?
   a. striving for superiority
   b. castration anxiety
   c. introversion-extraversion
   d. the collective unconscious

8. Much of the behavior that we call personality results from reinforcement and observational learning, according to:
   a. Jung
   b. Skinner
   c. Bandura
   d. Adler

9. Which of the following tends to emphasize freedom and personal growth in its view of human behavior?
   a. the psychoanalytic approach
   b. the biological approach
   c. the behavioral approach
   d. the humanistic approach

10. According to Rogers, what causes incongruence?
    a. an inherited sense of irony
    b. conditional acceptance or affection
    c. unconditional acceptance or affection
    d. unconditioned stimuli

11. Herb had the desire and potential to be a violinist but became, instead, a trader in hog futures. He decided never to touch the violin again. What is wrong with Herb, according to Maslow?
    a. He suffers from incongruence.
    b. He suffers from castration anxiety.
    c. He has not achieved self-actualization.
    d. He has an inferiority complex.

12. Which of the following views personality in terms of the adaptive significance to the Big Five traits?
    a. Abraham Maslow
    b. William James
    c. the behavioral approach
    d. the evolutionary approach

13. Recent studies of the personalities of identical and fraternal twins are surprising and important because they indicate that:
    a. personality is to some degree genetically determined
    b. environment is more important than heredity
    c. birth order is critical in personality formation
    d. monads and archetypes can be accounted for genetically

14. According to Mischel, what is the major factor that predicts human behavior?
    a. childhood experience
    b. specifics of the situation
    c. extraversion and introversion
    d. central and peripheral traits

15. You are asked to tell stories about a series of pictures. Which test is being administered to you?
    a. Rorschach
    b. MMPI
    c. TAT
    d. 16PF

Answers: 1. a **2.** d **3.** a **4.** b **5.** c **6.** d **7.** a **8.** c **9.** d **10.** b **11.** c **12.** d **13.** a **14.** b **15.** c.

13 Stress, Coping, and Health

THE NATURE OF STRESS

1. **Define stress and discuss the relationship between the severity of stress and its effects.**

   1-1. The text defines stress as any circumstances that threaten or are perceived to threaten one's well-being. This definition would indicate that stress is a very (<u>subjective</u>/objective) experience. Or to put it another way, stress lies in the mind of the _____.

   1-2. What effect did Lazarus find with respect to minor everyday hassles and mental and physical health?

   Answers: 1-1. subjective, beholder **1-2.** They can have significant harmful effects.

2. **Describe the key process and factors in our appraisal of stress.**

   2-1. When you appraise an event as either irrelevant, relevant but not threatening, or stressful, you are making a _____ appraisal.

   2-2. When you appraise an event as stressful and then you evaluate your coping resources and options, you are making a _____ appraisal.

   2-3. While a variety of factors influence stress evaluation, two are particularly important. Identify them in the situations described below.

      (a) A salesperson friend of mine is a frequent flyer, yet she still finds flying is stressful and can quickly tell you why this is so. What do you think she says?

(b) Why are natural disasters such as earthquakes and tornadoes particularly stressful?

Answers: **2-1.** primary **2-2.** secondary **2-3.** (a) She feels a lack of personal control when she flys. (b) Because they are unpredictable.

3. **Describe the four principal types of stress discussed in the text.**

    3-1.   The text lists four principal types of stress: frustration, conflict, change, and pressure. Identify these types of stress in the following situations.

        (a) You have three major exams coming up next week and you are also in charge of your sorority's fast-approaching homecoming celebration.

        (b) You leave your small home town and go off to a large city to enroll in a university.

        (c) You are late for an appointment and stuck in a traffic jam.

        (d) You are forced to choose between two good movies on television.

    3-2.   There are two kinds of pressure. One is the pressure to get things accomplished, or the pressure to _____. The other is the pressure to abide by rules, or the pressure to _____.

Answers: **3-1.** (a) pressure (b) change (c) frustration (d) conflict **3-2.** perform, conform.

4. **Identify the three basic types of conflict and discuss which types are most troublesome.**

    4-1.   Many persons do not want to pay their income taxes, but on the other hand they don't want to go to jail either. These persons are faced with an _____-_____ conflict.

    4-2.   Getting married has both positive and negative aspects that make it an excellent example of an _____-_____ conflict.

    4-3.   Consider the problem of the student who has to choose between scholarships for two different universities. Since she can't accept both she is faced with an _____-_____ conflict.

4-4. Now that you have identified the three basic types of conflict, list them below in their order of troublesomeness, beginning with the least troublesome.

(a) _____

(b) _____

(c) _____

Answers: 4-1. avoidance-avoidance **4-2.** approach-avoidance **4-3.** approach-approach **4-4.** (a) approach-approach (b) approach-avoidance (c) avoidance-avoidance.

5. Summarize evidence on life change as a form of stress.

5-1. The Social Readjustment Rating Scale (SRRS), measures the stress induced by _____ in daily living routines. The developers of this scale theorized that all kinds of life changes, both pleasant and unpleasant, would induce stress. Early research showed that high scores on the SRRS were correlated with physical _____ .

5-2. Later research began to indicate that high scores on the SRRS were primarily the result of (pleasant/ unpleasant) life changes. Other independent research has found that change by itself can induce stress, but the greatest stress appears to be induced by _____ life changes.

Answers: 5-1. changes, illness **5-2.** unpleasant, unpleasant.

RESPONDING TO STRESS

6. Identify some common emotional responses to stress and discuss the effects of emotional arousal.

6-1. The text describes three different dimensions of emotions that are particularly likely to be triggered by stress. Identify which of these dimensions is most likely to be present in the following situations.

(a) The emotions in this dimension are likely to be found as a person begins to feel more and more helpless and unable to cope with routine or profound setbacks.

(b) The emotions in this dimension are likely to be found as a person begins to feel increasingly frustrated, put upon, and treated unfairly.

(c) The emotions in this dimension are likely to be found as a person faces increasing degrees of conflict, pressure, and uncertainty.

6-2. According to optimal-arousal theories, what happens to the optimal arousal level as tasks become more complex?

Answers: 6-1. (a) dejection, sadness, and grief (b) annoyance, anger, and rage (c) apprehension, anxiety, and fear
6-2. The optimal arousal level decreases.

7. **Describe the three stages of the general adaptation syndrome.**

   7-1. Indicate which of the three stages of the General Adaptation Syndrome is being described in each of the following.

   (a) This is the initial stage in which the body prepares for the fight-or-flight response.

   (b) This is the second stage in which the body stabilizes its physiological changes as it begins to effectively cope with the stress.

   (c) This is the third stage in which the body's coping resources are becoming depleted and the resistance to many diseases declines.

   Answers: 7-1. (a) stage of alarm (b) stage of resistance (c) stage of exhaustion.

8. **Discuss the two major pathways along which the brain sends signals to the endocrine system in response to stress.**

   8-1. Fill in the missing parts in the diagram below detailing the two major pathways along which the brain sends signals to the endocrine system.

   CEREBRAL CORTEX

   (a) _____

   SYMPATHETIC NS   PITUITARY GLAND

                                               ACTH

   (b) _____ (GLAND)   (c) _____ (GLAND)

   CATECHOLAMINES   CORTICOSTEROIDS
   Increases heart rate &   Increases energy, inhibits
   respiration, etc.   tissue inflamation, etc.

   8-2. Which one of these two categories of hormones (catecholamines or corticosteroids) is involved in the fight-or flight response?

   Answers: 8-1. (a) hypothalamus (b) adrenal medulla (c) adrenal cortex **8-2.** catecholamines.

9. **Describe and evaluate aggression, giving up, and self-indulgence as behavioral responses to stress.**

   9-1. Answer the following questions regarding aggression, giving up, and self-indulgence as responses to stress.

   (a) Which of these responses is frequently, but not always, triggered by frustration?

(b) Which of these responses often results from a cognitive appraisal that one lacks control over problems?

(c) Which of these responses is illustrated by the saying, "When the going gets tough, the tough go shopping"?

Answers: 9-1. (a) aggression (b) giving up (c) self-indulgence.

10. Discuss defensive coping and constructive coping as mechanisms for dealing with stress.

10-1. Indicate whether each of the following situations illustrates defensive or constructive coping.

(a) This kind of coping is much more oriented to reality. _____

(b) This kind of coping is largely unconscious, although it can occur at conscious levels. _____

(c) This kind of coping uses self-deception to distort reality. _____

(d) This kind of coping is much more task-relevant and action oriented. _____

(e) This kind of coping avoids the problem and delays a possible solution. _____

10-2. What might be a useful defensive coping technique when faced with a temporary period of frustration that you can do little about?

Answers: 10-1. (a) constructive (b) defensive (c) defensive (d) constructive (e) defensive 10-2. Engage in creative fantasy.

THE EFFECTS OF STRESS ON PHYSICAL HEALTH

11. Describe the Type A behavior pattern and summarize the evidence linking it to coronary heart disease.

11-1. Tell whether the following characteristics are found in Type A or Type B persons.

____ (a) easygoing   ____ (d) patient

____ (b) competitive   ____ (e) argumentative

____ (c) quick to anger

11-2. Early research indicated that Type A persons were _____ times more likely to suffer from coronary heart disease than were Type B persons. Continuing research has since shown that the coronary risk is more (severe/moderate) than originally thought. It now appears that Type A persons are approximately _____ as likely to suffer from coronary heart disease compared to Type B persons.

Answers: 11-1. (a) Type B (b) Type A (c) Type A (d) Type B (e) Type A 11-2. six, moderate, twice.

12. **Discuss evidence linking stress to immunosuppression and a variety of physical illnesses.**

12-1. Research has found stress to be related to numerous diseases and disorders. What effect on the lymphocytes (the specialized white blood cells that are important in initiating the immune response) appears to be the link between stress and so many disorders?

12-2. While many studies have shown a relationship between stress and numerous physical illness, we can still not state definitely that stress leads to physical illnesses. Why is this?

Answers: **12-1.** Stress appears to suppress the proliferation of the lymphocytes (thus suppressing the immune system in general) **12-2.** Because almost all of the data are correlational (and you cannot infer cause and effect relationships from these kinds of data).

13. **Discuss how social support, optimism, and conscientiousness moderate individual differences in stress tolerance.**

13-1. What physical effect was found with students who had high social support during the stress of final exams?

13-2. What difference was found between optimists and pessimists with respect to physical health?

13-3. What trait was found to predict longevity in a long-term study that followed gifted children throughout most of their life span?

Answers: **13-1.** They had improved immunal functioning **13-2.** Optimists were more likely to enjoy good physical health **13-3.** conscientiousness.

HEALTH-IMPAIRING LIFESTYLES

14. **Discuss the negative impact of smoking, poor nutrition, and lack of exercise on physical health.**

14-1. Answer the following questions regarding the negative impact of smoking on physical health.

(a) How many fewer years can a 30-year-old smoker expect to live than a 30-year-old nonsmoker?

(b) What are the two most frequent diseases that kill smokers?

(c) What does evidence suggest to smokers who have tried and failed to stop smoking?

14-2. Answer the following true-false questions regarding the effects of poor nutrition and lack of exercise.

(a) The nutritional patterns in the United States are better than in most nations.

(b) Lack of regular physical exercise may increase chances of obesity.

(c) Physical fitness is associated with reduced risk of coronary disease and hypertension.

Answers: 14-1. (a) 8 years (b) lung cancer and heart disease (c) They should keep on trying to stop **14-2.** (a) false (b) true (c) true.

15. Discuss the relationship between behavioral factors and AIDS.

15-1. How is AIDS transmitted from one person to another?

15-2. What are the two principal behaviors that may lead to HIV infection?

15-3. Why can you not be sure that someone who shows no symptoms of AIDS does not have HIV infection?

Answers: 15-1. Through bodily fluids (particularly blood and semen) **15-2.** Sexual contact and the sharing of needles **15-3.** The symptoms may take years to develop after the initial HIV infection.

REACTIONS TO ILLNESS

16. Discuss individual differences in willingness to seek medical treatment and to comply with medical advice.

16-1. Indicate whether the following statements regarding individual differences in willingness to seek medical treatment are true or false.

(a) Delay in seeking treatment is perhaps the biggest problem here.

(b) The perception of pain and illness is highly subjective.

(c) Some persons seek treatment because they actually like the "sick role."

16-2. The text lists three reasons for failure to comply with medical advice. One is that patients often fail to completely _____ treatment instructions. A second is that the treatment may prove to be quite _____. The third reason is not directly related to either instructions or treatment, but rather to the attitude toward the _____. A negative attitude makes compliance (<u>more/less</u>) likely.

16-3. What appears to be of critical importance in increasing compliance with medical advice?

Answers: 16-1. (a) true (b) true (c) true **16-2.** understand, unpleasant (or aversive), physician or doctor, less **16-3.** The communication process between doctor and patient.

PUTTING IT IN PERSPECTIVE

17. Explain how this chapter highlighted two of the text's unifying themes (multifactoral causation and the subjectivity of experience).

    17-1. The fact that the amount of stress in any given situation primarily lies in the eyes of the beholder nicely illustrates the theme that experience is _____.

    17-2. The fact that stress interacts with numerous other factors that affect health illustrates the theme of _____ _____.

Answers: 17-1. subjective **17-2.** multifactoral causation.

APPLICATION: IMPROVING COPING AND STRESS MANAGEMENT

18. Summarize Albert Ellis's ideas about controlling one's emotions.

    18-1. The main idea behind Albert Ellis's rational-emotive therapy is that stress is largely caused by _____ thinking. Therefore, by changing one's catastrophic thinking and taking a more rational approach one can then reduce _____.

    18-2. Ellis illustrates this theory by postulating an A-B-C series of events. Describe below what is going on during each of these events.

    (A) activating event:

    (B) belief:

    (C) consequence:

18-3. Since the emotional turmoil in the A-B-C sequence is caused by the _____ sequence, effort must be directed towards changing irrational beliefs. Ellis proposes two techniques for doing this. One must first learn to _____ instances of irrational beliefs. Then one must learn to actively _____ these irrational beliefs.

Answers: 18-1. catastrophic, stress **18-2.** (A) The activating event that initiates the stress. (B) The belief about the event (C) The emotional consequences that result from the belief **18-3.** B, detect, dispute.

19. Discuss the adaptive value of humor and releasing pent-up emotions.

19-1. What dual role does humor play in easing stress in difficult situations?

19-2. Why might talking or writing about a problem with a sympathetic friend prove useful when experiencing stress?

Answers: 19-1. It allows for both redefining the problem in a less threatening way and the releasing of tension **19-2.** It may help to release pent-up tension.

20. Discuss the adaptive value of relaxation and exercise.

20-1. Complete the following statements regarding the adaptive value of relaxation and exercise.

(a) A quiet environment, a mental device, a passive attitude, and a confortable position are conditions that facilitate _____.

(b) Along with humor, releasing pent-up emotions, and relaxation, a regular exercise program may help to minimize physical _____.

Answers: 20-1. (a) relaxation (b) vulnerability.

REVIEW OF KEY TERMS

Acquired immune deficiency syndrome (AIDS)
Aggression
Approach-approach conflict
Approach-avoidance conflict
Avoidance-avoidance conflict
Biopsychosocial model
Catastrophic thinking
Conflict

Constructive coping
Coping
Defense mechanisms
Frustration
General adaptation syndrome
Health psychology
Immune response
Learned helplessness

Life changes
Optimism
Pressure
Rational-emotive therapy
Social support
Stress
Type A personality
Type B personality

_____ 1. Holds that physical illness is caused by a complex interaction of biological, psychological, and sociocultural factors.

_____ 2. Concerned with how psychosocial forces relate to the promotion and maintenance of health, and the causation, prevention, and treatment of illness.

_____ 3. Any circumstances that threaten or are perceived to threaten our well-being and thereby tax our coping abilities.

_____	4. Occurs in any situation in which the pursuit of some goal is thwarted.
_____	5. Occurs when two or more incompatible motivations or behavioral impulses compete for expression.
_____	6. Occurs when a choice must be made between two attractive goals.
_____	7. Occurs when a choice must be made between two unattractive goals.
_____	8. Occurs when a choice must be made whether to pursue a single goal that has both attractive and unattractive aspects.
_____	9. Any noticeable alterations in one's living circumstances that require readjustment.
_____	10. Expectations or demands that one behave in a certain way.
_____	11. A model of the body's stress response consisting of three stages: alarm, resistance, and exhaustion.
_____	12. An active effort to master, reduce, or tolerate the demands created by stress.
_____	13. Involves any behavior that is intended to hurt someone, either physically or verbally.
_____	14. Passive behavior produced by exposure to unavoidable aversive events.
_____	15. Largely unconscious reactions that protect a person from unpleasant emotions such as anxiety and guilt.
_____	16. Relatively healthy efforts to deal with stressful events.
_____	17. A behavior pattern marked by competitive, aggressive, impatient, hostile behavior.
_____	18. A behavior pattern marked by relaxed, patient, easy-going, amicable behavior.
_____	19. The body's defensive reaction to invasion by bacteria, viral agents, or other foreign substances.
_____	20. Various types of aid and succor provided by members of one's social network.
_____	21. A general tendency to expect good outcomes.
_____	22. An approach to therapy that focuses on altering clients' patterns of irrational thinking to reduce maladaptive emotions and behavior.
_____	23. Unrealistic and pessimistic appraisal of stress that exaggerates the magnitude of a problem.
_____	24. A disorder in which the immune system is gradually weakened and eventually disabled by the human immunodeficiency virus (HIV).

Answers: 1. biopsychosocial model **2.** health psychology **3.** stress **4.** frustration **5.** conflict **6.** approach-approach conflict **7.** avoidance-avoidance conflict **8.** approach-avoidance conflict **9.** life changes **10.** pressure **11.** general adaptation syndrome **12.** coping **13.** aggression **14.** learned helplessness **15.** defense mechanisms **16.** constructive coping **17.** Type A personality **18.** Type B personality **19.** immune response **20.** social support **21.** optimism **22.** rational-emotive therapy **23.** catastrophic thinking **24.** acquired immune deficiency syndrome (AIDS).

REVIEW OF KEY PEOPLE

Robin DiMatteo	Thomas Holmes & Richard Rahe	Hans Selye
Albert Ellis	Richard Lazarus	Shelley Taylor
Meyer Friedman & Ray Rosenman		

_____ 1. Observed that minor hassles were more closely related to mental health than were major stressful events.

_____ 2. These researchers developed the Social Readjustment Rating Scale.

_____ 3. Coined the word "stress" and described the General Adaptation Syndrome.

_____ 4. These researchers found a connection between coronary risk and what they called Type A behavior.

_____ 5. Showed several lines of evidence indicating that illusions may sometimes be adaptive for mental and physical health.

_____ 6. The developer of Rational-Emotive Therapy.

_____ 7. A leading expert on medical patient behavior.

Answers: 1. Lazarus **2.** Holmes & Rahe **3.** Selye **4.** Friedman & Rosenman **5.** Taylor **6.** Ellis **7.** DiMatteo.

SELF-QUIZ

1. Which of the following statements is correct?
   a. Stress is a subjective experience.
   b. Minor hassles can be as stressful as major ones.
   c. One should not seek to avoid all stress.
   d. All of the above.

2. You've been invited to dinner at a nice restaurant on the final night of a TV mini series you've been watching and thus find yourself confronted with:
   a. pressure
   b. frustration
   c. an approach-avoidance conflict
   d. an approach-approach conflict

3. The week of final exams subjects most students to what kind of stress?
   a. pressure
   b. change
   c. frustration
   d. conflict

4. High scores on the Social Readjustment Rating Scale were found to be correlated with:
   a. psychiatric disorders
   b. physical illness
   c. pessimistic attitudes
   d. Type A personality

5. According to optimal-arousal theories, which of the following situations would be least affected by a high optimal-arousal level?
   a. taking a psychology exam
   b. looking up a word in a dictionary
   c. buttoning a shirt
   d. explaining to your parents why you need more money

6. The General Adaptation Syndrome shows that the body eventually successfully adapts to long-term stress. This statement is:
   a. true
   b. false

7. Which of the following organs is involved in both of the body's two major stress pathways?
   a. the adrenal gland
   b. the sympathetic nervous system
   c. the pituitary gland
   d. the pineal gland

8. Aggression is frequently triggered by:
   a. helplessness
   b. frustration
   c. loneliness
   d. change

9. Which of the following characteristics is/are likely to be found with defensive coping?
   a. self-deception
   b. both conscious and unconscious awareness
   c. delay of a possible solution
   d. all of the above

10. One of the key links between stress and physical illness may be that the body's response to stress:
    a. increases the optimal-arousal level
    b. suppresses the immune system
    c. decreases the optimal-arousal level
    d. suppresses the adrenal gland

11. Smoking is to lung cancer as Type A behavior is to:
    a. coronary disease
    b. AIDS
    c. defensive coping
    d. mental disorders

12. A major idea behind Rational-Emotive Therapy is that stress is caused by:
    a. conflict
    b. frustration
    c. catastrophic thinking
    d. pressure

13. Social support and optimism are related to:
    a. the Type B personality pattern
    b. a low level of stress
    c. defensive-coping strategies
    d. good physical health

14. The best way to deal with stress is to:
    a. avoid it as much as possible
    b. learn defensive coping strategies
    c. learn constructive coping strategies
    d. avoid it as much as possible and learn defensive coping strategies

15. In comparison to Type B persons, Type A persons are more likely to be prone to:
    a. lung cancer
    b. arthritis
    c. coronary heart disorder
    d. vote Republican

Answers: 1. d **2.** d **3.** a **4.** b **5.** c **6.** b **7.** a **8.** b **9.** d **10.** b **11.** a **12.** c **13.** d **14.** c **15.** c.

14 PSYCHOLOGICAL DISORDERS

REVIEW OF KEY IDEAS

ABNORMAL BEHAVIOR: MYTHS, REALITIES, AND CONTROVERSIES

1. Describe and evaluate the medical model of abnormal behavior.

1-1. A model is a metaphor or theory that is useful in describing some phenomenon. For example, the computer is frequently used as a model of thinking. The *medical model* uses physical illness as a model of psychological disorders. Under the medical model, maladaptive behavior is referred to as mental _____.

1-2. The term "mental illness" is so familiar to all of us that we rarely think about the meaning of the concept and whether or not the analogy with disease is a good one. Among the model's detractors, Thomas Szasz asserts that words such as *sickness*, *illness*, and *disease* are correctly used only in reference to the _____, and that it is more appropriate to view abnormal behavior as a deviation from accepted social _____ than as an illness.

1-3. Other critics object to the disease model because they believe that the derogatory _____ inherent in medical diagnosis tends to carry a strong social stigma. People tend to be _____ against those who are labeled mentally ill.

1-4. Some critics also suggest that the medical model encourages sufferers to adopt the _____ role of patient, waiting for the doctor to produce a cure, rather than a more active role as problem solver.

1-5. The text takes an intermediate position: while there certainly are problems with the medical model it can be useful as long as one understands that it is just an _____ and not a true explanation. (For example, the medical concepts of diagnosis, etiology, and prognosis have proven useful in treatment and study of psychological disorders.)

Answers: 1-1. illness (disease, sickness) **1-2.** body, norms (behavior, standards) **1-3.** stigma, prejudiced (biased) **1-4.** passive **1-5.** analogy (model).

2. Explain the most commonly used criteria of abnormality.

2-1. What does abnormal mean? The three most commonly used criteria are deviance, maladaptive behavior, and personal distress. List the three criteria next to the descriptions below.

(a) _____: Does not conform to cultural norms or standards.

(b) _____: Behavior that interferes with the individual's social or occupational functioning.

(c) _____: Intense discomfort produced by depression or anxiety.

2-2. Following are three statements that describe a person with a particular type of disorder. Which criterion of abnormal behavior is illustrated by each statement? Place the letters from the list above in the appropriate blanks.

_____ Ralph washes his hands several dozen times a day. His handwashing interferes with his work and prevents him from establishing normal friendships.

_____ Even if Ralph's handwashing compulsion did not interfere with his work and social life, his behavior still would be considered strange. That is, most people do not do what he does.

_____ It is also the case that Ralph's skin is very raw, and he becomes extremely anxious when he does not have immediate access to a sink.

2-3. In some cultures, hearing voices or speaking with gods may be valued. In our culture, however, such behavior is likely to be considered abnormal. Thus, our judgments of abnormality are strongly influenced by our

_____. One of the problems involved in defining abnormality, then, is that there are no

_____-free criteria for psychological disorders.

2-4. Another complexity is that we all have *some* behaviors that interfere with our lives, that cause us discomfort, and that others may consider strange. Thus, the difference between normal and abnormal is not black and

white but exists along a _____.

2-5. In an interesting and controversial study, David Rosenhan arranged for "pseudopatients" to seek admission to

mental hospitals. They complained of one symptom, that they heard voices. While all of these individuals were

actually normal, _____ (what proportion?) were admitted to the facilities as mental

patients. The average length of stay was 19 days.

2-6. The major implication of this study is that it is (difficult/easy), even for mental health professionals, to discriminate between normality and abnormality.

Answers: **2-1.** (a) deviance, (b) maladaptive behavior, (c) personal distress **2-2.** b, a, c **2-3.** culture (values, society), value (culture) **2-4.** continuum **2-5.** all **2-6.** difficult.

3. List the five diagnostic axes of DSM-IV and discuss some of the controversial aspects of this classification system.

3-1. Below are descriptions of the five axes of the DSM-IV classification system. Label each with the correct axis number (I through V).

_____ Listing of physical disorders

_____ Diagnosis of personality or developmental disorders

_____ Diagnosis of the major disorders

_____ Estimates of the individual's current level of adaptive functioning

_____ Notes concerning the severity of stress experienced by the individual in the past year

3-2.   Before publication of the third edition of the DSM, different clinicians observing the same patient would frequently arrive at different, and incompatible, diagnoses. By making the descriptions of the disorder much more concrete and detailed, the DSM-III and DSM-IV brought a much-needed _____ to psychodiagnosis.

3-3.   The new DSM system has produced praise but some criticism as well. First, while consistency in diagnosis is a critically important step, it is important only to the extent that the diagnostic categories describe real conditions. Some critics have argued that consistency came at the price of sacrificing the _____ of the diagnostic category descriptions.

3-4.   Second, the recent DSMs include everyday problems that are not traditionally thought of as mental illnesses (such as nicotine-dependence disorder and gambling disorder). Although it may seem odd to include these in the DSM, what is the advantage of doing so?

Answers: 3-1. III, II, I, V, IV **3-2.** consistency (reliability, agreement) **3-3.** validity (accuracy) **3-4.** Since many health insurance policies reimburse only for treatment of disorders listed in the DSM, including these "everyday" problems may permit people to bill their insurance companies for treatment.

ANXIETY DISORDERS

4.   List four types of anxiety disorders and describe the symptoms associated with each.

4-1.   List the names of the four anxiety syndromes in the space below. As hints, the initial letters of some key words are listed at the left.

GAD: _____

PhD: _____

OCD: _____

PaA: _____ and _____

4-2.   Match the anxiety disorders with the symptoms that follow by placing the appropriate letters (from the previous question) in the blanks.

(a) _____   Sudden, unexpected, and paralyzing attacks of anxiety

(b) _____   Not tied to a specific object or event

(c) _____   Senseless, repetitive rituals

(d) _____   Brooding over decisions

(e) _____   Fear of specific objects or situations

(f) _____   Persistent intrusion of distressing and unwanted thoughts

(g) _____   Free-floating anxiety

(h) _____   Frequently includes fear of going out in public

Answers: 4-1. generalized anxiety disorder, phobic disorder, obsessive-compulsive disorder, panic disorder and agoraphobia **4-2.** (a) PaA (in this example, panic attacks) (b) GAD (c) OCD (d) GAD (e) PhD (f) OCD (g) GAD (h) PaA (in this case, agoraphobia).

5. **Discuss the contribution of biological, cognitive, personality, conditioning, and stress factors to the etiology of anxiety disorders.**

5-1. Recent research suggests that there are inherited differences between people in the extent to which they are predisposed to anxiety disorders. A major biological factor in anxiety seems to involve GABA, one of the body chemicals that functions as a _____ at the synapse. Similarly, the neurotransmitter _____ has been implicated in obsessive-compulsive disorder.

5-2. Conditioning or learning clearly plays a role as well. For example, if an individual is bitten by a dog, he or she may develop a fear of dogs through the process of _____ conditioning. The individual may then avoid dogs in the future, a response maintained by _____ conditioning.

5-3. People are more likely to develop a conditioned fear of snakes than of hot irons. Using Seligman's notion of preparedness, explain why.

5-4. Two types of anecdotal evidence do *not* support the conditioning point of view. For example, people with phobias (always can/frequently cannot) recall a traumatic incident, and people who have experienced extreme traumas (always/frequently do not) develop phobias.

5-5. As discussed in Chapter 6, the conditioning models have been extended to include a larger role for cognitive and other factors. For example, children probably acquire fears by _____ the behavior of anxious parents.

5-6. In addition, cognitive theorists indicate that certain *thinking styles* contribute to anxiety. For example, as indicated in your text, the sentence "The doctor examined little Emma's growth" could refer either to height or to a tumor. People who are high in anxiety will tend to perceive the (tumor/height) interpretation. People's readiness to perceive threat, in other words, appears to be related to their tendency to experience _____.

5-7. Personality also plays a role. Not surprisingly, people who score high on the _____ trait of the "big five" personality factors have an elevated prevalence of anxiety disorders and a poorer prognosis for recovery.

5-8. Finally, *stress* is related to the anxiety disorders. Studies described in your text indicate that stress is related both to _____ anxiety disorders and to the onset of _____ disorder.

Answers: **5-1.** neurotransmitter, serotonin **5-2.** classical, operant **5-3.** Preparedness is Seligman's notion that human beings are biologically prepared to be conditioned to some stimuli more than to others. We have evolved to be more afraid of snakes than of hot irons, the latter having appeared only relatively recently in our evolutionary history **5-4.** frequently cannot, frequently do not **5-5.** observing (modeling, imitating) **5-6.** tumor, anxiety **5-7.** neuroticism **5-8.** generalized, panic.

SOMATOFORM DISORDERS

6. **Compare and contrast the three somatoform disorders and discuss their etiology.**

6-1. For each of the following symptoms, indicate which disorder is described by placing the appropriate letters in the blanks: S for somatization, C for conversion, and H for hypochondriasis.

_____ Serious disability that may include paralysis, loss of vision or hearing, loss of feeling, and so on

_____ Many different minor physical ailments accompanied by a long history of medical treatment

_____ Cannot believe the doctors report that the person is not really ill

_____ Symptoms that appear to be organic in origin but don't match underlying anatomical organization

_____ Diverse complaints that implicate many different organ systems

_____ Usually does not involve disability so much as overinterpreting slight possible signs of illness

_____ "Glove anesthesia"; seizures without loss of bladder control

6-2. In the film *Hannah and Her Sisters* Woody Allen is convinced that certain minor physical changes are a sign of cancer. When tests eventually find no evidence of cancer, he is sure the tests have been done incorrectly. Which of the somatoform disorders does this seem to represent? _____

6-3. The somatoform disorders are associated with certain personality types, with particular cognitive styles, and with learning. Among personality types, the self-centered, excitable, and overly dramatic _____ personalities are more at risk for developing these disorders.

6-4. With regard to cognitive factors, focusing excessive attention on internal _____ factors, or believing that good health should involve a complete lack of discomfort, may contribute to somatoform disorders.

6-5. With regard to learning, the sick role may be positively reinforced through, for example, _____ from others or negatively reinforced by _____ certain of life's problems or unpleasant aspects.

Answers: **6-1.** C, S, H, C, S, H, C **6-2.** hypochondriasis **6-3.** histrionic **6-4.** physiological **6-5.** attention (kindness, etc.), avoiding (escaping).

DISSOCIATIVE DISORDERS

7. Describe the dissociative disorders and discuss their etiology.

7-1. The three dissociative disorders involve memory and identity. Two of the disorders involve fairly massive amounts of forgetting, dissociative _____ and dissociative _____.

7-2. People who have been in serious accidents frequently can't remember the accident or events surrounding the accident. This type of memory loss, which involves specific traumatic events, is known as dissociative _____.

7-3. An even greater memory loss, in which people lose their memories for their entire lives along with their sense of identity, is termed dissociative _____.

7-4. You may have seen media characterizations of individuals who can't remember who they are—what their names are, where they live, who their family is, and so on. While popularly referred to as amnesia, this type of dissociative disorder is more correctly called dissociative _____.

7-5. A few years ago there was a spate of appearances on talk shows by guests who claimed to have more than one identity or personality. This disorder is still widely known as _____-_____ disorder (MPD), but the formal name in the DSM-IV is _____ _____ disorder. The disorder is also often (<u>correctly/mistakenly</u>) called schizophrenia.

7-6. What causes dissociative disorders? Dissociative amnesia and dissociative fugue are related to excessive _____, but little else is known about why these extreme reactions occur in a tiny minority of people.

7-7. With regard to multiple-personality disorder, the diagnosis is controversial. Although many clinicians believe that the disorder is authentic, Spanos argues that it is the product of media attention and the misguided probings of a small minority of psychotherapists. In other words, Spanos believes that MPD (<u>is/is not</u>) a genuine disorder.

7-8. While the majority of people with multiple-personality disorders report having been emotionally and sexually _____ in childhood, little is known about the causes of this controversial diagnosis.

Answers: 7-1. amnesia, fugue **7-2.** amnesia **7-3.** fugue **7-4.** fugue **7-5.** multiple-personality, dissociative identity disorder, mistakenly **7-6.** stress **7-7.** is not **7-8.** abused.

MOOD DISORDERS

8. Describe the two major affective disorders: depressive disorder and bipolar mood disorder.

8-1. While the terms *manic* and *depressive* describe mood, they refer to a number of other characteristics as well, listed below. With one or two words for each characteristic describe the manic and depressive episodes. (Before you make the lists, it may be a good idea to review Table 14.2 and the sections on depressive and bipolar mood disorders.)

	Manic	*Depressive*
mood:	_____	_____
sleep:	_____	_____
activity:	_____	_____
speech:	_____	_____
sex drive:	_____	_____

8-2. Be sure to note that mania and depression are not the names of the two affective disorders. What is the name of the disorders accompanied only by depressive states? _____ _____ By both manic and depressive states? _____ _____ _____

Answers: 8-1. mood: euphoric (elated, extremely happy, etc.) vs. depressed (blue, extremely sad); sleep: goes without or doesn't want to vs. can't (insomnia); activity: very active vs. sluggish, slow, inactive; speech: very fast vs. very slow; sex drive: increased vs. decreased **8-2.** depressive disorder (or unipolar disorder), bipolar mood disorder (formerly manic-depressive disorder).

9. Explain how genetic and neurochemical factors may be related to the development of mood disorders.

9-1. Twin studies implicate genetic factors in the development of mood disorders. In a sentence, summarize the results of these studies.

9-2. While the exact mechanism is not known, correlations have been found between mood disorders and the activities of _____ such as norepinephrine, serotonin, and possibly also acetylcholine. Recent research suggests that of these, _____ may be most important.

Answers: **9-1.** For mood disorders, the concordance rate for identical twins is much higher than that for fraternal twins—about 67% for the former compared to 15% for the latter **9-2.** neurotransmitters (neurochemicals), serotonin.

10. Explain how cognitive factors, interpersonal factors, and stress may be related to the development of mood disorders.

10-1. People's *attributional styles* strongly affect their moods. Below are possible thoughts that a person might have after performing poorly on a test in school (or in an athletic event, social encounter, public speech, etc.). Following each thought are three dimensions of attributional style. Circle the one pole from each pair that best describes the sample cognition.

(a) "I've never been very good at this type of thing and I'm not doing well now."

internal ———————————————— external

stable ———————————————— unstable

global ———————————————— specific

(b) "I messed up the test this time because I was lazy, but next time I'll work harder."

internal ———————————————— external

stable ———————————————— unstable

global ———————————————— specific

(c) "I just can't ever seem to do anything well."

internal ———————————————— external

stable ———————————————— unstable

global ———————————————— specific

(d) "I messed up, but on the day of the event I had the flu and a high fever. I'm rarely sick."

internal ———————————————— external

stable ———————————————— unstable

global ———————————————— specific

10-2. Which of the above attributional styles (represented by a, b, c, or d) is most likely to characterize depressed people? _____ Least likely to characterize depressed people? _____

10-3. With regard to interpersonal factors, depressed people tend to lack _____ skills. How does this affect the ability to obtain reinforcers?

10-4. Why do we tend to reject depressed people?

10-5. What is the relationship between stress and the onset of mood disorders?

Answers: 10-1. (a) internal, stable, specific (b) internal, unstable, specific (c) internal, stable, global (d) external, unstable, specific **10-2.** c, d **10-3.** social (interpersonal); lack of social skills makes it difficult to obtain certain reinforcers, such as good friends and desirable jobs **10-4.** They are not pleasant to be around. Depressed people complain a lot, are irritable, and tend to spread their mood to others **10-5.** There is a moderately strong link between stress and the onset of mood disorders.

SCHIZOPHRENIC DISORDERS

11. Describe the general characteristics (symptoms) of schizophrenia.

11-1. Before we review the different types of schizophrenia, consider some general characteristics of the schizophrenic disorders, as follows.

(a) Irrational thought: Disturbed thought processes may include the false beliefs referred to as

_____ (e.g., the false belief that one is a world-famous political figure who is being pursued by terrorists).

(b) Deterioration of adaptive behavior: The deterioration usually involves social relationships, work, and neglect of personal _____.

(c) Distorted perception: This category may include hearing (or sometimes seeing) things that aren't really there. These sensory experiences are known as _____.

(d) Disturbed emotion: Emotional responsiveness may be disturbed in a variety of ways. The person may have little or no responsiveness, referred to as _____ affect, or they may show _____ emotional responses, such as laughing at news of a tragic death.

Answers: 11-1. (a) delusions (b) hygiene (cleanliness) (c) hallucinations (d) flat (flattened, blunted), inappropriate (erratic, bizarre).

12. Describe two classification systems for schizophrenic subtypes.

12-1. Write the names of the four recognized subcategories of schizophrenia next to the descriptions that follow.

(a) _____ type: Particularly severe deterioration, incoherence, complete social withdrawal, aimless babbling and giggling, delusions centering on bodily functions.

(b) _____ type: Muscular rigidity and stupor at one extreme, or random motor activity, hyperactivity, and incoherence at the other; now quite rare.

(c) _____ type: Delusions of persecution and grandeur.

(d) _____ type: Clearly schizophrenic, but doesn't fit other three categories.

12-2. Several critics have asserted that there are no meaningful differences among the categories listed above and have proposed an alternative classification system. Nancy Andreasen and others have described a classification system consisting of only two categories, one that consists of _____ symptoms and the other of _____ symptoms.

12-3. In Andreasen's system, "positive" and "negative" do not mean pleasant and unpleasant. Positive symptoms *add* something to "normal" behavior (like chaotic speech), and negative symptoms *subtract* something (like social withdrawal). Indicate which of the following are positive and which are negative by placing a P or an N in the appropriate blanks.

_____ flattened emotions

_____ hallucinations

_____ bizarre behavior

_____ social withdrawal

_____ apathy

_____ nonstop babbling

_____ doesn't speak

Answers: 12-1. (a) disorganized (b) catatonic (c) paranoid (d) undifferentiated **12-2.** positive, negative **12-3.** N, P, P, N, N, P, N.

13. Explain how genetic vulnerability, neurochemical factors, and structural abnormalities in the brain may contribute to the etiology of schizophrenia.

13-1. As with mood disorders, twin studies implicate genetic factors in the development of schizophrenia. In a sentence, summarize the general results of these studies.

13-2. As with mood disorders, neurotransmitter substances in the brain are implicated in the etiology of schizophrenia. Although the evidence is somewhat clouded, the neurotransmitter _____ is thought to be involved (because most of the drugs found useful in treating schizophrenia dampen down this particular neurotransmitter).

13-3. In addition to possible neurochemical factors, certain differences in brain structure may be associated with schizophrenia. What are these structural differences? Why is it difficult to conclude that these differences are definitely related to schizophrenia?

Answers: 13-1. For schizophrenia, as for mood disorders, the concordance rate for identical twins is much higher than that for fraternal twins (about 48% for identical twins and about 17% for fraternal twins. The respective percentages for mood disorders are 67% and 15%). **13-2.** dopamine **13-3.** Enlarged brain ventricles are associated with chronic schizophrenia. Enlarged ventricles are associated with a number of pathologies besides schizophrenia, however, so it is difficult to determine whether or not this brain abnormality is causally related to schizophrenia.

14. **Summarize evidence on how family dynamics and stress may be related to the development of schizophrenia.**

14-1. Families that communicate in an unintelligible manner (e.g., in vague, muddled, contradictory, or fragmented sentences) have a communication style that may be described as _____. Children brought up in these families are somewhat more likely to develop _____ than those brought up with a more normal communication pattern.

14-2. Expressed emotion refers to the extent to which a patient's relatives are overly critical or protective or are in other ways overly emotionally involved with the patient. Patients returning to families that are high in expressed emotion have a relapse rate that is much (<u>higher/lower</u>) than that of families low in expressed emotion.

14-3. What role does stress play in the etiology of schizophrenia? Stress is a fact of life, and it is obvious that not everyone who experiences stress develops schizophrenia. Current thinking is that stress may be a precipitating factor for people who are biologically or for other reasons already _____ to schizophrenia.

Answers: **14-1.** deviant (defective), schizophrenia **14-2.** higher **14-3.** vulnerable.

PSYCHOLOGICAL DISORDERS AND THE LAW

15. **Distinguish between the legal concepts of insanity and involuntary commitment.**

15-1. While the words *insane* and *schizophrenic* may in some cases apply to the same person, the terms do not mean the same thing. The term _____ is a legal term, while _____ is a descriptive term used in psychological diagnosis. For example, an individual troubled by hallucinations and delusions probably fits the category of _____. An individual who is judged by a court not to be responsible for his or her actions would be classified (under the M'naghten rule) as _____.

15-2. The following items concern the insanity defense. Mark True or False.

____ The insanity defense is used in fewer than 1% of homicide cases.

____ Available evidence suggests that in by far the majority of cases in which is it used, the insanity defense is a successful defense (i.e., wins the case).

15-3. More frequent than judgments of insanity are proceedings related to involuntary commitment to a psychiatric facility. Answer the following questions about involuntary commitment.

(a) What three criteria are used to determine whether an individual should be committed?

(b) What is required to temporarily commit an individual for one to three days?

(c) What is required for longer-term commitment?

Answers: 15-1. insane, schizophrenic, schizophrenic, insane **15-2.** true, false **15-3.** (a) In general, for people to be involuntarily committed, mental health and legal authorities must judge them to be (1) dangerous to themselves or (2) dangerous to others or (3) in extreme need of treatment. (b) Temporary commitment (usually 24 to 72 hours) may be done in emergencies by a psychologist or psychiatrist. (c) Longer-term commitments are issued by a court and require a formal hearing.

CULTURE AND PATHOLOGY

16. **Discuss the effects of culture on pathology.**

   16-1.   Your text divides viewpoints about culture and pathology into *relativists* and *panculturalists*. The

   _____ believe that there are basic standards of mental health that are *universal* across

   cultures. The _____ believe that psychological disorders *vary as a function of culture.*

   16-2.   Some data support the pancultural view. For example, most investigators agree that the three most serious categories of disorder, listed below, are universal:

   _____

   _____

   _____

   16-3.   On the other hand, some of the milder disturbances listed in the DSM, such as hypochondria, somatization, and

   generalized _____ disorder, (are/are not) considered full-fledged disorders in some cultures.

   16-4.   In addition, some disorders exist in some cultures and not others. For example, the obsessive fear about one's penis withdrawing into one's abdomen is found only among Chinese males in Malaya, and

   _____ nervosa is found only in affluent Western societies.

   16-5.   In summary, are psychological disorders universal, or do they vary across cultures?
   a.   Universal: The same standards of serious disturbance exist in all cultures.
   b.   Relative to the culture: Some disorders are recognized in some cultures and not others.
   c.   Both of the above: Some aspects of psychopathology are universal, some vary as a function of culture.

   Answers: 16-1. panculturalists, relativists **16-2.** schizophrenia, depression, bipolar disorder **16-3.** anxiety, are not **16-4.** anorexia **16-5.** c.

PUTTING IT IN PERSPECTIVE

17. **Explain how this chapter highlighted four of the text's unifying themes.**

   17-1.   Below are examples of the highlighted themes. Indicate which theme fits each example by writing the appropriate abbreviations in the blanks: MC for multifactorial causation, HE for the interplay of heredity and environment, SH for sociohistorical context, and C for the influence of culture.

   (a)   Mood and schizophrenic disorders will occur if one has a genetic vulnerability to the disorder *and* if one experiences a considerable amount of stress. ____

   (b)   Psychological disorders are caused by neurochemical factors, brain abnormalities, styles of child rearing, life stress, and so on. ____

   (c)   Bipolar disorder occurs in all societies; anorexia nervosa occurs only in affluent Western societies. ____

   (d)   Homosexuality is no longer classified as a disorder in the DSM. ____ and ____

   Answers: 17-1. (a) HE (b) MC (c) C (d) SH, C.

APPLICATION: UNDERSTANDING AND PREVENTING SUICIDE

18. **Summarize how age, sex, marital status, and occupational status are related to the prevalence of suicide.**

   18-1. Which marital status is associated with the fewest suicides?
   a. single
   b. divorced
   c. married
   d. bereaved

   18-2. Across which age range does the largest number of suicide *attempts* occur?
   a. 14 to 24
   b. 24 to 44
   c. over 55

   18-3. Suicide attempts are more common among _____; actual (successful) suicides are more common among

   _____.
   a. males, females
   b. females, males

   18-4. See Figure 14.17. After age 55 the suicide rate increases:
   a. only among men
   b. only among women
   c. for both men and women

   Answers: 18-1. c **18-2.** b **18-3.** b **18-4.** a.

19. **List four myths about suicidal behavior and summarize advice provided on preventing a suicide.**

   19-1. For each of the following statements, indicate whether it is true of false.

   _____ (a) Many suicidal individuals talk about committing suicide before they actually make the attempt.

   _____ (b) The majority of suicides are preceded by some kind of warning.

   _____ (c) A small minority of those who attempt suicide are fully intent on dying.

   _____ (d) Many people are suicidal for a limited period of time, not for their entire lives.

   19-2. While it is probably true that no one knows exactly what to do about suicide, your text makes some suggestions that may be useful if you ever find yourself face to face with someone contemplating suicide. Label statements *a* through *f* below with one of the following suggestions for dealing with a suicidal person.

   1. Take suicidal talk seriously.

   2. Provide empathy and social support.

   3. Identify and clarify the crucial problem.

   4. Suggest alternative courses of action.

   5. Capitalize on any doubts.

   6. Encourage professional consultation.

   (a) "Look, there's a number I want you to call, so that you can talk with someone about this and make an appointment for professional help."

   (b) "You say you're worried about how your family would react. You're right—this would be really tough for them."

(c) "You think no one cares. I know that I care, and that's why I'm here. I think I can understand what you've been going through, and I want to help."

(d) "O.K., let's really try to put a finger on what's the main issue here. Did you say that you think you've failed your family? Does that seem to be the main problem?"

(e) "Let's try to come up with some alternative possibilities about what to do to solve this situation. I've got some suggestions."

(f) "You've been talking about things that sound like they're related to suicide. Are you contemplating suicide? Because if you are, I want to talk to you about it."

Answers: 19-1. All of these statements are true and are thus contrary to the four myths of suicide **19-2.** (a) 6, Encourage professional consultation. (b) 5, Capitalize on any doubts. (c) 2, Provide empathy and social support. (d) 3, Identify and clarify the crucial problem. (e) 4, Suggest alternative courses of action. (f) 1, Take suicidal talk seriously.

REVIEW OF KEY TERMS

Agoraphobia
Anxiety disorders
Attributions
Bipolar mood disorder
Catatonic schizophrenia
Concordance rate
Conversion disorder
Culture-bound disorders
Delusions
Depressive disorders
Diagnosis
Disorganized schizophrenia

Dissociative amnesia
Dissociative disorders
Dissociative fugue
Dissociative identity disorder
Etiology
Generalized anxiety disorder
Hallucinations
Hypochondriasis
Insanity
Involuntary commitment
Medical model
Mood disorders

Multiple-personality disorder
Obsessive-compulsive disorder
Panic disorder
Paranoid schizophrenia
Phobic disorder
Prognosis
Psychosomatic diseases
Schizophrenic disorders
Somatization disorder
Somatoform disorders
Transvestism
Undifferentiated schizophrenia

medical model

Diagnosis

Etiology

Prognosis

transvestism

Anxiety disor.

Generalized AD

Phobic D.

Panic D.

_O-C-D._

1. Proposes that it is useful to think of abnormal behavior as a disease.

2. Involves distinguishing one illness from another.

3. Refers to the apparent causation and developmental history of an illness.

4. A forecast about the possible course of an illness.

5. A sexual disorder in which a man achieves sexual arousal by dressing in women's clothing.

6. A class of disorders marked by feelings of excessive apprehension and anxiety.

7. Disorder marked by a chronic high level of anxiety that is not tied to any specific threat.

8. Disorder marked by a persistent and irrational fear of an object or situation that presents no realistic danger.

9. Disorder that involves recurrent attacks of overwhelming anxiety that usually occur suddenly and unexpectedly.

10. Disorder marked by persistent uncontrollable intrusions of unwanted thoughts and urges to engage in senseless rituals.

_____Agoraphobia_____ **11.** A fear of going out in public places.

_____Somatoform_____ **12.** Physical ailments with a genuine organic basis that are caused in part by psychological factors.

_____Psychosomatic Dis._____ **13.** A class of disorders involving physical ailments that have no authentic organic basis and are due to psychological factors.

_____Somatization D._____ **14.** Disorder marked by a history of diverse physical complaints that appear to be psychological in origin.

_____Conversions_____ **15.** Disorder that involves a significant loss of physical function (with no apparent organic basis), usually in a single-organ system.

_____Hypocondria_____ **16.** Disorder that involves excessive preoccupation with health concerns and incessant worrying about developing physical illnesses.

_____Dissocative D._____ **17.** A class of disorders in which people lose contact with portions of their consciousness or memory, resulting in disruptions in their sense of identity.

_____amnesia_____ **18.** A sudden loss of memory for important personal information that is too extensive to be due to normal forgetting.

_____fugue_____ **19.** People's loss of memory for their entire lives along with their sense of personal identity.

_____multiple-personal_____ **20.** Older term, still widely used, that describes the coexistence in one person of two or more personalities.

_____Dissociative Identity_____ **21.** The new term that replaced multiple-personality disorder in the DSM-IV.

_____mood dis._____ **22.** A class of disorders marked by depressed or elevated mood disturbances that may spill over to disrupt physical, perceptual, social, and thought processes.

_____Unipolar depression dis._____ **23.** Disorders marked by persistent feelings of sadness and despair and a loss of interest in previous sources of pleasure.

_____bi polar_____ **24.** Disorder marked by the experience of both depressive and manic periods.

_____Concordance Rate_____ **25.** Statistic indicating the percentage of twin pairs or other pairs of relatives who exhibit the same disorder.

_____Attributions_____ **26.** Inferences that people draw about the causes of events, others' behavior, and their own behavior.

_____Syzo...nia_____ **27.** A class of disorders marked by disturbances in thought that spill over to affect perceptual, social, and emotional processes.

_____delusions_____ **28.** False beliefs that are maintained even though they clearly are out of touch with reality.

_____Hallucinating_____ **29.** Sensory perceptions that occur in the absence of a real, external stimulus, or gross distortions of perceptual input.

_____Paranoid_____ **30.** Type of schizophrenia dominated by delusions of persecution, along with delusions of grandeur.

_____Catatonic_____ **31.** Type of schizophrenia marked by striking motor disturbances, ranging from muscular rigidity to random motor activity.

_____disorganized_____ **32.** Type of schizophrenia marked by a particularly severe deterioration of adaptive behavior.

_____Undifferented_____ **33.** Type of schizophrenia marked by idiosyncratic mixtures of schizophrenic symptoms.

_____Insanity_____ **34.** A legal status indicating that a person cannot be held responsible for his or her actions because of mental illness.

_____Involuntary_____ **35.** Legal situation in which people are hospitalized in psychiatric facilities against their will.

## CHAPTER FOURTEEN

_____ **36.** Abnormal syndromes found only in a few cultural groups.

Answers: 1. medical model **2.** diagnosis **3.** etiology **4.** prognosis **5.** transvestism **6.** anxiety disorders **7.** generalized anxiety disorder **8.** phobic disorder **9.** panic disorder **10.** obsessive-compulsive disorder **11.** agoraphobia **12.** psychosomatic diseases **13.** somatoform disorders **14.** somatization disorder **15.** conversion disorder **16.** hypochondriasis **17.** dissociative disorders **18.** dissociative amnesia **19.** dissociative fugue **20.** multiple-personality disorder **21.** dissociative identity disorder **22.** mood disorders **23.** depressive disorders **24.** bipolar mood disorder **25.** concordance rate **26.** attributions **27.** schizophrenic disorders **28.** delusions **29.** hallucinations **30.** paranoid schizophrenia **31.** catatonic schizophrenia **32.** disorganized schizophrenia **33.** undifferentiated schizophrenia **34.** insanity **35.** involuntary commitment **36.** culture-bound disorders.

REVIEW OF KEY PEOPLE

Nancy Andreasen   Martin Seligman   Thomas Szasz
David Rosenhan

_____ 1. Critic of the medical model; argues that abnormal behavior usually involves a deviation from social norms rather than an illness.

_____ 2. Did a study on admission of pseudopatients to a mental hospital; concluded that our mental health system is biased toward seeing pathology where it doesn't exist.

_____ 3. Developed the concept of "preparedness"; believes that classical conditioning creates most phobic responses.

_____ 4. Proposed an alternative approach to subtyping that divides schizophrenic disorders into just two categories based on the presence of negative versus positive symptoms.

Answers: 1. Szasz **2.** Rosenhan **3.** Seligman **4.** Andreasen.

SELF-QUIZ

1. Which of the following concepts or people asserts that abnormal behavior is best thought of as an illness?
   a. the behavioral model
   b. the medical model
   c. Thomas Szasz
   d. Arthur Staats

2. This psychological disorder may produce serious disabilities, including paralysis, blindness, loss of hearing, etc.
   a. obsessive-compulsive disorder
   b. somatization disorder
   c. hypochondriasis
   d. conversion disorder

3. In Rosenhan's study involving admission of pseudopatients to psychiatric facilities, most of the "patients" were:
   a. diagnosed as seriously disturbed
   b. diagnosed as suffering from a mild neurosis
   c. dismissed within two days
   d. misdiagnosed by the ward attendants but correctly diagnosed by the professional staff

4. An individual gets sudden, paralyzing attacks of anxiety and fears going out in public away from her house. Which anxiety disorder does this describe?
   a. generalized anxiety disorder
   b. phobic disorder
   c. obsessive-compulsive disorder
   d. agoraphobia

5. Ralph cleans and scrubs the cupboards in his house seven times each day. Which anxiety disorder does this describe?
   a. generalized anxiety disorder
   b. phobic disorder
   c. obsessive-compulsive disorder
   d. panic disorder

6. Human beings may have evolved to be more easily conditioned to fear some stimuli than others. This is Seligman's notion of:
   a. preparedness
   b. anxiety differentiation
   c. somatization
   d. learned helplessness

7. Which of the following is included under the somatoform disorders?
   a. bipolar mood disorders
   b. hypochondriasis
   c. phobias
   d. schizophrenia

8. Paralysis or loss of feeling that does not match underlying anatomical organization is a symptom of:
   a. somatization disorder
   b. conversion disorder
   c. hypochondriasis
   d. malingering

9. Multiple personality is:
   a. an anxiety disorder
   b. a dissociative disorder
   c. a mood disorder
   d. a somatoform disorder

10. The disorder marked by striking motor disturbances ranging from rigidity to random motor activity and incoherence is termed:
    a. catatonic schizophrenia
    b. multiple personality
    c. dissociative disorder
    d. paranoid schizophrenia

11. The concordance rate for mood disorders has been found to be about 67% among identical twins and 17% among fraternal twins. These data suggest that the mood disorders:
    a. are caused primarily by stress
    b. have an onset at an early age
    c. are due primarily to family environment
    d. are caused in part by genetic factors

12. The attributional style of depressed people tends to be:
    a. external, unstable, global
    b. external, unstable, specific
    c. internal, stable, specific
    d. internal, stable, global

13. An individual thinks he is Jesus Christ. He also believes that, because he is Christ, people are trying to kill him. Which of the following would be the most likely diagnosis? (Assume that this individual is not correct—he is not Christ, and people are not trying to kill him.)
    a. multiple personality
    b. paranoid schizophrenia
    c. obsessive-compulsive disorder
    d. catatonic schizophrenia

14. A court declares that, because of a mental illness, an individual is not responsible for his criminal actions. The individual is:
    a. insane
    b. incompetent to stand trial
    c. psychotic
    d. schizophrenic

15. Among males suicide is committed most frequently:
    a. between the ages of 15 to 19
    b. between the ages of 20 to 24
    c. between the ages of 24 to 44
    d. after age 55

    Answers: 1. b **2.** d **3.** a **4.** d **5.** c **6.** a **7.** b **8.** b **9.** b **10.** a **11.** d **12.** d **13.** b **14.** a **15.** d.

# PSYCHOTHERAPY

REVIEW OF KEY IDEAS

THE ELEMENTS OF PSYCHOTHERAPY: TREATMENT, CLIENTS, AND THERAPISTS

1. Identify the three categories of therapy and discuss who seeks therapy.

1-1. Even though she already owns more than a thousand pairs of shoes, Imelba cannot resist the urge to buy more. She checks the Yellow Pages and calls three different psychotherapists regarding possible treatment for her compulsion.

    (a) One therapist tells her that treatment will require her to talk with the therapist so as to develop a better understanding of her inner feelings. This therapist probably belongs to the _____ school of psychotherapy.

    (b) Another therapist suggests that some form of medication may help alleviate her compulsion. This therapist probably pursues the _____ approach to psychotherapy.

    (c) The third therapist is of the opinion that her urge to buy shoes results from learning, and correcting it requires that she unlearn this compulsion. This therapist probably pursues the _____ approach to psychotherapy.

1-2. Indicate whether the following statements about people who seek and choose not to seek psychotherapy are true or false.

    _____ (a) The two most common presenting symptoms are excessive anxiety and depression.

    _____ (b) Persons seeking psychotherapy always have identifiable disorders.

    _____ (c) People without mental problems may seek therapy to further their personal growth.

Answers: 1-1. (a) insight (b) biomedical (c) behavioral **1-2.** (a) true (b) false (c) true.

2. Describe the various types of mental health professionals involved in the provision of psychotherapy.

2-1. Identify the following kinds of mental health professionals:

    (a) Medically trained persons (physicians) who generally use biomedical and insight approaches to psychotherapy.

(b) Persons with doctoral degrees who emphasize behavioral and insight approaches to psychotherapy in treating a full range of psychological problems (two types).

(c) Nurses who usually work as part of the treatment team in a hospital setting.

(d) These persons often work with both the patient and family to reintegrate the patient back into society.

(e) Persons who usually specialize in particular types of problems, such as vocational, drug, or marital counseling.

Answers: 2-1. (a) psychiatrists (b) clinical and counseling psychologists (c) psychiatric nurses (d) clinical social workers (e) counselors.

INSIGHT THERAPIES

3. **Explain the logic of psychoanalysis and describe the techniques by which analysts probe the unconscious.**

   3-1. Freud believed that psychological disturbances originate from unresolved conflicts deep in the unconscious levels of the mind. His theory of personality, which he called _____, would be classified as an _____ approach to psychotherapy. The psychoanalyst plays the role of psychological detective, seeking out problems thought to originate from conflicts left over from early _____.

   3-2. The psychoanalyst employs two techniques to probe the unconscious. One technique requires the patient to tell whatever comes to mind no matter how trivial. This technique is called _____ _____. The other technique requires the patient to learn to remember his or her dreams, which are then probed for their hidden meaning by the psychoanalyst. This technique is called _____ _____.

   Answers: 3-1. psychoanalysis, insight, childhood **3-2.** free association, dream analysis.

4. **Discuss resistance and transference in psychoanalysis.**

   4-1. Freud believed most people (<u>do/do not</u>) want to know the true nature of their inner conflicts and will employ various strategies so as to offer _____ to the progress of therapy. As therapy progresses, the patient often begins to relate to the therapist as though he or she was actually one of the significant persons (mother, father, spouse, etc.) in the patient's life. This phenomenon is called _____.

   Answers: 4-1. do not, resistance, transference.

5. **Identify the elements of therapeutic climate and discuss the therapeutic process in Rogers's client-centered therapy.**

   5-1. Client-centered therapy, as developed by Carl Rogers, holds that there are three important aspects necessary for a good therapeutic climate. These are genuineness, unconditional positive regard, and empathy. Match these terms with the correct definitions as given below.

   (a) The ability to truly see the world from the client's point of view and communicate this understanding to the client.

   (b) The therapist's openness and honesty with the client.

   (c) The complete and nonjudgmental acceptance of the client as a person without necessarily agreeing with what the client has to say.

   5-2. For client-centered therapy, the major emphasis is to provide feedback and _____ as the client expresses his or her thoughts and feelings. The idea here is that the client (<u>does/does not</u>) need direct advice. What is needed is help in sorting through personal confusion in order to gain greater _____ into true inner feelings.

   Answers: 5-1. (a) empathy (b) genuineness (c) unconditional positive regard **5-2.** clarification, does not, insight or understanding.

6. **Discuss the logic, goals, and techniques of cognitive therapy.**

   6-1. Answer the following questions regarding the logic, goals, and techniques of cognitive therapy.

   (a) What is the basic logic behind cognitive therapy? Or to put it another way, what is the origin of many psychological problems according to cognitive therapy?

   (b) What is the primary goal of cognitive therapy?

   (c) How do cognitive therapists go about trying to change a client's negative illogical thinking?

   (d) Cognitive therapy is actually a blend of insight therapy and behavior therapy. What technique from behavior therapy do cognitive therapists frequently employ?

   Answers: 6-1. (a) negative illogical thinking (b) to change the client's negative illogical thinking (c) through argument and persuasion (d) homework assignments.

7. **Describe how group therapy is generally conducted.**

7-1.   When conducting group therapy, the therapist generally plays a(an) (active/subtle) role, one that is primarily aimed at promoting _____ cohesiveness. Participants essentially function as _____ for each other, providing acceptance and emotional support.

Answers: 7-1. subtle, group, therapists.

8. **Discuss evidence on the efficacy of insight therapies.**

8-1.   Answer the following questions about the efficacy (effectiveness) of insight therapies.

(a)   What does the text conclude about the superiority of insight therapies over no treatment?

(b)   What does the text conclude about the efficacy of insight therapies over paraprofessional interventions such as peer self-help groups?

Answers: 8-1. (a) They are moderately superior. (b) The differences are often negligible.

BEHAVIOR THERAPIES

9. **Summarize the general principles underlying behavioral approaches to therapy.**

9-1.   In contrast to insight therapists who believe that pathological symptoms are signs of an underlying problem, behavior therapists believe that the _____ are the problem. Thus, behavior therapists focus on employing the principles of learning to directly change maladaptive _____. The two general principles underlying this approach are (1) one's behavior is a product of _____, and (2) what has been learned can be _____.

Answers: 9-1. symptoms, behavior, learning, unlearned.

10. **Describe the goals and procedures of systematic desensitization and aversion therapy.**

10-1.   State whether the following situations would be most applicable to systematic desensitization or to aversion therapy.

(a)   The treatment goal is to lessen the attractiveness of particular stimuli and behaviors that are personally or socially harmful.

(b)   The treatment goal is to reduce irrational fears such as found in phobias and other anxiety disorders.

(c)   The three-step treatment involves pairing an imagined anxiety hierarchy with deep muscle relaxation.

(d)   Treatment involves presenting an unpleasant stimulus, such as electric shock, while a person is engaged in performing a self-destructive, but personally appealing, act.

(e) This would be the treatment of choice for students who are unduly anxious about public speaking.

Answers: 10-1. (a) aversion therapy (b) systematic desensitization (c) systematic desensitization (d) aversion therapy (e) systematic desensitization.

11. Describe the goals and techniques of social skills training.

11-1. As the name implies, social skills training is a behavior therapy designed to improve a client's social or _____ skills. Three different behavioral techniques are employed. First, one is required to closely watch the behavior of socially skilled persons, a technique called _____. Next the client is expected to imitate and practice the behavior he or she has just witnessed, a technique called _____. Finally, the client is expected to perform in social situations requiring increasingly more difficult social skills, a technique called _____.

Answers: 11-1. interpersonal, modeling, rehearsal, shaping.

12. Discuss evidence on the effectiveness of behavior therapies.

12-1. Compared to the evidence in support of insight therapies, the evidence in favor of behavior therapy is somewhat (weaker/stronger). It is important to remember, however, that behavior therapies are best suited for treating (specific/general) psychological disorders and that all of the various behavioral techniques (are/are not) equally effective.

Answers: 12-1. stronger, specific, are not.

BIOMEDICAL THERAPIES

13. Describe the principal categories of drugs used in the treatment of psychological disorders.

13-1. Valium and Xanax, popularly called tranquilizers, are used to treat psychological disorders in which anxiety is a major feature. Thus, they are collectively called _____ drugs.

13-2. Another class of drugs is used to treat severe psychotic symptoms, such as hallucinations and confusion. These drugs are collectively called _____ drugs.

13-3. Three classes of drugs–tricyclics, MAO inhibitors, and selective serotonin reuptake inhibitors–have been found to be useful in alleviating depression. These drugs are collectively called _____ drugs.

13-4. A rather unique drug can function as both an antidepressant and antimanic agent. This drug is _____.

Answers: 13-1. antianxiety **13-2.** antipsychotic **13-3.** antidepressant **13-4.** lithium.

14. Discuss evidence on the effects and problems of drug treatments for psychological disorders.

14-1. Drug therapies have proven useful in the treatment of many psychological disorders. However, they remain controversial for at least two reasons. List these two reasons below.

Answers: 14-1. They alleviate rather than cure psychological distress and they are overprescribed and patients are over-medicated.

15. Describe ECT and discuss its therapeutic effects and its risks.

15-1. Answer the following questions about the nature, therapeutic effects, and risks of ECT.

(a) What is the physical effect of the electric shock on the patient?

(b) What general class of disorders warrant conservative use of ECT as a treatment technique?

(c) What does research evidence show regarding the effectiveness of ECT?

(d) What is the major risk of ECT?

Answers: 15-1. (a) It produces convulsive seizures (b) severe mood disorders (especially depression) (c) There is enough favorable evidence to justify conservative use at this time (d) It can produce both short-term and long-term intellectual impairment.

BLENDING APPROACHES TO PSYCHOTHERAPY

16. Discuss the merits of blending or combining different approaches to therapy.

16-1. A significant trend in modern psychotherapy is to blend or combine many different treatment approaches. Psychologists who advocate and use this approach are said to be _____. Multiple approaches are most likely when a (therapist/treatment team) provides the therapy. Evidence suggests that there is (some/no) merit in combining approaches to treatment.

Answers: 16-1. eclectic, treatment team, some.

CULTURE AND THERAPY

17. Discuss the barriers that lead to underutilization of mental health services by ethnic minorities and possible solutions to the problem.

17-1. The text lists four general barriers (cultural, language, access, and institutional) to mental health services for ethnic minorities. Indicate which of these barriers is represented in the following statements.

_____ (a) Many of the ethnic minorities are in low-paying jobs and without health insurance.

_____ (b) Very few mental health facilities are equipped to provide culturally responsive services.

_____ (c) There is a limited number of bilingual therapists.

_____ (d) Psychotherapy was developed by whites in the Western world to treat whites in the Western world.

17-2. What would be an optimal, but perhaps impractical, solution to the problems of language and cultural differences betweem therapists and clients?

17-3. What kind of training was recommended for therapists dealing with ethnic minorities?

Answers. 17-1. (a) access (b) institutional (c) language (d) cultural **17-2.** Ethnically match therapists and clients **17-3.** cultural sensitivity training.

INSTITUTIONAL TREATMENT IN TRANSITION

18. Explain why people grew disenchanted with mental hospitals.

18-1. After more than a century of reliance on state mental hospitals, the evidence began to grow that these institutions were hurting more than helping many patients. What condition unrelated to funding was said to be partly responsible for this state of affairs?

Answer: 18-1. The removal of patients from their communities separated them from essential support groups.

19. Describe the deinstitutionalization trend and evaluate its effects.

19-1. The transferring of mental health care from large state mental hospitals to community-based facilities is what is meant by the term _____. As a result of deinstitutionalization, the number of patients in large mental hospitals has (increassed/decreased) remarkably. The opening of community-based treatment facilities and the emergence of effective _____ therapies were the major factors that accounted for this remarkable decline.

19-2. While deinstitutionalization has resulted in a decrease in the number of patients, the number of admissions to psychiatric hospitals has actually _____. This is because of a large number of readmissions for short-term care, which the text calls "the _____ _____ problem." Another problem brought about by deinstitutionalization is that a large number of discharged patients who have meager job skills and no close support groups make up a sizeable portion of the nation's _____ persons.

Answers: 19-1. deinstitutionalization, decreased, drug **19-2.** increased, revolving door, homeless.

PUTTING IT IN PERSPECTIVE

20. Explain how this chapter highlighted two of the text's unifying themes.

20-1. How has theoretical diversity influenced psychotherapy?

20-2. The approaches to psychotherapy discussed in this chapter are not universally accepted or used, and some are actually counterproductive in many cultures. Why is this?

Answers: 20-1. It has resulted in better treatment techniques **20-2.** Because of cultural influences and differences.

APPLICATION: LOOKING FOR A THERAPIST

21. Discuss where to seek therapy and the potential importance of a therapist's sex, theoretical approach, and professional background.

   21-1. In addition to private practice, schools, and work places, the text lists three other places where one might seek therapy. List them below.

   21-2. The text concludes that the kind of degree and theoretical approach held by the psychotherapist is (less/more) important than the therapist's personal skills, although a verifiable degree indicating some kind of professional training is important. The sex of the therapist should be chosen according to the feelings of the _____; it is unwise to engage a therapist whose sex makes the client feel uncomfortable.

Answers: 21-1. community mental health centers, hospitals, human service centers **21-2.** less, client (patient).

22. Summarize what one should look for in a prospective therapist and what one should expect out of therapy.

   22-1. The text lists three areas to evaluate when looking for a therapist. Complete the following statements describing these areas.

   (a) Can you talk to the therapist _____?

   (b) Does the therapist appear to have _____?

   (c) Does the therapist appear to be _____?

   22-2. What did the Ehrenbergs say about what to expect from psychotherapy?

Answers: 22-1. (a) openly (in a candid, nondefensive manner) (b) empathy and understanding (c) self-confident
22-2. It takes time, effort, and courage.

REVIEW OF KEY TERMS

Antianxiety drugs
Antidepressant drugs
Antipsychotic drugs
Aversion therapy
Behavior therapies
Biomedical therapies
Client-centered therapy
Clinical psychologists
Cognitive therapy

Counseling psychologists
Deinstitutionalization
Dream analysis
Electroconvulsive therapy (ECT)
Free association
Group therapy
Insight therapies
Interpretation
Lithium

Mental hospitals
Psychiatrists
Psychoanalysis
Psychopharmacotherapy
Resistance
Social skills training
Tardive dyskinesia
Transference

_____ **1.** Two groups of professionals with doctoral degrees in psychology that specialize in the diagnosis and treatment of psychological disorders and everyday behavioral problems.

_____ **2.** Physicians who specialize in the treatment of psychological disorders.

_____ **3.** Therapies that involve verbal interactions intended to enhance client's self-knowledge and thus produce healthful changes in personality and behavior.

_____ **4.** An insight therapy that emphasizes the recovery of unconscious conflicts, motives and defenses through techniques such as free association and dream analysis.

_____ **5.** A technique in which clients are urged to spontaneously express their thoughts and feelings with as little personal censorship as possible.

_____ **6.** A technique for interpreting the symbolic meaning of dreams.

_____ **7.** A therapist's attempts to explain the inner significance of a client's thoughts, feelings, memories, and behavior.

_____ **8.** A client's largely unconscious defensive maneuvers intended to hinder the progress of therapy.

_____ **9.** Process that occurs when clients start relating to their therapist in ways that mimic critical relationships in their lives.

_____ **10.** An insight therapy that emphasizes providing a supportive emotional climate for clients who play a major role in determining the pace and direction of their therapy.

_____ **11.** An insight therapy that emphasizes recognizing and changing negative thoughts and maladaptive beliefs.

_____ **12.** The simultaneous treatment of several clients in a group.

_____ **13.** Therapies that involve the application of learning principles to change a client's maladaptive behaviors.

_____ **14.** A behavior therapy used to reduce clients' anxiety responses through counterconditioning.

_____ **15.** A behavior therapy in which an aversive stimulus is paired with a stimulus that elicits an undesirable response.

_____ **16.** A behavior therapy designed to improve interpersonal skills, that emphasizes shaping, modeling, and behavioral rehearsal.

_____ **17.** Therapies that use physiological interventions intended to reduce symptoms associated with psychological disorders.

_____ **18.** The treatment of mental disorders with drug therapy.

_____ **19.** Drugs that relieve tension, apprehension, and nervousness.

_____ **20.** Drugs that gradually reduce psychotic symptoms.

_____ 21. A neurological disorder marked by chronic tremors and involuntary spastic movements.

_____ 22. Drugs that gradually elevate mood and help bring people out of a depression.

_____ 23. A chemical used to control mood swings in patients with bipolar mood disorder.

_____ 24. A treatment in which electric shock is used to produce cortical seizure accompanied by convulsions.

_____ 25. The treatment of mental disorders with medication.

_____ 26. A medical institution specializing in the provision of inpatient care for psychological disorders.

_____ 27. Transferring the treatment of mental illness from inpatient institutions to community-based facilities that emphasize outpatient care.

Answers: 1. clinical and counseling psychologists **2.** psychiatrists **3.** insight therapies **4.** psychoanalysis **5.** free association **6.** dream analysis **7.** interpretation **8.** resistance **9.** transference **10.** client-centered therapy **11.** cognitive therapy **12.** group therapy **13.** behavior therapies **14.** systematic desensitization **15.** aversion therapy **16.** social skills training **17.** biomedical therapies **18.** psychopharmacotherapy **19.** antianxiety drugs **20.** antipsychotic drugs **21.** tardive dyskinesa **22.** antidepressant drugs **23.** lithium **24.** electroconvulsive therapy (ECT) **25.** psychopharmacotherapy **26.** mental hospitals **27.** deinstitutionalization.

REVIEW OF KEY PEOPLE

Aaron Beck   Carl Rogers   Joseph Wolpe
Sigmund Freud

_____ 1. Developed a systematic treatment procedure that he called psychoanalysis.

_____ 2. The developer of client-centered therapy.

_____ 3. Noted for his work in the development of cognitive therapy.

_____ 4. The developer of systematic desensitization.

Answers: 1. Freud **2.** Rogers **3.** Beck **4.** Wolpe.

SELF-QUIZ

1. Which approach to psychotherapy is most likely to use medication as part of the treatment package?
   a. insight
   b. biomedical
   c. behavioral
   d. group

2. Which of the following is not a true statement?
   a. Some persons seek psychotherapy for personal growth.
   b. The two most common problems that lead to psychotherapy are sexual problems and depression.
   c. Persons seeking psychotherapy don't always have identifiable problems.
   d. All psychotherapists are not equally effective.

3. Which of the following mental health professional is most likely to employ both biomedical and insight approaches to psychotherapy?
   a. psychiatrists
   b. clinical psychologists
   c. psychiatric nurses
   d. counselors

4. Psychoanalysis is an example of what kind of approach to psychotherapy?
   a. insight
   b. learning
   c. biomedical
   d. a combination of learning and biomedical

5. A client who begins to relate to her psychoanalyst as she would her mother would be said to be exhibiting:
   a. transference
   b. free association
   c. catharsis
   d. restructuring

6. The major emphasis in client-centered therapy is to provide the client with:
   a. interpretation of unconscious thinking
   b. cognitive restructuring
   c. feedback and clarification
   d. good advice

7. Which of the following is likely to be commonly found in behavior therapy?
   a. free association
   b. emphasis on non-verbal cues
   c. transference
   d. social skills training

8. Which of the following is not likely to be found in cognitive therapy?
   a. a search for automatic negative thoughts
   b. reality testing
   c. an emphasis on rational thinking
   d. dream interpretation

9. Which kind of therapists are likely to play the least active (most subtle) role in conducting therapy?
   a. behavior therapists
   b. cognitive therapists
   c. group therapists
   d. psychoanalytic therapists

10. Which of the following therapies is most likely to see the symptom as the problem?
    a. psychoanalysis
    b. Gestalt
    c. behavior
    d. cognitive

11. Which of the following behavior therapy techniques would most likely be used to treat a fear of flying?
    a. systematic desensitization
    b. aversive conditioning
    c. modeling
    d. rehearsal

12. In comparison to other forms of therapy, behavior therapy is most applicable to all kinds of psychological disorders. This statement is:
    a. true
    b. false

13. Electroconvulsive therapy (ECT) is now primarily used to treat patients suffering from:
    a. anxiety
    b. phobia
    c. depression
    d. psychosis

14. Psychotherapists who combine several different approaches in their approach to therapy are said to be:
    a. enigmatic
    b. eclectic
    c. unspecific
    d. imaginative

15. The trend toward deinstitutionalization largely came about because large mental institutions:
    a. were becoming too expensive
    b. were actually worsening the condition of many patients
    c. could not be properly staffed
    d. relied too much on drugs

Answers: 1. b **2.** b **3.** a **4.** a **5.** a **6.** c **7.** d **8.** d **9.** c **10.** c **11.** a **12.** b **13.** c **14.** b **15.** b.

## CHAPTER FIFTEEN

# 16 SOCIAL BEHAVIOR

REVIEW OF KEY IDEAS

PERSON PERCEPTION: FORMING IMPRESSIONS OF OTHERS

1. **Describe how various aspects of physical appearance may influence our impressions of others**.

   1-1. In general, we attribute _____ characteristics to good-looking people. We tend to view attractive people as warmer, friendlier, better-adjusted, and more poised. Although differences are not as great for competence, we are also inclined to see attractive people as (<u>less/more</u>) intelligent and successful than less attractive people.

   1-2. While good looks in general have relatively little impact on judgments of honesty, people do tend to view baby-faced individuals (large eyes, rounded chin) as more ___ _____ _____ than others but also as more helpless and submissive. (Hey, what about the notorious criminal Baby-faced Nelson? Well, it's a general rule of thumb, not an absolute principle.)

   Answers: 1-1. positive (desirable, favorable) characteristics (e.g., more friendly, sociable, poised, warm, and well-adjusted) **1-2.** honest.

2. **Explain how schemas, stereotypes, and other factors contribute to subjectivity in person perception.**

   2-1. Briefly define the following:

   (a) schemas:

   (b) stereotypes:

2-2. Men are competitive, women are sensitive: these are stereotypes. Stereotypes frequently are broad generalizations that tend to ignore the _____ within a group. While most people who hold stereotypes do not assume that all members of a group behave in the same way, they probably do assume that group members are more _____ than others to share a particular set of characteristics.

2-3. Whether probabilistic or absolute, schemas in general and stereotypes in particular direct our perception, so that we tend to see the things we expect to see. Such selective perception results in an over estimation of the degree to which our expectations match actual events, a phenomenon referred to as _____ correlation.

2-4. In one study discussed in the text subjects watched a videotape of a woman engaged in various activities (including drinking beer and listening to classical music). For one set of subjects she was described as a librarian and for another as a waitress. What effect did the occupational labels have on subjects' recall of the woman's *activities*?
   a.   Subjects in the "librarian" condition tended to recall her listening to classical music.
   b.   Subjects in the "waitress" condition tended to recall her drinking beer.
   c.   Both of the above.

2-5. The study just described illustrates subjectivity in person perception. Our schemas, in this case the _____ that we have about categories of people, affect how we perceive and what we remember.

Answers: **2-1.** (a) Social schemas are cognitive structures or *clusters of ideas* about people and events. (b) Stereotypes are a type of schema about groups or categories of people **2-2.** diversity (variability), likelihood (probability) **2-3.** illusory **2-4.** c **2-5.** stereotypes.

3. Explain the evolutionary perspective on bias in person perception.

3-1. How does one explain bias or prejudice in terms of evolution? To explain anything in terms of evolution one assumes that the particular characteristic or trait had _____ value in our evolutionary past. For example, the bias in favor of physical attractiveness might have signaled health, which was associated with reproductive potential in _____ and the ability to acquire resources in _____.

3-2. Evolutionary theorists also assert that we needed a quick way to categorize people as friend or enemy or, in more technical terms, as members of our _____ or members of the _____.

3-3. The question still remains: how could prejudice and bias be adaptive? It must be clear that what was adaptive in our evolutionary past (is also/may not be) adaptive now. Nonetheless, from the point of view of evolutionary theory, cognitive mechanisms involving bias have been shaped by natural _____.

Answers: **3-1.** adaptive (survival), women, men **3-2.** ingroup, outgroup **3-3.** may not be, selection.

ATTRIBUTION PROCESSES: EXPLAINING BEHAVIOR

4. Explain what attributions are, and why and when we make them.

4-1. Why are you reading this book? The search for causes of events and of our own and others' behavior is termed

_____. For example, you might _____ your behavior to an upcoming test (or to personal interest, lust for knowledge, fear, etc.).

4-2. Attributions are inferences that people make about the _____ of events and about their own and others' behavior.

4-3. Why do we make attributions? We seem to have a strong need to _____ our experiences.

Answers: 4-1. attribution, attribute **4-2.** causes (origin, source, explanation) **4-3.** understand (explain, make sense of).

5. Describe the distinction between internal and external attributions, and summarize Weiner's theories of attribution.

5-1. Which of the following involve internal and which external attributions? Label each sentence with an I or an E.

_____ He flunked because he's lazy.

_____ Our team lost because the officials were biased against us.

_____ The accident was caused by poor road conditions.

_____ He achieved by the sweat of his brow.

_____ Criminal behavior is caused by poverty.

_____ His success is directly derived from his parents' wealth and influence.

5-2. Weiner proposed that attributions are made not only in terms of an internal-external dimension but also in terms of a stable-unstable dimension. Suppose that Sally makes a high score on an exam. Her score could be attributed to the fact that she worked hard, an (internal/external) factor. If she *always* works hard, the factor is also (stable/unstable). If she does not always work hard the factor is (stable/unstable).

5-3. Or, Sally's high score might be attributed to an easy test, an (internal/external) factor. If the tests are always easy, then this factor is (stable/unstable). If the tests are sometimes easy and sometimes difficult, then the factor is (stable/unstable).

Answers: 5-1. I, E, E, I, E, E **5-2.** internal, stable, unstable **5-3.** external, stable, unstable. (For more practice with these concepts see Chapter 14 of this study guide.)

6. Describe several types of attributional bias and cultural differences in attributional tendencies.

6-1. Define or describe the following:

(a) fundamental attribution error:

(b) actor-observer bias:

(c) defensive attribution:

(d) self-serving bias:

6-2. Recent research has indicated that the attributional biases described above may not apply to all cultures. Since collectivist societies emphasize accomplishing the goals of the group over individual achievement, collectivist cultures are (less/more) likely to attribute others' behavior to personal traits. In other words, people from collectivist cultures tend to be (less/more) prone to the fundamental attribution error.

6-3. Some evidence also indicates that people from collectivist societies would be more likely to attribute their *successes* to (the ease of a task/unusual ability). Similarly, they would be more likely to attribute their *failures* to (bad luck/lack of effort). Thus, in contrast with people from individualistic societies, people from collectivist cultures appear to be (less/more) prone to the self-serving bias.

Answers: 6-1. (a) the tendency for observers to attribute an individual's behavior to *internal* rather than *external* factors (b) the tendency for observers to attribute an actor's behavior to internal rather than external factors *and the tendency for actors to attribute their own behavior to external causes* (Yes, there is overlap between these two concepts. The fundamental attribution error is part of the actor-observer bias.) (c) the tendency to attribute other people's misfortunes to internal causes, that is, the tendency to blame the victim (d) the tendency to attribute our *successes* to internal factors and our *failures* to situational factors. (We tend to explain others' failures in terms of internal factors and our own in terms of external factors, as the actor-observer bias indicates. However, as the self-serving bias indicates, we tend to attribute our successes to internal factors and our failure to external factors, an exception to the actor-observer rule.) **6-2.** less, less **6-3.** the ease of a task, lack of effort, less.

CLOSE RELATIONSHIPS: LIKING AND LOVING

7. Summarize evidence on four key factors in attraction discussed in the text.

7-1. In the blanks below list four key factors associated with attraction, then briefly explain what each concept means and how it is related to attraction.

(a) _____:

(b) _____:

(c) _____:

(d) _____:

7-2. What is the matching hypothesis?

Answers: 7-1. (a) proximity: We are more likely to form friendships with people who are spatially close to us, people who live, shop, sit, or work nearby. (b) physical attractiveness: We prefer to date, marry, and form friendships with people who are physically attractive. (c) similarity: We tend to like others who are like us (in attitudes, personality, social background, etc.). (d) reciprocity: We tend to reciprocate liking; in other words, we tend to like others who like us. **7-2.** The matching hypothesis proposes that people tend to date and marry others of the opposite sex who are *approximately equal* to themselves in physical attractiveness.

8. **List several myths about love and describe efforts to analyze love into components.**

   8-1.   List the three myths about love described in your text.

   8-2.   Hatfield and Berscheid divide love into two types: _____ love, which involves a complete absorption in another and is characterized by intense emotion, and _____ love, described as a warm, tolerant, and trusting affection.

   Answers: 8-1. When you fall in love you'll know it. Love is a purely positive experience. True love lasts forever
   8-2. passionate, companionate.

9. **Discuss cross-cultural research on romantic relationships and evolutionary analyses of mating patterns.**

   9-1.   According to David Buss, males and females do not emphasize the same attributes in prospective mates. Buss's data indicate that _____ are more interested in mates who have or can acquire financial resources (e.g., who are ambitious, hard-working, or rich) while _____ are more interested in mates who are beautiful and youthful. These gender differences in mate preference appear to occur (<u>cross-culturally/only in the West</u>).

   9-2.   While there is cross-cultural similarity in mate selection, there are differences between cultures in their views of the relationship between romantic love and marriage. The idea that people should be in love in order to marry is in large part an 18th-century invention of (<u>Eastern/Western</u>) culture.

   Answers: 9-1. women, men, cross-culturally (The song *Summertime* from *Porgy and Bess* sums it up like this: "Oh, your daddy's rich, and your ma is good looking.") **9-2.** Western. (Like another song says: love and marriage go together—like a horse and carriage. But this is not a universally accepted idea.)

ATTITUDES: MAKING SOCIAL JUDGMENTS

10. **Discuss evidence on the hypothesized relationship between love and attachment.**

   10-1.   In Chapter 11 we discussed types of attachment between infants and their caregivers. What *general* conclusion did Hazen and Shaver reach about infant attachment and the later love relationships of adults?

   10-2.   Write the names of the three infant attachment styles next to the appropriate letters below.

   S: _____

   A-A: _____

   A: _____

10-3. Using the letters from the previous question, identify the types of romantic relations predicted by the infant attachment styles.

_____ As adults these people have difficulty getting close to others and describe their relationships as lacking intimacy.

_____ These adults are preoccupied with love, expect rejection, and describe their relationships as volatile and marked by jealousy.

_____ These individuals easily develop close relationships and describe their relationships as trusting.

Answers: 10-1. The three types of infant-caretaker attachments tend to predict characteristics of the love relationships that children have as adults **10-2.** secure, anxious-ambivalent, avoidant **10-3.** A, A-A, S.

11. Describe the components of attitudes and the relations between attitudes and behavior.

11-1. Attitudes are said to be made up of three components: cognition, affect, and behavior. What do the words _cognition_ and _affect_ refer to? List synonyms (one or two words for each) in the blanks below.

cognition: _____

affect: _____

11-2. The behavioral component refers, of course, to behavior. When expressed, it is the component we can readily observe, but it is not always expressed. Thus, this component is described in terms of behavioral

_____ or tendencies.

11-3. People can have attitudes toward almost anything—political views, art, other people, cottage cheese. Take cottage cheese. List the three components of attitudes illustrated next to the examples below.

_____ He hates cottage cheese.

_____ If cottage cheese touches his plate he scrapes it into the garbage.

_____ He thinks: "Cottage cheese seems kind of lumpy."

Answers: 11-1. (a) beliefs (or thoughts, thinking) (b) emotion (or feelings) **11-2.** predispositions **11-3.** affect, behavior, cognition. (Note that the components may be remembered as the ABCs of attitude—affect, behavioral predispositions, and cognition.)

12. Summarize evidence on source factors, message factors, and receiver factors that influence the process of persuasion.

12-1. If you are the _source_ of a communication, the message giver:

(a) What factors mentioned in your text would you use to make yourself more _credible_?

_____ and _____

(b) What else would you hope to emphasize about yourself? _____

12-2. With regard to _message_ factors:

(a) Which is generally more effective, a one-sided message or a two-sided message? _____

(b) In presenting your argument, should you use every argument that you can think of or emphasize just the stronger arguments? _____

(c) Is simple repetition a good strategy, or should you say something just once? _____

(d) Do fear appeals tend to work? _____ When? _____

12-3. With regard to *receiver* factors in persuasive communications:

    (a) If you know that someone is going to attempt to persuade you on a particular topic you will be (harder/easier) to persuade. This is the factor referred to as _____.

    (b) Resistance to persuasion is greater when an audience holds an attitude incompatible with the one being presented. In this case the receiver will also tend to scrutinize arguments longer and with more skepticism, an effect referred to as (confirmation/disconfirmation) bias.

    (c) People will be persuaded only if the message is not too different from their original position. This *range* of potentially acceptable positions is referred to as people's _____ of acceptance.

Answers: 12-1. (a) expertise, trustworthiness (b) likability (for example, by increasing your physical attractiveness or emphasizing your similarity with the message receiver) **12-2.** (a) In general, two-sided (That's the kind of speech Mark Antony gave over the body of Caesar in Shakespeare's *Julius Caesar*.) (b) stronger only (c) repetition (causes people to believe it's true, whether it is or isn't) (d) yes, *if* they arouse fear (and especially if the audience is persuaded that the effects are exceedingly unpleasant, likely to occur, and avoidable) **12-3.** (a) easier (b) disconfirmation (c) latitude.

13. Explain how cognitive dissonance can account for the effects of counterattitudinal behavior and effort justification.

    13-1. (Dissonance is a truly complicated theory, but the following exercise should help. First read over the text, then see how you do on these questions. Here's a hint: Both problems that follow are contrary to commonsense ideas of reward and punishment; dissonance theory prides itself on making predictions contrary to these commonsense ideas. Item 13-1 indicates that we like behaviors accompanied by less, not more, reward; item 13-2 indicates that we like behaviors accompanied by more, not less, discomfort.)

    Ralph bought a used car. However, the car uses a lot of gas, which he doesn't like because he strongly supports conserving energy. He rapidly concludes that conserving fuel isn't so important after all.

    (a) Ralph has engaged in counterattitudinal behavior. What were the two contradictory cognitions? (One is a thought about his *behavior*. The other is a thought about an important *attitude*.)

    (b) Suppose the car was a real beauty, a rare antique worth much more than the price paid. Alternatively, suppose that the car was only marginally worth what was paid for it. In which case would dissonance be stronger? In which case would the attitude about gas guzzling be more likely to change?

    13-2. Suppose Bruce decides to join a particular club. (1) One possible scenario is that he must travel a great distance to attend, the club is very expensive, and he must give up much of his free time to become a member. (2) Alternatively, suppose that the traveling time is short, the club is inexpensive, and he need not give up any free time. In which case (1 or 2) will he tend to value his membership more, according to dissonance theory? Briefly, why?

Answers: 13-1. (a) I know I bought the car. I'm against the purchase of cars that waste gas. (b) The additional reward in the first situation produces less dissonance and will tend to leave Ralph's original attitude about gas consumption intact. Ralph's attitude about gas consumption will change more when there is less justification (in terms of the value of the car) for his action. As described in your text, we tend to have greater dissonance, and greater attitude change, when *less reward* accompanies our counterattitudinal behavior. **13-2.** According to dissonance theory, he will value the membership more under alternative 1, even if the benefits of membership are slight, because people attempt to *justify the effort* expended in terms of the benefits received. (While dissonance is a true phenomenon with many of the characteristics that Festinger described in 1957, several other variables are operating, so it is difficult to predict when dissonance will occur.)

14. Relate learning theory and the elaboration likelihood model to attitude change.

14-1. Following are examples that relate learning theory to attitude change. Indicate which type of learning—classical conditioning (CC), operant conditioning (OC), or observational learning (OL)—is being illustrated.

_____ Ralph hears a speaker express a particular political attitude that is followed by thunderous applause. Thereafter, Ralph tends to express the same attitude.

_____ Advertisers pair soft drinks (and just about any other product) with attractive models. The audience likes the models and develops a stronger liking for the product.

_____ If you express an attitude that I like, I will agree with you, nod, say "mm-hmm," and so on. This will tend to strengthen your expression of that attitude.

14-2. To illustrate the elaboration likelihood model: Suppose that you are to travel in Europe and must decide between two options, renting a car or traveling by train (on a Eurailpass). In the blanks below indicate which persuasive route, central (C) or peripheral (P), is referred to in these examples.

____ On the basis of train brochures showing apparently wealthy and dignified travelers dining in luxury on the train while viewing the Alps, you opt for the train.

____ Your travel agent is an expert who has advised many of your friends, and she strongly recommends that you take the train. You decide on the train.

____ A friend urges you to consider details you hadn't previously considered: traffic, waiting in line, additional cab fare, and so on. After weighing the relative expenses and conveniences for four traveling together you decide to rent a car.

14-3. In the elaboration likelihood model, the route that is easier, that involves the least amount of thinking, is the _____ route. The route in which relevant information is sought out and carefully pondered is the _____ route. Elaboration, which involves thinking about the various complexities of the situation, is more likely to occur when the _____ route is used.

14-4. Elaboration leads to (<u>more enduring/transient</u>) changes in attitudes. In addition, elaboration (i.e., the more central route) is (<u>more/less</u>) likely to predict behavior.

Answers: 14-1. OL, CC, OC **14-2.** P, P, C **14-3.** peripheral, central, central **14-4.** more enduring, more.

CONFORMITY AND OBEDIENCE: YIELDING TO OTHERS

15. Describe Asch's work on conformity.

15-1. Briefly summarize the general procedure and results of the Asch line-judging studies.

15-2. Conformity increased as number of accomplices increased, up to a point. At what number did conformity seem to peak? _____

15-3. Suppose there are five accomplices, one real subject, and another accomplice who dissents from the majority. What effect will this "dissenter" have on conformity by the real subject?

Answers: 15-1. Subjects were asked to judge which of three lines matched a standard line, a judgment that was actually quite easy to make. Only one of the subjects was a real subject, however; the others were accomplices of the experimenter, who gave wrong answers on key trials. The result was that a majority of the real subjects tended to conform to the wrong judgments of the majority on at least some trials **15-2.** 7 **15-3.** Conformity will be dramatically reduced (to about one-fourth of its peak).

16. Describe Milgram's study on obedience to authority and the ensuing controversy.

16-1. Two individuals at a time participated in Milgram's initial study, but only one was a real subject. The other "subject" was an accomplice of the experimenter, an actor. By a rigged drawing of slips of paper the real subject became the _____ and the accomplice became the _____. There were a total of _____ subjects, or "teachers," in the initial study.

16-2. The experimenter strapped the learner into a chair and stationed the teacher at an apparatus from which he could, supposedly, deliver electric shocks to the learner. The teacher was to start at 15 volts, and each time the learner made a mistake the teacher was supposed to _____ the level of shock by 15 volts—up to a level of 450 volts.

16-3. What percentage of the subjects continued to obey instructions, increasing the shock all the way to 450 volts? _____

16-4. What is the major conclusion to be drawn from this study? Why are the results of interest?

16-5. As you might imagine, Milgram's studies on obedience were controversial, producing both detractors and defenders. Following are two categories of objections raised against the Milgram studies. Beneath each are possible *counter-arguments* asserted by either Milgram or his supporters. Complete the counter-arguments by filling in the blanks.

   (a) "Subjects in an experiment expect to obey an experimenter, so the results don't generalize to the real world."

      The flaw in this argument, according to Milgram's defenders, is that in many aspects of the real world, including the military and business worlds, obedience (is not/is also) considered appropriate. So, Milgram's results (do/do not) generalize to the real world.

   (b) "Milgram's procedure, by which subjects were allowed to think that they had caved in to commands to harm an innocent victim, was potentially emotionally damaging to the subjects. Milgram's experiment was unethical."

      Milgram's defenders assert that the brief distress experienced by the subjects was relatively (slight/great) in comparison with the important insights that emerged.

Answers: 16-1. teacher, learner, 40 **16-2.** increase **16-3.** 5, none, 65 percent **16-4.** The major conclusion is that ordinary people will tend to obey an authority even when their obedience could result in considerable harm (and perhaps even death) to others. The result is of interest because it suggests that such obedience as occurs in war atrocities (e.g., in World War II, at Mai Lai in Vietnam, and throughout history) may not be due so much to the evil *character* of the participants as to pressures in the *situation*. (Milgram's results are also of interest because most people would not expect them: even psychiatric experts predicted that fewer than 1% of the subjects would go all the way to 450 volts.) **16-5.** (a) is also, do (b) slight. (Many psychologists today share the critics' concerns, however, and the study has not been replicated in the United States since the 1970s.)

17. Discuss cultural variations in conformity and obedience.

17-1. As with other cross-cultural comparisons, replications in other countries yield some similarities and some differences. Indicate true (T) or false (F) for the following statements.

_____ The obedience effect found by Milgram seems to be a uniquely American phenomenon.

_____ In replications of the Milgram studies in several European countries, obedience levels were even higher than those in the United States.

_____ Replications of the Asch line-judging studies suggest that cultures that emphasize collectivism are somewhat more conforming than are those that emphasize individualism.

Answers: 17-1. F, T, T.

BEHAVIOR IN GROUPS: JOINING WITH OTHERS

18. Discuss the nature of groups and the bystander effect.

18-1. The word *group* doesn't have the same meaning for social psychologists that it does for everyone else. As I look out across my social psychology class on a Tuesday morning, I might say to myself, "Hm, quite a large group we have here today." Actually, my class is *not* a group in social psychological terms because it lacks one, and perhaps two, of the essential characteristics of a group. A group consists of two or more individuals who (a) _____ and (b) are _____.

18-2. Which of the following are groups, as defined by social psychologists?

_____ A husband and wife.

_____ The board of directors of a corporation.

_____ A sports team.

_____ Spectators at an athletic event.

_____ Shoppers at a mall.

18-3. What is the bystander effect?

18-4. Why does the bystander effect occur?

Answers: 18-1. (a) interact (b) interdependent 18-2. The first three are groups and the last two are not
18-3. When people are in groups (or at least in the presence of others), they are less likely to help than when they are alone. Or, the greater the number of onlookers in an emergency, the less likely any one of them is to assist the person in need. 18-4. One reason the bystander effect occurs is because of diffusion of responsibility (the idea that "Someone else will do it," or that "We're all equally responsible").

19. Summarize evidence on group productivity and group decision making.

19-1. One reason that individuals working in groups may be less productive is that they are less *efficient*. How could working in a group decrease efficiency? Give an example.

19-2. Another reason for decreased productivity in groups involves decreased *effort*. Describe the phenomenon of social loafing.

19-3. Social loafing and the bystander effect seem to share a common cause: _____ of responsibility.

19-4. This problem should help you understand the concept of group polarization. Suppose that a group of five corporate executives meet to decide whether to *raise or lower* the price of their product, and by how much. Before they meet as a group, the decisions of the five executives (expressed as a percentage) are to *raise* the price as follows: +32%, +17%, +13%, +11%, and +2%. After they meet as a group, which of the following is most likely to be the result? Assume that group polarization occurs.

a. +30%, +10%, +3%, +3%, and +2%

b. +32%, +29%, +22%, +15%, and +20%

c. +3%, +13%, +11%, +9%, and +2%

d. −10%, −7%, −3%, 0%, and +7%

19-5. What is group polarization?

19-6. Have you ever been in a group when you thought to yourself, "This is a stupid idea, but my best friends seem to be going along with it, so I won't say anything." If so, you may have been in a group afflicted with groupthink. Groupthink is characterized by, among other things, an intense pressure to _____ to group opinions accompanied by very low tolerance for dissent.

19-7. According to Janis, the major cause of groupthink is high group _____, the *degree of liking* that members have for each other and for the group, a "we" feeling. While the groupthink theory has intuitive appeal, evaluation research support for Janis's conclusions has been mixed.

Answers: 19-1. Individuals in a group may be less efficient because they can't coordinate their work, as when the efforts of one person duplicate or interfere with those of another **19-2.** Social loafing is the reduction in effort expended by individuals working in groups as compared to people working alone **19-3.** diffusion **19-4.** b **19-5.** Group polarization is the tendency for a group's decision to shift toward a more extreme position in the direction that individual members are already leaning. As the research on risk and caution indicate, the shifts may occur toward either extreme, depending on the original position of the group **19-6.** conform **19-7.** cohesiveness.

PUTTING IT IN PERSPECTIVE

20. Explain how the chapter highlighted three of the text's unifying themes.

20-1. This chapter again illustrates psychology's commitment to empirical research. When people hear the results of psychological studies they frequently conclude that the research just confirms commonsense. Dispute this view by listing and describing *at least one study* with results that are not predictable from common sense assumptions.

20-2. Cross-cultural differences and similarities also reflect one of the unifying themes. People conform, obey, attribute, and love throughout the world, but the manner and extent to which they do so are affected by cultural factors. Important among these factors is the degree to which a culture has an _____ or _____ orientation.

20-3. Finally, the chapter provides several illustrations of the way in which our view of the world is highly subjective. For example, we tend to make ability and personality judgments based on people's physical _____; see what we expect to see as a result of the cognitive structures termed social _____; distort judgments of physical lines based on pressures to _____; and make foolish decisions when we become enmeshed in the group phenomenon known as _____.

Answers: 20-1. This chapter has described at least three studies that defy the predictions of common sense or of experts. (1) Concerning *Milgram's studies*, psychiatrists incorrectly predicted that fewer than 1% of the subjects would go to 450 volts. (2) Results from *cognitive dissonance* studies are frequently the opposite of common sense. For example, common sense would suggest that the more people are paid, the more they would like the tasks for which they receive payment; dissonance researchers found that the opposite is true; people paid *more* liked the tasks *less*. (3) Common sense might predict that the larger the number of people who see someone in need of help, the more likely any one is to offer help. Research on the *bystander effect* consistently finds the opposite result **20-2.** individualistic, collectivistic **20-3.** attractiveness (appearance), schemas, conform, groupthink.

APPLICATION: UNDERSTANDING PREJUDICE

21. Relate person perception and attributional bias to prejudice.

21-1. Prejudice is a negative _____ toward others based on group membership.

21-2. The cognitive component of prejudice is comprised of schemas about groups. This type of schema is frequently referred to as a _____.

21-3. Stereotypes are part of the *subjectivity* of person perception. People tend to see what they expect to see, and when stereotypes are activated people see and remember information that (is/is not) congruent with their stereotype.

21-4. Stereotypes are highly accessible and frequently are activated automatically, so that even though people reject prejudiced ideas, stereotypes (can not/may still) influence behavior.

21-5. People's *attributional biases* are also likely to maintain or augment prejudice. For example, observers tend to attribute success in men to (ability/luck) but success in women to (ability/luck).

21-6. People are also predisposed to attribute other people's behavior to internal traits, the bias referred to as the _____ attribution error. Thus, when people experience adversity, we are likely to attribute their misfortune to (personal traits/environmental events).

Answers: 21-1. attitude **21-2.** stereotype **21-3.** is **21-4.** may still **21-5.** ability, luck **21-6.** fundamental, personal traits.

22. Relate principles of attitude formation and group processes to prejudice.

22-1. Attitudes are to a large extent learned. For example, if someone makes a disparaging remark about an ethnic group that is followed by approval, the approval is likely to function as a _____ that increases that person's tendency to make similar remarks in the future. This is the learning process known as _____ _____. Or, if someone simply *observes* another person making such a remark, the observer may acquire the tendency to make similar remarks through the process known as _____ _____.

22-2. Ingroup members perceive themselves differently from outgroup members. One difference in perception involves the tendency of ingroup members to evaluate outgroup members (less/more) favorably. In addition, the more strongly one identifies with one's ingroup, the (less/more) prejudiced one tends to be toward the outgroup.

22-3. Another important difference in the perception of outgroups by ingroups is termed the *illusion of outgroup homogeneity*. Explain this concept.

Answers: 22-1. reinforcer, operant conditioning, observational learning (modeling) **22-2.** less, more **22-3.** We overestimate the similarity or homogeneity of people in outgroups. That is, we tend to think that they all look alike, and they tend to think that we all look alike. It goes beyond appearance—ingroups tend to view outgroup members as similar in behavior and attitudes as well.

REVIEW OF KEY TERMS

Attitudes	Group polarization	Person perception
Attributions	Groupthink	Prejudice
Bystander effect	Illusory correlation	Proximity
Channel	Individualism	Receiver
Cognitive dissonance	Ingroup	Reciprocity
Collectivism	Internal attributions	Self-serving bias
Companionate love	Interpersonal attraction	Social loafing
Conformity	Latitude of acceptance	Social psychology
Discrimination	Matching hypothesis	Social schemas

External attributions
Fundamental attribution error
Group
Group cohesiveness

Message
Obedience
Outgroup
Passionate love

Source
Stereotypes
Validity effect

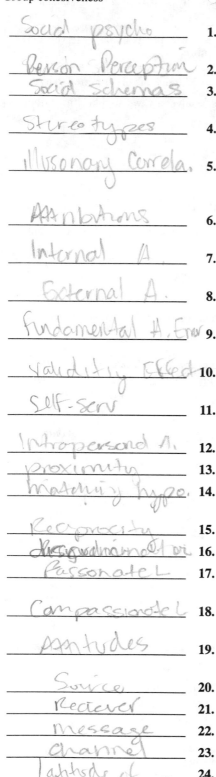

Social psycho 1. The branch of psychology concerned with the way individuals' thoughts, feelings, and behaviors are influenced by others.

Person Perception 2. The process of forming impressions of others.

Social schemas 3. Clusters of ideas about categories of social events and people that we use to organize the world around us.

Stereotypes 4. Widely held beliefs that people have certain characteristics because of their membership in a particular group.

Illusonary Correla. 5. Error that occurs when we estimate that we have encountered more confirmations of an association between social traits than we have actually seen.

Attributions 6. Inferences that people draw about the causes of events, others' behavior, and their own behavior.

Internal A. 7. Attributing the causes of behavior to personal dispositions, traits, abilities, and feelings.

External A. 8. Attributing the causes of behavior to situational demands and environmental constraints.

Fundamental A. Error 9. The tendency of an observer to favor internal attributions in explaining the behavior of an actor.

Validity Effect 10. The finding that simply repeating a statement causes it to be perceived as more valid or true.

Self-serv 11. The tendency to attribute our positive outcomes to personal factors and our negative outcomes to situational factors.

Interpersonal A. 12. Liking or positive feelings toward another.

proximity 13. Geographic, residential, and other forms of spatial closeness.

matching hypo. 14. The observation that males and females of approximately equal physical attractiveness are likely to select each other as partners.

Reciprocity 15. Liking those who show that they like us.

discrimination or 16. Behaving differently, usually unfairly, toward the members of a group.

Passionate L 17. A complete absorption in another person that includes tender sexual feelings and the agony and ecstasy of intense emotion.

Compassionate L 18. A warm, trusting, tolerant affection for another whose life is deeply intertwined with one's own.

Attitudes 19. Responses that locate the objects of thought on dimensions of judgment; have cognitive, behavioral, and emotional components.

Source 20. The person who sends a communication.

Reciever 21. The person to whom the message is sent.

message 22. The information transmitted by the source.

channel 23. The medium through which the message is sent.

lattitude of 24. A range of potentially acceptable positions on an issue centered around one's initial attitude position.

Cognitive diss 25. Situation that exists when related cognitions are inconsistent.

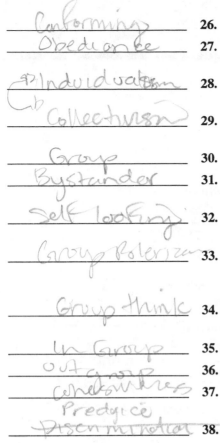

Conforming   **26.** Yielding to real or imagined social pressure.

Obedience   **27.** A form of compliance that occurs when people follow direct commands, usually from someone in a position of authority.

(a) Individualism   **28.** Involves putting group goals ahead of personal goals and defining one's identity in terms of the group one belongs to.

(b) Collectivism   **29.** Involves putting personal goals ahead of group goals and defining one's identity in terms of personal attributes rather than group memberships.

Group   **30.** Two or more individuals who interact and are interdependent.

Bystander   **31.** The apparent paradox that people are less likely to provide needed help when they are in groups than when they are alone.

Self loafing   **32.** A reduction in effort by individuals when they work together as compared to when they work by themselves.

Group Polariza   **33.** Situation that occurs when group discussion strengthens a group's dominant point of view and produces a shift toward a more extreme decision in that direction.

Group think   **34.** Phenomenon that occurs when members of a cohesive group emphasize concurrence at the expense of critical thinking in arriving at a decision.

In Group   **35.** The group one belongs to and identifies with.

Out group   **36.** People who are not a part of the ingroup.

cohesiveness   **37.** The strength of the liking relationships linking group members to each other and to the group itself.

Prejudice / Discrimination   **38.** A negative attitude held toward members of a group.

Answers: 1. social psychology **2.** person perception **3.** social schemas **4.** stereotypes **5.** illusory correlation **6.** attributions **7.** internal attributions **8.** external attributions **9.** fundamental attribution error **10.** validity effect **11.** self-serving bias **12.** interpersonal attraction **13.** proximity **14.** matching hypothesis **15.** reciprocity **16.** discrimination **17.** passionate love **18.** companionate love **19.** attitudes **20.** source **21.** receiver **22.** message **23.** channel **24.** latitude of acceptance **25.** cognitive dissonance **26.** conformity **27.** obedience **28.** collectivism **29.** individualism **30.** group **31.** bystander effect **32.** social loafing **33.** group polarization **34.** groupthink **35.** ingroup **36.** outgroup **37.** group cohesiveness **38.** prejudice.

REVIEW OF KEY PEOPLE

Solomon Asch   Elaine Hatfield   Harold Kelley
Ellen Berscheid   Fritz Heider   Stanley Milgram
Leon Festinger   Irving Janis   Bernard Weiner

_____   **1.** Was the first to describe how people make attributions in terms of internal or external factors.

_____   **2.** With Hatfield did research describing two types of romantic love: passionate and companionate.

_____   **3.** Originator of the theory of cognitive dissonance.

Asch   **4.** Devised the "line-judging" procedure in pioneering investigations of conformity.

Milgram   **5.** In a series of "fake shock" experiments studied the tendency to obey authority figures.

_____   **6.** Developed the concept of groupthink.

_____   **7.** Under the name of Walster did early study on dating and physical attractiveness; with Berscheid, described types of romantic love.

SELF-QUIZ

1. Which of the following characteristics do we tend to attribute to physically attractive people?
   a. low intelligence
   b. friendliness
   c. unpleasantness
   d. coldness

2. Cognitive structures that guide our perceptions of people and events are termed:
   a. attributions
   b. stigmata
   c. schemas
   d. denkmals

3. Inferences that we make about the causes of our own and others' behavior are termed:
   a. attributions
   b. stigmata
   c. schemas
   d. denkmals

4. Bruce performed very well on the examination, which he attributed to native ability and hard work. Which attributional bias does this illustrate?
   a. the fundamental attribution error
   b. the actor-observer bias
   c. the self-serving bias
   d. illusory correlation

5. According to evolutionary theory, as described by David Buss, men want mates who:
   a. are young and beautiful
   b. have the ability to acquire resources
   c. are similar to them in attitudes
   d. have a good sense of humor

6. Which of the following could be an example of the fundamental attribution error?
   a. Ralph described himself as a failure.
   b. Ralph thought that the reason he failed was that he was sick that day.
   c. Jayne said Ralph failed because the test was unfair.
   d. Sue explained Ralph's failure in terms of his incompetence and laziness.

7. Bruce had what could be described as a secure attachment to his parents during his infancy. What kind of relationship is he likely to develop as an adult?
   a. trusting and close
   b. jealous
   c. volatile and preoccupied with love
   d. difficult

8. Which of the following is, in general, likely to reduce the persuasiveness of a message?
   a. The receiver's viewpoint is already fairly close to that of the message.
   b. The receiver has been forewarned about the message.
   c. A two-sided appeal is used.
   d. The source is physically attractive.

9. Subjects in Group A are paid $1 for engaging in a dull task. Subjects in Group B are paid $20 for the same task. Which theory would predict that Group A subjects would enjoy the task more?
   a. balance
   b. cognitive dissonance
   c. self-perception
   d. observational learning

10. In making a decision you rely on the opinion of experts and the behavior of your best friends. According to the elaboration likelihood model, which route to persuasion have you used?
   a. central
   b. peripheral
   c. attributional
   d. 66

11. Which of the following is the best statement of conclusion concerning Milgram's classic study involving the learner, teacher, and ostensible shock?
   a. Under certain circumstances, people seem to enjoy the opportunity to be cruel to others.
   b. People have a strong tendency to obey an authority even if their actions may harm others.
   c. The more people there are who observe someone in need of help, the less likely any one is to help.
   d. Aggression seems to be a more potent force in human nature than had previously been suspected.

12. Which of the following is most likely to function as a group?
   a. shoppers at a mall
   b. the audience in a theater
   c. the board of trustees of a college
   d. passengers in an airplane

13. Vanessa witnesses a car accident. In which of the following cases is she most likely to stop and render assistance?
   a. Only she saw the accident.
   b. She and one other individual saw the accident.
   c. She and 18 others saw the accident.
   d. The other observers are pedestrians.

14. Suppose the original decisions of members of a group are represented by the following numbers in a group polarization study: 9, 7, 5, 5, 4. The range of numbers possible in the study is from 0 to 9. Which of the following possible shifts in decisions would demonstrate polarization?
   a. 2, 3, 3, 4, 5
   b. 7, 7, 6, 5, 5
   c. 5, 4, 0, 2, 3
   d. 9, 9, 7, 7, 5

15. According to Janis, what is the major cause of groupthink?
   a. strong group cohesion
   b. weak group cohesion
   c. the tendency of group members to grandstand
   d. group conflict

   Answers: 1. b 2. c 3. a 4. c 5. a 6. d 7. a 8. b 9. b 10. b 11. b 12. c 13. a 14. d 15. a.

APPENDIX B STATISTICAL METHODS

REVIEW OF KEY IDEAS

1. **Describe several ways to use frequency distributions and graphs to organize numerical data.**

   1-1. Identify the following methods that are commonly used to present numerical data.

   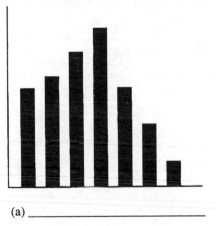 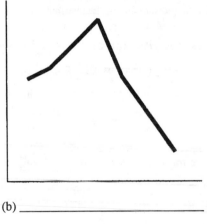

   (a) _____ (b) _____

   1-2. What data are usually plotted along the:

   (a) horizontal axis?

   (b) vertical axis?

   1-3. What is the purpose of these kinds of descriptive statistics?

Answers: 1-1. (a) histogram (b) frequency polygram **1-2.** (a) the possible scores (b) the frequency of each score
1-3. They are used to organize and summarize data.

2. Describe the measures of central tendency and variability discussed in the text.

2-1. State which measure of central tendency, the mean, median, or mode, would be most useful in the following situations.

    (a) Which measure would be best for analyzing the salaries of all workers in a small, low-paying printshop that includes two high-salaried managers? Explain your answer.

    (b) Which measure would be best for selecting a single ice cream flavor for an upcoming party?

    (c) Which measure would be best for pairing players at a bowling match, using their individual past scores, so that equals play against equals?

    (d) Where do most of the scores pile up in a positively skewed distribution?

Answers: 2-1. (a) The median, because the high salaries of the two management persons would distort the mean (b) the mode (c) the mean (d) at the bottom end of the distribution.

3. Describe the normal distribution and its use in psychological testing.

3-1. Answer the following questions regarding the normal distribution.

    (a) What is the general shape of the normal distribution?

    (b) Where are most of the scores located in a normal distribution?

    (c) What is the unit of measurement in a normal distribution?

    (d) What percentage of scores falls above 2 standard deviations in a normal distribution (see Fig. B-6 in the text)?

    (e) If your percentile ranking on the SAT was 84, what would your SAT score be (see Fig. B.7 in the text)?

Answers: 3-1. (a) It is a bell-shaped curve (b) near the center (c) the standard deviation (d) 2.14% (e) 600 (approximately).

4. **Explain how the magnitude and direction of a correlation is reflected in scatter diagrams and how correlation is related to predictive power.**

    4-1.   Answer the following questions about the magnitude and direction of a correlation as reflected in scattergrams.

        (a) Where do the data points fall in a scattergram that shows a perfect correlation?

        (b) What happens to the data points in a scattergram when the magnitude of correlation decreases?

        (c) What does a high negative correlation indicate about the scores on variable X are high?

    4-2.   Answer the following questions regarding the predictive power of correlations.

        (a) How does one compute the coefficient of determination?

        (b) What does the coefficient of determination tell us?

        (c) What could we say if the sample study used in the text showed a correlation of -.50 between SAT scores and time watching television?

Answers: 4-1. (a) In a straight line (b) They scatter away from a straight line (c) Scores on variable Y would be low
4-2. (a) By squaring the correlation coefficient (b) It incidates the percentage of variation in one variable that can be predicted based on the other variable (c) Knowledge of TV viewing habits allows one to predict 25% of the variation on SAT scores (.50 X .50 = .25).

5. **Explain how the null hypothesis is used in hypothesis testing and relate it to statistical significance.**

    5-1.   Answer the following questions regarding the null hypothesis and statistical significance.

        (a) In the sample study correlating SAT scores and television viewing, the findings supported the null hypothesis. What does this mean?

        (b) What level of significance do most researchers demand as a minimum before rejecting the null hypothesis?

(c) What is the probability of making an error when a researcher rejects the null hypothesis at the .01 level of significance?

Answers: 5-1. (a) We cannot conclude that there is a significant negative correlation between SAT scores and television viewing (b) the .05 level (c) 1 in 100.

REVIEW OF KEY TERMS

Coefficient of determination
Correlation coefficient
Descriptive statistics
Frequency distribution
Frequency ploygon
Histogram
Inferential statistics

Mean
Median
Mode
Negatively skewed distribution
Normal distribution
Null hypothesis
Percentile score

Positively skewed distribution
Scatter diagram
Standard deviation
Statistics
Statistical significance
Variability

_____ 1. The use of mathematics to organize, summarize, and interpret numerical data.

_____ 2. An orderly arrangement of scores indicating the frequency of each score or group of scores.

_____ 3. A bar graph that presents data from a frequency distribution.

_____ 4. A line figure used to present data from a frequency distribution.

_____ 5. Type of statistics used to organize and summarize data.

_____ 6. The arithmetic average of a group of scores.

_____ 7. The score that falls in the center of a group of scores.

_____ 8. The score that occurs most frequently in a group of scores.

_____ 9. A distribution in which most scores pile up at the high end of the scale.

_____ 10. A distribution in which most scores pile up at the low end of the scale.

_____ 11. The extent to which the scores in a distribution tend to vary or depart from the mean.

_____ 12. An index of the amount of variability in a set of data.

_____ 13. A bell-shaped curve that represents the pattern in which many human characteristics are dispersed in the population.

_____ 14. Figure representing the percentage of persons who score below (or above) any particular score.

_____ 15. A numerical index of the degree of relationship between two variables.

_____ 16. A graph in which paired X and Y scores for each subject are plotted as single points.

_____ 17. The percentage of variation in one variable that can be predicted based on another variable.

_____ 18. Statistics employed to interpret data and draw conclusions.

_____ 19. The hypothesis that there is no relationship between two variables.

_____ 20. Said to exist when the probability is very low that observed findings can be attributed to chance.

Answers: 1. statistics **2.** frequency distribution **3.** histogram **4.** frequency polygon **5.** descriptive statistics **6.** mean **7.** median **8.** mode **9.** negatively skewed distribution **10.** positively skewed distribution **11.** variability **12.** standard deviation **13.** normal distribution **14.** percentile score **15.** correlation coefficient **16.** scatter diagram **17.** coefficient of determination **18.** inferential statistics **19.** null hypothesis **20.** statistical significance.

Take the guesswork out of succeeding in college with . . .

College Survival Guide:
Hints and References to Aid College Students,
Fourth Edition
by Bruce Rowe, Los Angeles Pierce College

> *How can I finance my college education?*
> *Can I get credit through examination?*
> *What can I do to get better grades on my exams?*

You'll find the answers to these questions and more in Bruce Rowe's 77-page paperback. If you're like many students just starting out at college, the whole experience can be somewhat overwhelming. By the time you've figured out what you need to know to succeed, you've already wasted a lot of time and money going in wrong directions!

Now, for just $11.95, you can get a concise guide that will give you practical information on such topics as:

- How to manage your time
- How to study for and take exams
- How to use the Internet to do research for assigned papers
- How to finance your education
- How to maintain your concentration
- How to get credit through examination
- How and when to use the credit/no credit option
- And much more!

You can purchase the manual for $11.95 by calling toll free (800) 354-9706, or by filling out and returning the coupon provided on the back of this page.

ORDER FORM

Yes, I want to purchase: *College Survival Guide: Hints and References to Aid College Students, Fourth Edition* (ISBN: 0-534-35569-2)

Residents of: AL, AZ, CA, CT, CO, FL, GA, IL, IN, KS   _____ **Copies x $11.95** _____
KY, LA, MA, MD, MI, MN, MO, NC, NJ,   **Subtotal** _____
NY, OH, PA, RI, SC, TN, TX, UT, VA, WA,   **Tax** _____
WI must add appropriate state sales tax.   **Handling** $4.00
Total Due _____

Payment Options

_____ Check or money order enclosed *or*

Bill my _____ VISA _____ MasterCard ____ American Express

Card Number: _____

Expiration Date: _____

Signature: _____

Please ship my order to:

Name _____

Institution _____

Street Address _____ _____

City _____ State _____ Zip+4 _____ + _____

Telephone ( ) _____

Your credit card will not be billed until your order is shipped. Prices subject to change without notice. We will refund payment for unshipped out-of-stock titles after 120 days and for not-yet-published titles after 180 days unless an earlier date is requested in writing from you.

Mail to: Wadsworth Publishing Company
Source Code 9WWPY004
Ten Davis Drive
Belmont, California 94002-3098
Phone: (800) 354-9706
Fax: (800) 522-4923

Photocopy, fold, close, and return with payment